Robert Peebles Nevin

Black-robes

or Sketches of Missions and Ministers in the Wilderness and on the Border

Robert Peebles Nevin

Black-robes
or Sketches of Missions and Ministers in the Wilderness and on the Border

ISBN/EAN: 9783337010379

Printed in Europe, USA, Canada, Australia, Japan

Cover: Foto ©ninafisch / pixelio.de

More available books at **www.hansebooks.com**

BLACK-ROBES,

OR

SKETCHES

OF

MISSIONS AND MINISTERS

IN THE WILDERNESS AND ON THE BORDER.

BY

ROBERT P. NEVIN.

PHILADELPHIA:
J. B. LIPPINCOTT & CO.
1872.

Entered according to Act of Congress, in the year 1872, by
J. B. LIPPINCOTT & CO.,
In the Office of the Librarian of Congress at Washington.

CONTENTS.

THE JESUIT.

		PAGE
I.—The Priest and the Parson of Two Hundred Years Ago	.	7
II.—The Missionary among the Savages of Superior	. .	16
III.—Marquette, his Cotemporaries and Successors, and what they accomplished	. . . .	33
IV.—The Legend of the Defeat of the Eries	. . .	53
V.—The Faith on the Pennsylvania Border and in the Valleys of La Belle Rivière	. . . . . .	66

THE MORAVIAN.

I.—The Moravians in Eastern Pennsylvania	. . . .	87
II.—The "Place of Hogs" on the Upper Alleghany	. .	98
III.—The "Village of Peace" on the Beaver	. . .	109
IV.—The Journey through the Wilderness	. . .	123
V.—Trouble at Work in the Tents on the Muskingum	.	136
VI.—Captain Pipe plans New Mischief, and what came of his Schemes	. . . .	151
VII.—The Dispersion of the Congregation; its Restoration, and its Return to the Muskingum	. . . . .	171

THE METHODIST.

I.—The Methodist Preacher of the Border—Nascitur, non fit	.	185
II.—The Arrest, Awakening, Conviction, Conversion, and the Call of the Preacher	. . . . . .	198
III.—The Preacher in the Pulpit	. . . . .	210
IV.—In the Saddle and on the Circuit	. . . .	230
V.—The Cane-Ridge Revival	. . . . . .	248
VI.—Mentionable Men among the Preachers of the Border	.	265

(iii)

THE PRESBYTERIAN.

		PAGE
I.—	Old Redstone—its People and its Presbytery	281
II.—	The Parson of Seventy-five Years Ago	299
III.—	The Sabbath-day, and how it was sanctified	314
IV.—	The Long Sabbath, and the Great Buffalo Sacrament	334
V.—	The Early Laborers in the Border Vineyard	348

THE JESUIT.

THE JESUIT.

I.

THE PRIEST AND THE PARSON OF TWO HUNDRED YEARS AGO.

ATTRIBUTE the fact to whatever motive we please, accord to it whatever degree of deserving, one way and the other, our several prejudices may incline to, it is nevertheless indisputable that the Roman Catholic Church has always moved far in advance of all other Christian denominations in missionary enterprise. Inspired by a sublime devotion, the self-denying priest has never hesitated to respond to a conviction of duty, nor paused to consider the hinderances in the way of its discharge. No field of labor has been so remote, no intervening stretch of wilderness and solitude so vast, but that to attain the one, he has bade willing defiance to the toils, the trials, and the perils of the other. Pestilence has not stayed him, famine has not restrained him, fire and sword have not dismayed him. Outstripping the march of civilization, distancing even the enterprise of the few, made famous by the feat, who, led by desire of traffic, or the love of wild adventure, have accomplished their bolder advances, penetrating far, over long-extending leagues of pathless way, into the heart of savage wastes, he has assumed the more marvelous achievement, nor rested content until, traversing the weary reaches between, of forest, plain, desert, and mountain, he has journeyed from sea to sea, and made the passage of a continent.

In 1626, Jean de Brébeuf, of the order of Jesus, starting from Quebec, entered upon his first missionary labor, fixing his station among the Huron Indians, on the Canada shore of the lake of that name, nearly a thousand miles from the point of his embarkation on the St. Lawrence River. Ten years later, the exiled preacher, Roger Williams, the foremost venturer among his Puritan brethren, sought out a scene for his personal toils—and for a new settlement—among the Narragansetts in Rhode Island, but the enterprise took him scarcely beyond sound of the axe of the pioneer in the clearings on the frontier of the Plymouth settlements. In 1648, John Eliot, the most noted of evangelical apostles among the Indians, officiating on a salary of fifty pounds per annum, had extended his labors into the backwoods, perhaps half a dozen miles outside of Boston harbor. Seven years before, the canoe that bore them landed Fathers Jogues and Raymbault among the Ojibwas, or Chippewas, on the banks of the Saut Ste. Marie, close upon the waters of Lake Superior, midway almost between shore and shore of the opposite oceans. Whole generations later, and within memory of living men, when ministers, under auspice of the domestic missionary societies, first went out to serve among the mixed populations, native and imported, of Western (peninsular) Michigan, they found the orchards, grown old and crumbled from decay, which were planted by the Jesuit fathers nearly a century and a half before.

If a comparison be instituted between the teachings and the preachings of the Papist and the Puritan, in the time of which we treat, the contrast will be marked, and strikingly at variance with a prevailing conviction respecting the fact. The instructions under which the follower of Loyola entered upon his work demanded an exclusive devotion to the one specific object of his errand,—to proclaim Christ and his Cross to the benighted savages of the New World. The Christian virtues were to be held in strict observance. He was to be meek, patient, forgiving, temperate, charitable, and of untiring affection. He was to conform, as nearly as possible, to the manners and customs of the tribes among which he might be thrown; loving them as brothers; tendering a cheerful proffer of all courtesies and civilities, even the most trifling; partaking with them of their fare,—a hard task for graceful performance, but one claimed as a sacred due of hospitality,—no matter how rude or how repulsive it might be; all, that identifying himself with them thus intimately, he might the more readily win them over to the embrace of the Faith which it was his mission to preach.

The Puritan, on the other hand, took upon him his office independently, and in boasted contempt of higher human authority. With the Bible for his rule and conscience for his guide, only to God would he hold himself accountable. His peculiar dogmas regarding forms of belief and of worship, of government ecclesiastical and civil, and of individual conduct, made up mainly his religion. In his preaching he preferred to discourse upon points of doctrine; to denounce the Divine Right of Bishops; to discuss the question whether Sanctity of Life is Evidence of Justification, or to deliver a solemn protest against the Eating of Mince-pies on Christmas. Thus it happened that while Roger Williams was proclaiming vehemently against the cross in the English standard, to the spiritual edification of his hearers, and while, with his ready right hand, Endicott was defiantly cutting it out, Father Jogues, a tortured, mutilated prisoner, far away in a camp of the Iroquois, in the fullness of a more amiable zeal, was carving the same sacred symbol, and with it tracing out the adorable name of IESUS in the bark of the trees. And so it was, that while the "Apostle of the Indians" found topics quite up to his taste, for pulpit deliveries, in such themes as "The Wearing of Wigs and Long Hair," and "The

Use of Tobacco," Charles Garnier, the gentle disciple of Ignatius, was proclaiming the compassionate lessons of his divine Master in his own inspired utterances; preaching repentance and faith to the Huron and the Iroquois, and administering the saving sacrament of baptism to his converts,—all the while, and everywhere, steadily pursuing, through hazard and through hardship, his appointed task; that task which was to find its requital at last in the crown of martyrdom, for which, in his moods of ecstasy, he was used to petition so fervently.

The religion of the Puritan may be said to have been a religion of the head, characteristically cold, rigid, and vindictive. Charity with him was an unfamiliar virtue. His ministry was devoted to the rooting out of heresies, and to the instillation of "wholesome spiritual doctrine." The Law furnished him with his texts and his proofs, rather than the Gospel, as Moses was his master of inspiration rather than the Messiah. To keep a salutary espionage over the consciences of his fellow-communicants,—to disfranchise Wheelright, and to banish Mrs. Hutchinson, for the very fault (none else than non-conformity) which had made himself an exile from his native land,—was a more praiseworthy service than would have been the conversion of a Mohican or a Wampanoag. He seemed to act upon the presumption that the truth could make its own way among the Gentiles, and that the exclusive office of the teacher or pastor was to see that the "professor" lived up to the line of Congregational orthodoxy. His function was to call the righteous, not sinners, to repentance. It was nothing out of the way that Parris should take it as worthy a heavenly benediction when he "preached and prayed" against deaf Rebecca Nurse, and had her hanged by the neck, one summer's day, till she was dead. Cotton Mather thought that he was winning a peculiar claim to celestial favor when he harangued the crowd whose unsanctified instincts threatened to tempt them to the rescue of the condemned preacher, Burroughs, as he stood on the scaffold, and with a comfortable conscience could thank God "for justice being so far executed among us,"—the governor and the president of Harvard College responding "Amen" to it,—as his miserable victim was launched, strangled, into eternity.

The religion of the Jesuit, on the other hand, was eminently a religion of the heart. Love was the cardinal element of his faith. Christ, with him, was all and in all. Calvary was the sacred mountain to which he turned for his oracles, rather than Sinai. The injunction of his adorable Lord he put literally in practice,—taking up his cross and following him. He never tarried to discuss mooted questions in theological science, receiving the dogmas of his church without cavil, and confessing to its mysteries dutifully, satisfied, as he was, in the terms of old and approved acceptance, to understand as he believed, and not to fetter and imperil himself by assuming only to believe as he understood. Freed thus from the necessity of lingering at home to watch against the upgrowth of schism, he was at liberty to take up the more benevolent and consistent offices of his vocation, and wherever souls were to be snatched from perdition,— the more distant and dangerous, the more inviting the mission,—thither to force his way, or—for with his face once set upon an errand he never turned back—to perish in the attempt.

"O my Jesus," said the pious Gabriel Lallemand, "it is necessary that Thy blood, shed for the savages as well as for us, should be efficaciously applied to their salvation. It is on this account that I desire to co-operate with Thy grace, and to immolate myself for Thee." "What shall I render to Thee, O my Lord Jesus," reads the vow of the noble Jean de Brébeuf, "for all that I have received from Thee? I will accept Thy chalice; I will call upon Thy name. And now I vow, in presence of Thine eternal Father, and of the Holy Ghost,— before the angels, the apostles, and the martyrs,— that if, in Thy mercy, Thou shalt ever offer unto me, Thy unworthy servant, the grace of martyrdom, I will not refuse it. From this hour I offer unto Thee, with all my will, O Thou my Jesus, my body, my blood, my soul, so that, by Thy permission, I may die for Thee who hast deigned to die for me.

So, Lord, will I accept Thy chalice and invoke Thy name, O Jesus, Jesus, Jesus!"

This was the spirit of the Jesuit's devotion, and these types of the illustrious company of those who, like René Menard, Chabanel, Garreau, Le Maistre, Du Poisson, Antoine Daniel, and their fellows, dedicated themselves to martyrdom, that the faith to which they were plighted, with its saving grace, might be implanted in the hearts of the heathen.

As to the merits of the one order of these ecclesiastical functionaries, and of the other, it may readily be conceived that a decided opinion prevailed in the minds of the savages. "You saw me," said one of them, representing his people before the Governor of Massachusetts, "long before the French did; yet neither you nor your ministers ever spoke to me of prayer or of the Great Spirit. They saw my furs and my beaver-skins, and they thought of them only. These were what they sought. When I brought them many I was their great friend. That was all. On the contrary, one day I lost my way in my canoe, and arrived at last at an Algonquin village, where the Black-Robes taught. I had hardly arrived when a Black-Robe came to see me. I was loaded with peltries. The French Black-Robe disdained even to look at them. He spoke to me at once of the Great Spirit, of Paradise, of Hell, and of the Prayer which is the only path to heaven. I heard him with pleasure.

At length prayer was pleasing to me. I asked for baptism, and I received it. Then I returned to my own country, and told what had happened to me. They envied my happiness,—and set out to find the Black-Robe, and asked him to baptize them. If, when you first saw me, you had spoken to me of prayer, I should have had the misfortune to learn to pray like you, for I was not able then to find out if your prayer was good. But I have learned the prayer of the French. I love it, and will follow it till the earth is consumed."

While the labors of the early Catholic missionaries were devoted chiefly to the natives inhabiting the wildernesses of Canada, they were not so to the exclusion of a more extended exercise. Their enterprise led them beyond the boundaries of that province, and brought them within borders of a strange land, which, lying south of the chain of lakes, away in the rear of the Plymouth settlements, reached, with its broad ranges of forest and prairie, from the Alleghany Mountains to the Mississippi River. It is of their attempts, as the pioneers of Christianity in these regions,—the regions of "the West," as the term had its application and limitation down to within a score or two of years ago,—that this sketch proposes to treat.

II.

THE MISSIONARY AMONG THE SAVAGES OF SUPERIOR.

THE Ottawa, Menomonee, Chippewa, Illinois, and other Indian nations inhabiting the regions bordering upon the waters of Superior and Michigan, formed part of the great Algonquin family, which, having its connecting links through other intermediate tribes, extended along the line of lakes to the eastern seaboard, including and terminating with the powerful clans of the Abenakis in Maine. Within this belt of territory, and edging upon the lake which bears their name, lay the possessions of the Hurons or Wyandots, a people deriving their lineage and language from the Iroquois, but bound to the Algonquins, as was inevitable from their geographical position, by the more reliable ties of sympathy and interest.

Voyages for the purposes of trade were common between the Ottawas and the other kindred tribes of the West, and their allies, the Hurons, of the East. Straggling parties would make the excursion at almost any season of the year, except, perhaps, in the dead of winter; but the great tours happened more rarely, and were undertaken when the months were propitious, offering fair skies, a genial atmosphere, open water, and the promise of supplies, in the game and the growth of the woods, for subsistence on the way. From sixty to a hundred or more canoes would gather at some convenient harbor on Green Bay, or on the Saut Ste. Marie, into which would be packed the cargoes of peltries and copper, their chief articles of export, when the flotilla, manned with some five persons to each bark, forming altogether quite a numerous party, would start upon their voyage. After the Old World had sent over its colonies to the New, and the settlements that sprang up on the seacoast and along the rivers began to exhibit their superior attractions, these voyages were continued farther down the St. Lawrence, until at length Quebec, the frontier town of the French, became the terminus of the trade. Here the native foresters could supply themselves at a cheap rate, according to their estimate of values, with the foreign commodities that suited their simple tastes,—beads, bits of glass, ribbons, rings, and the like,—while the barterers with whom they dealt were disposed to believe that they had not been outbargained in the furs and skins received in exchange.

While tarrying at port, social intercourse was not neglected between dealers and customers, and while the Frenchman excited the admiration and taxed the credulity of his visitor with descriptions of the marvels of his native land, the Indian, ambitious to maintain his national importance as well, would reciprocate with stories of the wonders of the distant interior where he inhabited,—of its mighty rivers and fresh-water seas, of its illimitable prairies, and of the populous tribes that filled the region. Tempted by these representations, Nicolet, one of the earliest and most adventurous pioneers of New France, determined upon a voyage of exploration. A ready familiarity with the Algonquin tongue qualified him peculiarly for the undertaking. He made the expedition, visiting the "Sea Tribe," in the neighborhood of Green Bay, and having returned, offered his own testimony in confirmation of the statements made by the native traders.

Among the national festivals of the Algonquins was one of peculiar solemnity, entitled the Feast of the Dead, recurring, periodically, every tenth year, and held at some chosen locality in the country of the Hurons. On these events, delegations from all the tribes, far and near, were accustomed to assemble, bearing with them the bones of their dead of the last decade, dug from their graves, and brought for final sepulture in the one common depository consecrated to that use, but more particularly attracted, no doubt, by the feasts, the songs and dances, the games, and the torch-light processions which were the ceremonial accompaniments of the occasion. The period for a return of this festival happened in 1641, and was attended, among the rest, by a representation of Chippewas from the Saut Ste. Marie.

The Jesuit missionaries were not slow to take advantage of so promising an opportunity to urge the claims of the Faith upon these strange barbarians. So eloquently did they press their appeals, and such was their gentle and winning manner, that they found favor in the eyes of the savages, who made earnest entreaty that some of their number should accompany them in the backward voyage to their lodges in the far land. Ever since the return of Nicolet, several years previously, the good fathers had contemplated the establishment of a mission in that quarter, and now that Providence had opened a way, they promptly and thankfully accepted the invitation. Preliminarily to a positive occupation of the ground, Fathers Jogues and Raymbault were appointed to undertake the journey, explore the country, and fix upon a station. Coasting Lake Huron in their canoes, after a voyage of seventeen days, made peculiarly pleasurable by the charming scenery that skirted their progress, and the genial summer atmosphere, redolent with the rich balm of pines, through which they floated, they arrived on the 4th of July at the Saut, to be met with the hearty welcome of two thousand Indians.

The wonders narrated by the old traders at Quebec were repeated. The missionaries were told of the great plains that stretched south and west, away from the lakes, and of the populous tribes—the Miamis, the Sacs and Foxes, the

Kickapoos, and the Pottawotamies—by which they were inhabited. Rumors, too, were rehearsed of vaster regions lying still farther beyond; of the river of rivers,—the MESIPI they called it,—that had its broad course there, and of the Nadowessi, mighty and terrible, a nation of hunters and of a thousand warriors, that occupied the land. The missionaries were filled with wonder at the recital. Their hearts overflowed with compassion for the multitudes living and perishing thus in ignorance, and instantly would they have committed themselves to the work of their enlightenment, only that, as yet, the laborers were too few in the field of the Hurons, and the successes established there, through so much toil, too precious, to allow of the risk to the spiritual perseverance of the newly elect, that might ensue upon their withdrawal. But there was to be no final abandonment of the ground. They tarried for some days, sharing the hospitalities of their Chippewa friends, planted a cross on the site near the river where now stands the Cathedral of St. Mary, as the distinguishing emblem of their creed, and for evidence to such as might follow that they had been before, and were entitled to come again, to hold and to possess for the French and for the Faith, and then, launching their canoes, they glided out into the rapids of the Ste. Marie and floated away on their homeward-bound voyage. They never returned. Raymbault died, perishing from exposure. Jogues followed ultimately, hurried to his reward by the murderous blow of an Iroquois assassin.

A party of Ottowas, under guidance of a pair of wandering traders, who, in pursuit of their calling, some two years before had strayed upon them, visited the Hurons in 1656, and made request for a Black-Robe to join them on their return. Two of the fathers, Leonard Garreau and Gabriel Druilletes,—that man of "incomparable charity,"—were accordingly commissioned for that purpose. Upon starting they took with them a company of Frenchmen, with the view of planting a white settlement among the natives at the Saut. The attending Frenchmen, soon wearying of the society of their savage *co-voyageurs*, and perhaps not uninfluenced by a regard for their personal safety, withdrew in a body from the enterprise. The missionaries were not to be deterred by the spiritless example of the deserters, but manfully continued their advance. Paddling their way against the tide of the river, they had proceeded as far as the island of Montreal, when they were suddenly attacked by a party of Iroquois, lurking secretly in await for them. Garreau fell fatally wounded under the first fire. The Ottowas deserted their canoes and took to the shore. Here, gathering behind defenses hastily thrown up, they sheltered themselves until escape was practicable, when they stole away, abandoning Druilletes, whom they would not allow to go with them, to whatever fate might overtake him.

But when the Jesuit resolved he accomplished. In his lexicon there was no such word as fail. Did persecution, armed with tortures, interpose to prevent him? He might writhe under its inflictions, but he would not be hindered. Did certain death lie visibly before him in the way? No matter to the devotee whose daily invocation was that he might be found worthy, if the reward were not beyond his desert, to win the crown of martyrdom.

The establishment of the Saut Ste. Marie mission was deferred, but not abandoned, because of the disaster at Montreal Island. In 1660 another trading fleet of sixty canoes, laden with the ordinary freightage, arrived from Superior at Quebec. Three hundred Ottowas manned the expedition. They reiterated the request which had been urged by their brethren four years before, that a servant of the "God of the Prayer" should go back with them on their return. The Superior, Father Lallemand, listened to their prayer, and cast his eyes around to find the fitting candidate for the embassy. Among the enlisted in the sacerdotal service was a veteran, who, in earlier years, had toiled with Brébeuf, Jogues, Garnier, and Bressani, of saintly remembrance, and participated in all their trying experiences, save only the last, by which their earthly connection had been severed. Hard service had done its equal share with the frosts of fifty-six winters to whiten his hair, and the keen-edged weapons of his enemies had left their deeper grooves than the well-marked furrows of time, on his cheek. Sixteen years' devotion to it had not diminished his ardor in the cause to which he was plighted. His physical frame, constitutionally delicate, would have rendered him incompetent for missionary duty, save that its energies, through a severe and uninterrupted process of discipline, had been trained to extraordinary endurance. His manners were those of a rarely accomplished, highly polished Christian gentleman. He was zealous in his Master's cause, but his zeal was of a temperate type, kept evenly quick and warm by the "live coals," rather than stimulatively ardent by the fitful flashes from off the altar.

René Menard was the man for the post. If the Superior, after having indicated his choice, hesitated on account of the age and infirmities of the priest to confirm it, "Fear not," said the worthy associate of the old martyrs. "He who feeds the young raven, and clothes the lily of the field, will take care of his servants." The venerable father was nominated, and forthwith started upon the mission.

The savage traders had been liberal in their offers of kind treatment. No sooner had they got fairly under way with their fleet, however, than the native treachery of their hearts began to betray itself. Indignities were heaped upon the gray-headed priest, especially by Le Brochet, a principal chief of the party, whose example failed not to provoke a like behavior on the part of his inferiors.

He was made to perform their most menial services. He was compelled to toil at the oar from dawn till dark, and to contribute his more than equal share in the transportation of their burdens at the portages. He was forbidden his accustomed devotions; made the object of mockery and derision; robbed of his breviary, which the ruffianly wretches hurled into the water; yet patiently he endured it all, "and like a lamb dumb before his shearer, so opened he not his mouth." Famine overtook the party on its way, when all were reduced to the extremity of subsisting on berries, barks, roots, acorns, and the *tripe de roche*, a woodland moss, gathered as they might find it, here and there, on the rocks.

Arrived at the Saut at last, the Indians cast the unhappy missionary ashore, and left him provisionless, shelterless, barefooted, and with only the tatters of his threadbare robe for protection against the weather. Yet the soul of the heroic old man did not fail him. As of wont, his daily orisons ascended to heaven. As of wont, his lips gave breath to praise, the recesses of the woods wakening as they had never wakened before, to the strange song of the New Adoration,—the *Salve Regina*,—and the floods clapping their hands to the glad music of the *Ave Maris Stella*. For several days he was reduced for sustenance to the use of dry bones crushed to a coarse powder between stones and thus made edible. Some of his red-skin companions at length relented, sought him out, and conducted him to where their wigwams were pitched, miles away at Keweenaw Bay.

Upon their extermination as a tribe, in 1649, by the Iroquois, a crippled remnant of the Hurons took refuge with the Ottowas. Ten years' exposure to the old superstitions may have dimmed, but had not obliterated, the religious impressions of these unfortunate exiles. As soon as Father René appeared among them, these sheep of the old flock gathered fondly about him, and with the stray wanderers of the scattered cote of St. Mary's on the Wye, he formed the nucleus of a new fold at St. Theresa's Bay,—as designated by him,—on Lake Superior. Such was the establishment of the first permanent mission in the Far West. Menard was not to be allowed, without dispute, to administer to the spiritual wants of his flock. The Ottowa people, under unworthy example of their chiefs, who were violent in their opposition to the faith of "the Prayer," drove the pious father from their cabins. He constructed for himself a rude shelter of fir-branches, through which the winds had almost unobstructed passage, and this was his lodge through the long, bitter months of a northern winter,—this his only protection against its storms, and snows, and cold. His labors were limited to the sick and equally suffering with himself among the unfriendly tribe, but were not without their recompense. Several baptisms are mentioned among the fruits of his efforts.

In the spring, having learned of a group of refugee Wyandots, inhabiting an island in Green Bay, he determined upon a visit to that quarter. The route was ascertained to be an exceedingly difficult and dangerous one. His friends advised him against the undertaking. "God calls me thither," he replied. "I must go if it cost me my life." Embarking in a canoe accordingly, attended by his proved friend the *Donné*, John Guérin, together with a small party of Hurons, he started upon the hazardous voyage. The way was long, following the devious current of the Menomonee, and laborious from the many crossings overland necessary, in order to avoid the various rapids in the river. Before having proceeded very far, the Indians, with accustomed infidelity, deserted the missionaries, who with wonted perseverance, however, continued to press on. At one of the portages, Guérin started in advance of his aged companion. The latter, with a dubious trail to follow, drifted out of the true course and lost his way. Guérin, more fortunate, made the crossing successfully, and awaited anxiously the arrival of the priest. He never appeared. Diligent search was made for him. The bag he carried, his breviary, and portions of his apparel were found long afterwards in the huts of some of the savages, but never a trace of the body of the missionary. René Menard, the last surviving of the Fathers in the Faith who had been first to bear the tidings of Redemption to the barbarians of the New World, had followed, by the same path whither they had gone, and the company of apostles on earth stood again complete as the circle of martyrs in Paradise.

But the Cross had been planted in the soil of the tribes on the Great Lake, and it was not to be abandoned. Claudius Allouez was appointed to fill the place made vacant by the loss of the venerable René. He accepted the commission cheerfully, joined the Ottowa flotilla at Montreal, in the summer of 1665, and by the month of September was in his allotted field of labor. His first tarrying-point was at the bay of St. Theresa, where he was met and welcomed by some of the native converts of Menard. Thence he coasted along the lake, until, early in October, he had reached the charming bay of Chegoimegon. Here he encountered an assemblage of savages, representing the various clans of Algonquins, gathered in from their several cantons along the coast, and wrought up to a high pitch of enthusiasm, in view of a contemplated descent upon the encampments of their common enemy, the Sioux. The priest looked on with feelings of painful regret. It was a matter of prime importance for his purpose that the martial fever should be quieted, and, if possible, the threatened warfare obviated. While the more youthful warriors, therefore, with their battle-songs and dances, were busy adding fuel to the fire of excitement, the prudent missionary invited their elders apart,

—the sachems and experienced veterans of the clans,—and labored to convince them of the inexpediency of the proposed adventure. His counsels prevailed, and the undertaking was abandoned.

Allouez then built a chapel, on a spot which he designated as *La Pointe du Saint Esprit*, and thus prepared himself for the opening of his work among the tribes.

The difficulties which he had to encounter were many, and hard to overcome. The superstitions of the Indian—dear to him as the traditional inheritance of his fathers—were most to his choice, moreover, because their mysteries, of a type in their sublimation with the real circumstances of his life, lay within the range and aptitude of his unsophisticated habits of thinking. His objects of worship had to be plainly visible somehow, in the shadow at least, if not in the substance. The idea of a spirit imperceptible to sense, and unidentified with some special feature or other of nature, such as the sun, the winds, the water, the woods, was one beyond his grasp of comprehension. When the missionary, therefore, undertook to tear to pieces the structure of the old religion, he had the prejudices, firmly rooted as the growth of ages in a congenial soil could make them, to contend against; while when, on the other hand, he sought to substitute a knowledge of the faith of his Master, he encountered the harder task of attempting to build up without the material for reconstruction,

—the language of the savage being destitute of terms to represent the abstractions of his creed.

Then there were the social and domestic usages to correct; favorite practices not inconsistent with the native conception of morality, but scarcely comporting with the ethics of the new doctrine. Marriage, in its sacramental sense, was an unknown institution among the people. Man and woman, with perhaps a gift of wampum passed between them,—as a "consideration" for the longer or shorter term of accommodation that might follow, rather than as the pledge of a permanent compact, —would take to the same wigwam, but the relation thus contracted might be dissolved at any time as caprice decided, and either, or both, of the parties remain at liberty to enter into new alliances upon the same convenient terms. When the pair thus associating happened to have outlived the ardencies of youth, they usually kept up the companionship for years,—perhaps for life; but this fidelity was maintained from motives of convenience commonly rather than from tenderness of attachment, the woman acting pretty much in the capacity of slave, hoeing the corn, cracking the hominy, and attending generally to the domestic drudgery, while the man, making his amusements his occupation, provided the luxuries of the chase for the larder, or "filled his red-stone pipe for smoking," and took his ease in his cabin.

Polygamy, besides, was prevalent. Indeed, their

customs—and their customs were their law—allowed the almost unrestricted indulgence of desire, and their grossness in this respect was so open, so shameless, so abominable, that the very brutes that roamed their forests were paragons of decency in comparison.

But Father Allouez did not despair of his mission. The chapel which he had erected, the novel appointments of its interior, the unaccustomed services, and the strange doctrines of the new religion, all combined to excite the curiosity of the natives; and from far and near, Nepissings and Kikapoos, Saulteurs and Pottawottamies, they gathered in to see the Black-Robe, and to listen to the marvelous tidings which he proclaimed. His attention being invited to these various tribes, he undertook a pilgrimage through their several territories, distributing his lessons of counsel and instruction in all their villages. As the fruit of his first winter's labor he was able to report the baptism of eighty-four subjects, principally children, but including several adults. Having continued at his work through two years, he returned to Quebec, tarried for two days, reported to his Superior, laid in a small stock of such supplies as were more pressingly needed at his Western post, engaged the services of an assistant, Father Louis Nicholas, and turned his face again towards Chegoimegon.

In his old field once more, Allouez applied himself with new industry to his labors. Missions were permanently established among the Ottowas, Chippewas, and Nepissings. But his efforts were not restricted to these tribes. He established his posts in the communities of the Miamis; built his oratories of mats and bark among the Sacs and Winnebagoes; and thus, season by season, migrated from scene to scene, until the news of redemption had been declared to twenty-five tribes, and eighty souls had been gathered by baptism into the fold of Christ. The Kiskakons, as a nation, under his preaching, adopted the faith of the Cross. From Lapointe Allouez proceeded to Green Bay, and his first mass being celebrated on the festival of St. Francis Xavier, the post was designated by that title. From that point as a centre he kept up an active intercourse with the various tribes of the region, explained the mysteries of the Prayer, opened chapels for instruction, waited upon the sick, and discharged the practical duties of his office in such a manner as secured the confidence of the natives, gave force to his influence, and aided him materially in the profitable prosecution of his labors. Hundreds were baptized, including chiefs and others of the distinguished among the people, some of whom, like Kekakoung, a converted Kiskakon, became preachers themselves of the creed of their adoption. *Our Father*, translated into their tongue, grew to be the familiar prayer of the wigwam, and *Kyrie Eleison* the accustomed chant at their devotions. Schools were instituted, where the children were taught the form of worship, and indoctrinated in the rudimentary elements of the Christian confession.

After the death of Marquette, Allouez, in 1676, went, under commission, to the Illinois tribe, to fill the place of that deceased missionary. He reached their territory in April, and at once took possession of the quarters which had been occupied by his illustrious predecessor. Since Marquette's time the population, gathered in from their temporary migrations, had multiplied materially, so that where he had found but one race and seventy-four cabins, his successor discovered three hundred and fifty-one lodges, accommodating eight tribes. On the day of the Feast of the Invention of the Holy Cross, the missionary planted a model of the emblem appropriate to the day, twenty-five feet high, which continued to stand long years afterwards as a monument to his zeal and enterprise. With occasional intervals, Allouez remained with this people till 1679, when, relinquishing the charge, he returned to Mascoutens.

III.

MARQUETTE, HIS COTEMPORARIES AND SUCCESSORS, AND WHAT THEY ACCOMPLISHED.

IN the spring of 1668, James Marquette, accompanied by Le Boesme, a worthy brother of the Order of Jesus, took boat at Quebec and launched out upon the long journey to the Northwest. After the usual voyage along the romantic coast of Lake Huron, accomplished without incident worthy of mention, the reverend adventurers, entering the Saut Ste. Marie, and winding their course amid the isles that gem its channel, reached their point of destination, and disembarked on its southern shore, at the foot of the rapids. Here they erected a station, and, without delay, Marquette commenced the exercise of his priestly functions. His fame had preceded him in that distant wilderness, so that the savages poured in from every quarter to hear him. The assemblies that gathered at the summons for services were large, attentive, and apparently interested, so that sanguine expectations were entertained of fruitful results to his labor. But his hopes were not to be realized. Curiosity—their chief attracting motive—once gratified, his hearers gradually dropped off, or, if they lingered, betrayed no evidence of any impression that might be regarded as profitable or hopeful. Despairing of success, he determined to change his scene of operations, and accordingly, in the early autumn of the year following, removed to the mission opened by Allouez, at Lapointe, after a weary and trying passage of thirty days' continuance, made through desolate reaches of snow and ice. The inhabitants of two of the villages which were planted in the neighborhood, old converts of the Hurons in exile, received him kindly. Long estrangement from the influence of enlightened teachers had caused the decay of religion among them, and a partial relapse into the old superstitions; but, although not without opposition, especially from the tribes of adjoining settlements, the lost ground was speedily recovered.

Marquette had listened to the legends that were told of the river of incomparable magnitude that rolled away to the west, and of the formidable nation—the Dacotahs—that swarmed the vast lands beyond. The spirit of adventure stirred sympathetically in his bosom with the zeal of the *religieuse*, and he resolved that, so soon as opportunity pointed the way, he would meet its hazards and put the rumor to the proof. The Winnebagoes, a tribe of the Dacotahs, and the only one east of the Mississippi, occupied the region bordering on the western extremity of Lake Superior. As a helpful preliminary to the grand project held in view, the missionary was anxious to secure the friendly favor of this people, and opened up negotiations which he hoped would result in an invitation to visit them; but, when on the eve of accomplishment, his plans were suddenly foiled. Some treachery of the Hurons offended their neighbors, and gave rise to a war which eventuated in their forced retreat to the quarter formerly occupied by them at Mackinaw. Marquette was compelled to retire with his friends. Here, amid the group of cabins in the new settlement, he erected a chapel and established the mission of St. Ignatius. But the spot was a dreary, inhospitable one, and offered indifferent prospect of good to be accomplished.

While yet at Lapointe, the eminent father had taken advantage of the presence of a prisoner from that tribe to have himself instructed in the dialect of the Illinois. That nation, an extensive and powerful one, occupied the country lying between Lake Michigan and the Mississippi River, contiguous to the territory of the Dacotahs on the west, and, save by the partial interposition of the Miami district, reaching between the southern limit of Lake Michigan and Lake Erie, by the Iroquois on the east, both dreaded enemies, between the opposite pressure of which they were doomed to be finally crushed out of existence. Defeated in his original plan of opening up a way of approach to the Dacotahs, or Sioux, through the Winnebagoes, Marquette determined to make the trial by a more southerly route through the territory of the Illinois. Accordingly, as early as was practicable in the spring of 1673, armed for his only defense with cross, beads, and breviary, he turned his face towards the setting sun, and started forth upon his enterprise. Mascoutens was the first point of attainment fixed upon, but finding the place deserted, he resumed his course, pushing westwardly until striking the Wisconsin, he embarked upon its waters in a canoe, and committing himself to the protection of the Blessed Virgin Immaculate, commenced his voyage. Day after day his frail craft glided on with the flow of the current; distance after distance, traced lingeringly along the winding channel of the stream, was measured, until, after a week of time and one hundred and twenty miles of progress, on the memorable 17th of June the mouth of the tributary was reached, and the successful explorer found himself afloat on the broad bosom of the Mississippi.

Upon his return from that distinguished adventure, instead of retracing his course by the Wisconsin, he struck into the Illinois, and ascended that river until having reached a settlement of the Peorias he decided, at their earnest solicitation, to tarry a few days in their town. He next proceeded to the Kaskaskias, another clan of the Illinois, who received him with a welcome so cordial that he promised, as soon as possible, to revisit their village and establish a mission there. After a brief stay with this hospitable people, amply rewarded by the privilege of conferring the rite of baptism upon a dying child, he bade them an affectionate adieu, and having crossed the intervening prairie, returned by lake to Mackinaw.

The severe exposures to which he had been subjected in this expedition told seriously upon the health of the enterprising missionary. He had been attacked with dysentery in his travels. Resisting the remedies applied for its correction, the disease assumed a chronic type, and was rapidly wearing away his strength. That his end was approaching was painfully evident. But the purpose upon which he was bent was not to be thwarted by any hinderance short of death. Had he not pledged himself to the benighted Kaskaskian savages that he would return to declare to them the glad news of Redemption? Let consequences happen as they might, the promise must be made good.

Thirteen months after his arrival at Mackinaw, in the month of October, suffering painfully still from his malady, but with a spirit active and unyielding as ever, he set out upon the arduous undertaking. Winter overtook him on the way, and impeded by the ice which had closed up the Chicago River, he was compelled to suspend progress, comforting himself as he best could with such protection as a rude hut, put up by his own hands, might afford against the inclemencies of the season. With the opening of the river in the early spring he resumed his way, reaching his destination at length on the 8th of April. After having spent some time in passing from lodge to lodge, instructing the inmates separately in the Faith, he invited them to assemble in a body at an appointed place, near at hand, on the prairie. Here he erected an altar to the "Unknown God," and before an eager audience of over two thousand hearers, "declared Him unto them."

At this newly-established mission Marquette continued his labors for some two weeks, when, with his health utterly shattered, and under a self-conviction now that "the time of his departure was at hand," he decided to return to Mackinaw, that he might die there, cheered in the "putting on of immortality" by the familiar presence of his brethren. Many of the Indians, to whom he had endeared himself by his amiable and unselfish example, accompanied him on the way, bidding him adieu, reluctantly and with their warmest expressions of sympathy, as, with his pair of associates, he took his canoe, launched from the beach, and glided away along the eastern and hitherto untraversed coast of Lake Michigan. As they made advance by day, he reclined painfully, but uncomplainingly, in the narrow confinement of his frail vessel. At night he was carried ashore and laid to rest on the ground, with the moss, gathered from the decaying forest-wood, for his couch, and the leaves of the living trees for his covering. And so they journeyed on. As near high noon of a beautiful day in May they approached a river, which empties about midway of its length into Lake Michigan, he ordered his oarsmen to pause, and indicating an elevated spot on the river-shore, he said that there was to be his grave. His companions urged him to let them take advantage of the propitious weather and row on, but he refused, and was carried to the land. "Say adieu to my Superiors," he whispered, as they laid him gently on the ground, the dews of death settling on his brow the while. "Bid farewell to my fellow-disciples of the Faith. As for yourselves, you are weary—rest; I shall never forget you." Then lifting his eyes to heaven, he murmured, devoutly, "*Sustinuit anima mea in verba ejus,—Mater Dei, memento mei!*" After an hour of silent communion with God, he solemnly repeated the Creed, thanked the Almighty that he was permitted to die in that distant solitude, a brother of the Order of Jesus, and a victim of his devotion to the Cross. Then, with the name of his Redeemer on his lips, he bowed his head and gave up the ghost. His body was buried as he directed,—on the bluff by the shore of the river that is known by his name. His companions erected a rude cross over the spot of his interment, where, after a fervent appeal for his saintly intercession with God in their behalf, they left him to his rest.

Two years later a party of Kiskakons, members

of his old charge, dug up the missionary's bones, and, joined on the way by canoe-loads of Iroquois, bore them with religious care to the station at Mackinaw. Here they were met by the villagers of the place, led in a body by the priests Pierson and Nouvel, who, to the chant of *De Profundis*, landed the remains, and with becoming ceremony bore them to the chapel for final burial. Gabriel Richard, a Sulpitian, stationed long years afterwards at Detroit, who was a deputy to Congress, and who enjoys the higher reputation of having established the first printing-press in Michigan, visiting the locality where Marquette had died, and where he presumed his relics still to be, raised on the spot a wooden cross, and with his penknife carved upon it the inscription,—

"Fr. Jh. Marquet
Died here 9th May, 1675."

This is the only monument which has ever been reared to his memory; but the fame of his name cannot perish from history, nor the renown of his sanctity from the traditions of the faith which he so nobly exemplified and so brilliantly adorned.

Father Druilletes, a veteran apostle of the Jesuits, stands conspicuous among the distinguished missionaries of the Northwest. He enjoyed a special reputation because of the marked sanctity of his life. During the prevalence of an epidemic among the Indians, miraculous cures were accredited to him, which at once established for him a name and an authority highly potent and influential. Under his administration the Indians of the Ste. Marie were, as a nation, converted to Christianity. The decree enunciatory of this revolution in their form of faith was issued on the 11th of October, 1670. "The God of the Prayer," said the declaration, "is the Master of life;" and the young men, walking the streets of the village, proclaimed, "The Saut prays; the Saut is Christian." A twelvemonth's service was rewarded with the baptism of three hundred subjects. His miraculous power operated materially in his favor. Very many, influenced by that distinguishing proof of more than common virtue, were led to conviction. Polygamy was renounced; other depraved vices were abandoned; the medicine-men were repudiated; the children were brought to receive the benediction of the priests; the first fruits of their gathering were laid at the altar of the New God; and when starting upon the war-path,—that emergency which, in view of its hazardous contingencies, is the best test of true religious conviction,—their prayers were now addressed to the Divinity of the Black-Robe.

A party of Sioux came to the Saut, in 1674, to negotiate a peace with the Algonquins at that place. At a council held at the mission-house to discuss the measures in dispute between the tribes, a member of the conference, becoming excited, sprang up, drew his knife, and brandished it defiantly in the face of a Dacotah. Angered at the outrage, the Sioux leaped to his feet, drew a blade from his hair,—the usual place of carrying that weapon,—shouted his war-cry, which immediately called his clansmen about him, rushed upon the Algonquins and drove them from the house. The expelled party retaliated by setting the building on fire. The Sioux ambassadors were all burned to death. This was a severe blow to the missionary. His chapel and his home were reduced to ashes. The Dacotahs were enraged, the Algonquins exposed to continual chastisements from their enemies, so that betwixt the aggressions of the one and the reprisals of the other there was little space left for the cultivation of spiritual grace. But Druilletes continued at his work, not without profit, until, after a long and faithful service, "broken by age, hardship, and infirmity," he returned to Quebec, where a few months afterwards he died.

During a suspension of the labors of Allouez among the Illinois, brought about by the visit of La Salle, who entertained little regard for his order, and less for this particular brother of the Jesuits, Fathers Gabriel de la Ribourde, Zenobius Membré, and Louis Hennepin of the Recollects, who had accompanied the celebrated explorer on his expedition, opened a mission, in 1679, at Peoria. They were anxious to acquire the language of the natives, and, at the same time, as far as possible, to promote the spiritual aim of their mission. For both these purposes, having been adopted into the families of two of the chiefs, they had every facility; but, greatly to their discouragement, the dialect was beyond their skill of acquisition, and the people seemed to be wedded to their idols irreclaimably. Baptism was administered to a dying warrior, but almost before the priest had retired from the performance of the rite, the old superstition resumed its sway, and the chieftain expired an apostate amid the incantations of his own medicine-men. Father Membré despaired utterly. In hope of accomplishing some good, he shifted the scene of his operations to another neighborhood, only to meet with like disappointment. Still, he and his colaborers toiled on, however, until hostilities broke out between the Illinois and the Iroquois, which resulted in the dispersion of the former. The missionaries, left without protection, decided to return to Green Bay. On the way, encountering an accident as they floated along the Illinois River, they got ashore, two of the party tarrying to repair a damage to their canoe, while the other, old Father Gabriel, walked some distance apart to repeat his breviary. While thus engaged, he was surprised by a raiding band of Kikapoos, and mercilessly murdered. After a fruitless search for him, his associates resumed their voyage, and finally reached Green Bay in safety. Thus began, and so disastrously ended, the Mission of the Recollects among the Illinois.

The Jesuits determined to reoccupy the field from which they had retired in favor of the Recollects, and accordingly, in the spring of 1692, and in the person of Sébastien Rale, the mission at Peoria was reopened. Upon his arrival the excellent father was greeted cordially by the Indians of the various villages. They attended worship respectfully; they sent their children to receive instruction; the Prayer found favor in their eyes, and the morals taught in the articles of the new creed met with undivided approval,—all save the doctrine, so universally distasteful, that the man must be the husband of but one wife. They would not repudiate polygamy. Two years' toil was productive of little profit, and Rale, abandoning the field, withdrew to his original charge among the Abenakis in Maine.

James Gravier, who had previously made a passing visit to the post, returned to supply the vacancy created by the retirement of Rale. The labors of his predecessors, although unsuccessful on the whole, had not been expended entirely in vain. About fifty Peorians and Kaskaskias were either converts or favorably inclined towards Christianity, but the large majority were devoted to the superstitions of their fathers. The forms of chapel-service had been maintained by the faithful with due observance since the departure of Rale, a venerable chief assuming the priestly vicarship for the time,—himself making the tour of the village, morning and evening, to invite the attendance of worshipers. Deprived of a competent spiritual leader, however, and exposed to the active antagonism of the medicine-men, there was imminent risk of an early relapse into heathenism. This native school of prophets had witnessed with alarm the progress of a confession which, once accepted, must prove ruinous to their occupation, and, unhappily countenanced by the licentious soldiery of the French fort close by, were using their best endeavors to arrest its further advance. It was, therefore, with feeling of joyful gratitude that the handful of persevering neophytes hailed the arrival of the missionary. The prophets immediately organized in array against this their new and formidable adversary. They assailed him with misrepresentation, mockery, and maltreatment. They ridiculed the ceremonies of his office; they charged that his charities were but mischiefs in disguise; that his rosaries were charms for pernicious practices; that the baptismal water was a distillation of venom, which it was death to be bedewed with, and—an epidemic having begun to prevail among them—that he had created the infection, relief from which could only be had through his expulsion from their village. Nevertheless, the patient but fearless father continued to labor on, sustained by the consciousness of fulfilling his duty, if not comforted by the results attending his efforts But the day of recompense was at hand.

Michael Ako, a Frenchman, who had served with Hennepin in his Upper Mississippi voyage of exploration, withdrew from his comrades on their return, and retired to Peoria, where he remained, conducting a small but lucrative trade at that settlement. He was a man of unquestionable energy, but notoriously profligate in his habits. Among his associates at the fort he enjoyed the distinction of an intimacy with the chief of the Kaskaskias. This chief had a daughter, most attractive, as attraction ran among the dusky maidens of the villages, who, having been reared under training of the priests, and in the clearer illumination of the True Light than was vouchsafed to her sisterhood of the clans, had knelt at the Cross and offered her vows at the shrine of the Beautiful Devotion. The libertine Ako met the lovely Kaskaskian, was captivated by her charms, and solicited her hand in marriage of her father. The sachem, gratified with the proposal, promptly indicated his approval; but Mary, when the suit of her lover was preferred, declined the overture. She had heard how the virgins of the French, who were ardent in the faith, were wont to renounce all meaner attachments, and banded together in seclusion from the world, to expend their lives, for Christ's sake and that of the Blessed Mother of Purity, in works of charity and mercy. Stirred by their generous example, she had determined upon a like dedication of herself. The father, angered at her refusal, tore the clothing from her person, and drove her naked from his lodge into the street. Then convoking a council of the chiefs, he made known his grievance, charged the responsibility of it on the French missionary, and asked, and obtained, an order prohibiting attendance at his services. But the priest fearlessly threw open the doors of his chapel, and the few whose fealty had stood the test of similar proscriptions before, and who were not to be intimidated now, followed to the sanctuary according to custom, in defiance of the prohibition. The disaffected then attempted to blockade the approaches to the chapel; and finally, finding even that expedient ineffectual, one of the leaders rushed into the building, brandishing his tomahawk, and threatening death to all unless they instantly withdrew. Gravier stood firmly at his post; not one of his flock manifesting the slightest disposition to desert him, until abashed by their behavior, the intruder had withdrawn. The garrison at the fort, instead of offering that protection to the missionary which the common sympathies of race and religion ought to have commanded, joined with the savages in their abuse and violence.

While the feud was still raging, the chief's daughter herself interposed, waited upon Father Gravier, and offered that if the surrender might quiet the disturbance of the people, she was willing, with his permission, to forego her choice and submit to the proposed sacrifice. " If I consent to the marriage," said she, " my father will listen to you, and induce the rest to do so. I desire to please God, and will yield for love of Him." The missionary gave his approval, and, "more a victim than a bride," Ako led the Kaskaskian maiden to the altar.

This episode in the domestic life of the chief, which threatened while it lasted the very existence of the mission, proved, in the end, the most fortunate incident that could have happened. The bride of Ako, a young woman of more than ordinary force of character, was conscientious and earnest in her convictions. The impressions which had resulted in her conversion, while keenly defined on the sensitive surface, were deeply stamped as well into the very substance of her heart; so that with more than the enthusiasm, as was natural, of her priestly teachers, she had all of their depth and determination of feeling. What was denied to her as a novice in a convent, she undertook as a wife in a wigwam, enforcing persuasively the claims of religion as she had opportunity. Ako was the first to succumb to her influence, and, from the profligate that he had been, was reformed into a model of piety. Her father followed next, and the bitter agent of persecution became, like Saul of Tarsus, the vigorous champion of the faith.

A great feast was prepared, to which the leading men of the villages of the clan were invited. The chief arose in their midst, and, expressing contrition for past offenses, declared openly his renunciation of heathenism, calling upon his guests to go and do likewise. While the chief counseled the men, the young wife exhorted the women. The force of their leader's example, and of his daughter's eloquence, did not fail of effect. Gravier devoted himself to the instruction of his now willing hearers. Mary, taking for her themes the pictures which the priests had provided, and by which she had been taught herself,—pictures illustrative of interesting passages in the life of Jesus,—told over the touching stories which they represented,—the story of the birth in the manger at Bethlehem, of the opening of the eyes of the Blind Beggar of Jericho, of the raising of the Dead Man of Bethany, of the Cross, and of the Resurrection. Her clanfolk listened, wondered, and relented. Men and women began to pray; children laid aside their implements of play, and, wandering by in groups, sang the hymns which the missionary composed for them, in the streets of the village, so that within the space of eight months this gracious awakening resulted in the baptism of two hundred and six souls.

Gravier remained at, and in the neighborhood of, Peoria until 1699, when he was recalled to Mackinaw. The next year he made the voyage of the Mississippi, following it to its mouth. Thence he returned to his station on the Illinois, resumed his labors, roused again, unluckily, the hostility of the medicine-men, and in a fray excited by these antagonists, received a severe wound, from the effects of which he died.

The first attempts at the erection of a mission in Southern Michigan, according to the testimony of the few of the tribe of the Pottawottamies still to be found on the spot, was made, perhaps, as early as 1675. The successful achievement of the project was accomplished in 1680. Father Allouez, in that year, attended by Dablon, after having coasted Lake Michigan from Green Bay, entered the St. Joseph River, so called in honor of the patron saint of Canada, and making advance against its tide, proceeded until, some twenty-five miles (fifty by the river) from its mouth, he reached the locality now the seat of the inviting town of Niles. About half a mile up-stream from the heart of the town—a narrow belt of boggy lowland lying between it and the river—rises a semicircular bluff, at the base of which, and through the soil of the marshy level, runs a brook which empties its slender contribution of supply into the St. Joseph. On this bluff, up till within twenty-five years since, if not now, the traces were plainly distinguishable of a fortification, the cross planted at the time of its construction, and still to be seen, in the rear of it, indicating by whom, and for what use, it was built. Here, conveniently established between an encampment of Miamis on one side of the river, and three several settlements—one at Pokegan, a second on

the shores of what are now known as the Notre
Dame Lakes, and the third and principal one, close
by the fort—of the Pottawottamies on the other,
Alloucz built a chapel (a brewery occupies the site
now), and near by, a log cabin for his own accommodation.
His labors were carried on successfully, and
without the occurrence of any extraordinary event
to invest them with special interest. After a faithful
service of several years, he died in the summer
of 1690. His ashes repose in the graveyard of the
Catholic mission at Niles. The establishment was
kept up, part of the time under the ministry of
Chardon, "a man wonderful in the gift of tongues,
speaking fluently nearly all the Indian languages
of the Northwest," until 1759. In that year the
French garrison of Fort St. Joseph was attacked
by a party of English soldiers, the engagement resulting,
after a fierce contest, in the defeat of the
French. The survivors of the garrison, including
the priests, were carried away, prisoners, to Quebec.
The mission, thus violently dissolved, was not reorganized
for nearly a hundred years. In 1830,
Father Stephen Badin pitched his tent in the
vicinity, revived the faith among the Pottawottamies,
built a chapel on the little St. Mary's Lake,
near South Bend, bought a section of land, which,
conveyed to the Bishop of Vincennes, through him
was dedicated, in the interests of education, to the
church, and is now the seat of that notable institution
of learning—the University of Notre Dame.

We have noticed the labors of the earliest, and most prominent, of the Jesuit fathers concerned in the leading missionary movements of the Northwest. These distinguished pioneers were not left to struggle alone. As the exigencies of service called, willing hearts were ready to respond, and recruit after recruit followed until the Black-Robe became a presence common and familiar among the tribes of the region. While Marest and Guignas penetrated the vast wastes west of Lake Superior, and bordering on the Mississippi, proclaiming redemption to the Sioux, Mermet made his pilgrimage across the intervening prairies, and planted the standard of faith, where a colony of Mascoutens had formed a lodgment, on the banks of the Ohio. While Louis André made his canoe his habitation, and visited, one by one in regular circuit, the villages clustering around Green Bay, Aubert toiled amid the snow-fields bordering upon the boundaries of the Far Northwest,—how faithfully, and at what sacrifice, the Indians tarrying there to-day attest, as they lead the visitor to an island in the Lake of the Woods, and, repeating the melancholy story of his end, point out the blood-stained rock on which he was slaughtered.

Thus by the feet, the beautiful feet of them that bring glad tidings of good things, were borne the messages of the gospel. Thus did the energetic Jesuit press his ministry, till not a village,—not a camp, on plain or water-course, where flitting clansmen pitched their tents, while through a summer's noon, or a winter's, they followed the chase or dipped their nets in quest of food,—not a wigwam in all the wilderness was left in which his presence was not known, and where his spiritual counsels were not heard.

IV.

THE LEGEND OF THE DEFEAT OF THE ERIES.

THAT portion of the West, including the meadows and uplands watered and drained by the upper Ohio and its tributaries, seems, down to a comparatively recent date, to have been, almost entirely, an uninhabited waste, ranged over, no doubt, in their hunting tours, by bands of Indians from the north, but without a fixed population of its own. Of these game-seeking adventurers, those that frequented the valleys and hills of the Alleghany River were likely of the Iroquois tribe, while the wider extent of territory lying to the west, most probably, constituted the sporting-ground of the Eries. The settlements of the Iroquois clustered along the Mohawk Valley and about the several lakes, Oneida, Onondaga, Cayuga, and Seneca, in New York, while those of the Eries, beginning with Tu-shu-wa, which occupied the site of the present city of Buffalo, extended westward along the whole length of the southern shore of the lake that bears their name. The Eries were a strong, proud, and warlike people,—ambitious to preserve that eminence among the tribes which their valor had won, and which their vigilance thus far in their history had protected.

There is a story told as to how, at their own seeking, the prowess of which they boasted was put to the test, followed with the detail of the catastrophe, fearful and fatal, which attended the experiment, and thus runs the legend:

Daganoweda, a wise man of the Onondaga nation, aroused to the conviction that the practice of secession so common among the tribes, where, at pleasure, whole clans were wont to detach themselves and seek out new settlements for the planting of new organizations, was the secret of the weakness of a people, set himself at work not merely to correct the custom, but to carry out the opposite theory naturally suggested, and effect, if possible, a general consolidation of the several neighboring tribes of his region. He laid his scheme, carefully and shrewdly prepared to its minutest details, both as touching the form of union, and the laws by which its affairs should be regulated, before some of the leading minds of the respective nations; brought about a convention, on the banks of the Ga-nun-ta-a, or Onondaga Lake, of the prominent sages of each; carried through the project successfully, and effected the erection of the formidable Confederacy of the Ho-de-no-sau-nee, or Five Nations.

When the tidings of this coalition was carried to their towns, the Eries, or Sag-a-neh-gi, became alarmed. Right confidently, nay eagerly, would they have taken to the war-path against Seneca singly, or Cayuga, Onondaga, Oneida, or Mohawk, but the forces united of the five, numbered an array too commanding in its proportions to be regarded with feelings of indifference. The object of the combination was readily conjectured; but, new bond and all, were not the Sag-a-neh-gi, even though numerically inferior, still, in activity, skill, bravery,—all the elements, indeed, that go to make up the finished warrior,—their more than peers? As a matter of prudent precaution—for where were they left with their proud *prestige* as Lords of the Lake departed?—they decided to put the question to the test.

A runner was dispatched to the Ho-nan-ne-ho-onts, or Senecas, the border tribe of the confederates, with a friendly challenge to meet them at Tu-shu-wa in a friendly game of ball—a hundred chosen men against a hundred—for a wager of such value as might be mutually agreed upon. The messenger was honorably received by the Senecas; the proposition laid before the council, discussed, voted upon, and rejected. The Eries, elated with this implied admission, as they chose to interpret the answer, of their superior prowess, renewed the challenge. It was again considered by their neighbors, and again declined. When the *défi* was delivered for the third time, the older heads of the council would have given a final refusal, but the younger warriors began to murmur at the action of their elders. Who were these vain braggarts,—these burrowers in the banks of the Great Lake,—that they should creep from their holes to fling insolence in the faces of the Warders of the Threshold of the Long House? The deliberate judgment of the counselors gave way to the pressure. The challenge was accepted.

A hundred athletes, of faultless proportion, and approved in wind and limb, were selected for the contest. Armed, each one, with his implement of play,—a slender hickory sapling, cut of suitable length, bowed at one end like a battledoor, and having the hoop stoutly laced athwart-wise with the dried and twisted sinews of the deer,—they formed into file, took up their march, and cheered by the wild applause of their clansmen as they left, were soon lost to view in the shadows of the forest. A fleet-footed messenger was sent in advance to notify the Sag-a-neh-gis of their coming. Arrived at the spot,—an open space put carefully in order for the occasion, close by the village, and near the lake,—the Seneca champions produced their valuables—belts of finely-carved and polished wampum, bracelets and rings of silver and copper, moccasins trimmed with crimsoned moose hair, and embroidered with painted quills of the porcupine, shells of purple and gold, with pearls of the purest water—and assorted them in heaps upon the ground. The Eries produced their trinkets of greatest rarity, beauty, and value, and placed them in corresponding piles, side by side with the others.

The hour of contest arrived. The game opened briskly, and was conducted with great skill by both parties, but resulted in the triumph of the Senecas. The victors behaved with a modest propriety scarcely to be expected under the circumstances; indulging in no parade of exultation, but quietly collecting the trophies won in the strife, and proceeding to re-invest themselves in their loose robes, laid aside while at exercise, preparatory to their departure. Nettled at the issue, and anxious to win a revenge for their discomfiture, the Sag-a-neh-gis invited their competitors to tarry over another day and have a new trial of merit at a foot-race. The invitation was accepted. Ten men were selected from each of the parties by their respective chieftains, and next morning were led to the course appointed for the contest. Again were the Eries defeated. The chagrin which they naturally felt at the result was materially heightened from the fact that the Kaukwas, a neighboring clan present as invited guests, were witnesses of the failure.

To redeem, if possible, their lost honors, a wrestling match was proposed, and agreed to, upon the terms that the successful champion in each trial should cleave the skull of his fallen adversary, and carry away his scalp, to be worn in his belt as a trophy of the victory. The savage stipulation was distasteful to the Senecas, but to take exception to it would be to expose themselves to the charge of cowardice,—a charge which native pride could never brook; they, therefore, interposed no objection, but, after consultation, decided that in case of success on their side, they would retire from the field without inflicting the murderous penalty. The day following was the time appointed, and, at their invitation, the village of the Kaukwas, some eighteen miles distant, the place for the contest. When the parties had assembled and the signal was given, a Seneca stepped promptly into the ring. He was as promptly met by a champion of the Eries. After a short struggle the Sag-a-neh-gi was brought to the ground, but the victorious Ho-nan-ne-ho-ont, refusing to inflict the mortal penalty upon his prostrate competitor, turned on his heel, and, amid their hearty applause, retired to the circle of his friends. The chief of the Eries no sooner witnessed the movement than, with a bound, he leaped to the side of his fallen clansman, and with a blow of the tomahawk that buried the blade of the weapon to its haft in his head, left him dead on the spot where he had fallen.

A second and a third encounter followed with a like result, each defeated champion being brained in turn, and his lifeless remains dragged from the arena, to clear the space for a new contestant and a fresh victim of sacrifice. Excitement, intense at first among the Sag-a-neh-gi, grew wilder and fiercer with each succeeding catastrophe. Fearful of still more fatal consequences if the dueling were kept up, the leader of the Senecas, after the third engagement, called his partisans around him, stated his apprehensions, and advised an immediate retirement from the field. Acting upon the suggestion, the force of which was fully appreciated, they quietly fell back from their position, till, without awakening suspicion as to their intent, they had gotten beyond arrow-flight of pursuit, when, taking to the cover of the woods, they were off at a leap, and presently far away on the trails that led to their native lodges. Taken by surprise at the unexpected manœuvre, and perhaps restrained by the reflection that, as invited guests, the Senecas were honorably entitled to safe departure, the Sag-a-neh-gis did not attempt to follow, but gathering up the bodies of their slain, returned crestfallen and dejected to their wigwams at Tu-shu-wa.

The result of the contest was well calculated to create uneasiness in the minds of the Eries. They had failed, signally failed, in all the exercises—

exercises of their own choosing—in which they had been engaged. Their adversaries had proved themselves not only men of nerve and substance, but schooled, moreover, to dexterous and vigorous action. On the war-path it would be no holiday pastime to come to clubs against them. If so much might be argued of a single member, what was not to be apprehended of the united house of the new confederacy? That hostile designs were in reserve, sooner or later, to be put in force against the outside, unaffiliated nations by the league, was a settled conviction, for upon no other argument, according to savage ratiocination, could the novel and extraordinary compact be accounted for. The wise men of the tribe took the question into consideration. After due deliberation it was resolved that to guard against the contingencies likely to arise, it became them to adopt decisive measures, and that rather than await an invasion of the enemy, it was their surer policy themselves to assume the aggressive. The plan agreed upon was to bring out their whole force, make a sudden descent upon the Senecas, then, if successful in their surprise-assault, to advance against the Cayugas, and so successively against the Onondagas, Oneidas, and Mohawks, until all were annihilated. The scheme was bold, but if secretly and expeditiously dispatched, entirely practicable.

Among the women of the tribe was one, a childless widow, by parentage and early belonging a Seneca, but who, in one of their former forays, had been captured by a party of Eries, with whom she had since dwelt as the wife, while he lived, and afterwards as the widow, of one of their warriors. New associations and attachments had left her content with her captivity, but not to the forgetfulness of the old home on the slopes of the Nunda-war-o-noh-gi or of her kindred. When the decision of the council had transpired, under a quick realization of the fearful calamity in store for her people, she determined to interfere for its prevention. When the darkness of night had fairly settled over the village, and its inhabitants were wrapped in slumber, she stole cautiously from her lodge, and wending her way along the irregular avenues of the town, soon found herself beyond its limits. Following the course of the Niagara River, she hurried on through the gloom of the forests, with only such light to guide her steps as falling from the stars dropped winkingly through the thick leaves overarching her path, until, as the dawn peeped over the waters, she found herself on the shore of Lake Ontario. Some wanderer early abroad, or perhaps a benighted hunter in the woods, had left his canoe, tied to a tree, on the margin of the lake. She undid the astening, leaped into the vessel, and shoved out into the water. Coasting the lake she plied her oar with unflagging energy, and by nightfall reached a settlement of the Senecas at the mouth of the Oswego River. She hastened to the wigwam of one of the principal chiefs, and there unfolded the scheme of treachery which had been plotted in the councils of the Sag-a-neh-gis.

Swift-footed messengers were dispatched, without delay, to carry the intelligence to the tribes of the confederacy. Speedily, as if borne on the wings of a bird, was the news communicated through the length and breadth of the land. The fire was kindled on the shore of the Onondaga, the great League-Fire of the Ho-de-san-no-ge-ta, the Custodians of the Council Brand, and at the summons gathered in from their remotest settlements—from the meadows of the Mohawk,—from the sylvan abodes on the Oneida and Cayuga—the wise men and the warriors of the Nation. The conference was brief. With the prompt action characteristic of the confederates, it was decided to instantly marshal their forces, move into the menaced territory of the Senecas, and there await the invasion of the enemy. The march, five thousand men in file, began. At Canandaigua Lake report was had, through their runners, that the Eries had crossed the Genesee, and were rapidly moving eastward. Unconscious of the betrayal of their plans, they were pressing on, briskly and eagerly, in full confidence of success.

The armies met at Honeoye, a little lake at half distance between Canandaigua and the Genesee, separated only by a narrow sluice, the bed of the streamlet through which the surplus water of the lake was discharged. No sooner did the Sag-a-neh-gis discover the presence of their foe than, with a yell that pierced the forest to its remotest solitude, they sprang to the conflict. The shock of the onset was terrific. Midway in the channel of the stream they came together. Knife met knife in the hand-to-hand grapple; their blades, now lifted for the stroke flashed in the light, now descended after the fatal blow, dripping with crimson. The brook ran red with blood. The confederates could not resist the impetuous headway of the attack. Inch by inch, until they were forced back some distance from the bed of the rivulet, did they retreat; the Eries, encouraged by success, pushing forward with redoubled spirit, and filling the air with whoops of triumph. Victory seemed within grasp of the assailants when the complexion of affairs experienced a change.

In arranging their plan of assault, the confederates had detached from their main body a company of a thousand youths, neophytes as yet in warlike service, who were ordered to make a detour through the woods, and, throwing themselves behind the enemy, to open an attack on their rear. The movement was accomplished, and just in time for opportune relief at the critical juncture referred to. The customary yell attending the charge into action was the first indication had of their presence and purpose. The Eries were taken greatly by surprise; nevertheless, although the circumstance served to chill the ardor of their hopes materially, they recoiled not from the odds, but battled on with unabated energy. But the fiery zeal of the youths, who had their virgin laurels to win, as well as the honor and integrity of the Long House to strike for, was an added element in the contest, which even the most stubborn resistance was not equal to. The valiant Sag-a-neh-gis maintained their high reputation well. They fought, they fell, they died, but they would not yield; and it was only over the strewn carcasses of the slain, and through a way hewn wearily out by stroke of tomahawk and knife, that the confederates were able to gain back, foot by foot, the ground which they had lost.

The result of a conflict where personal fortitude, address, and power of endurance were evenly balanced, and where superiority in numerical strength must determine the issue, may be anticipated. When the clash of battle ceased at last, and the wild acclaims of victory pealed from the lips of the exultant Ho-de-no-sau-nee, it was the outburst of a jubilation that could provoke no response; for of all the gallant array that had striven so valiantly for honor and conquest, save here and there a solitary craven who, during the fray, had taken to flight, not a living warrior was left to be moved to mortification or resentment, or to breathe defiance against the conquerors. The

Sag-a-neh-gi, as a name among the nations, was blotted out forever.

As the ancients of the tribes—the broken remnant of the old nation of renown—sit in the sunshine at their cabin-doors, stringing their beads or plaiting their braids for the tawdry trinkets in which they traffic, in these latter degenerate days, such is the tale with which they talk away a summer's hour for the entertainment of idlers that choose to loiter and listen. Let the preliminary details of the tradition meet with what acceptance they may, the crowning fact of the catastrophe is undeniably authentic. The battle between the Eries and the Iroquois took place in or about the year 1654, and resulted, as the narrative sets forth, in the complete extermination of the former. Their broad lands became a possession of the confederates,— the first of a series of acquisitions that were to go on until the empire of the Ho-de-no-sau-nee reached from Carolina to Canada, and from the seashore to the Mississippi.

V.

THE FAITH ON THE PENNSYLVANIA BORDER AND IN THE VALLEYS OF LA BELLE RIVIÈRE.

ALTHOUGH the annihilation of the Eries left the Iroquois in undisputed ownership of the territory, there was no permanent occupation of the upper Ohio valley region for many years afterwards. The labors of the early Jesuit missionaries, therefore, among this people, were limited to their original settlements on the lakes. Twelve years before the date of the defeat of the Eries—that event so remote as to be without a positive history, mummied, as it were, amid the obscurities of traditional times—the Black-Robe had crossed the St. Lawrence, and planted the Cross in the wilds of Western New York. In the summer of that year Father Jogues, together with René Goupel—the "Good René,"—and Ahistari, a converted chief of the Hurons, were captured by a party of Mohawks, on their return from a successful raid into the Canada country. Jogues, after having his finger-nails torn out, his fingers gnawed to the bone, and been forced to run the "narrow path to Paradise," as he terms the gauntlet, was hurried along to one of the nearest villages of his captors. Here he found a scaffold erected, on which were placed a number of Hurons, prisoners like himself, destined apparently for instant execution. Several of these were catechumens, who, in happier days, had received instruction from his lips in the lodges on their native lakes.

Forgetful of his own afflictions, the generous father at once entered upon his priestly duty, offering whatever of spiritual consolation he could impart to the captives, enlightening the ignorant, confessing the faithful, and qualifying the convert for the redeeming rite of baptism. There were those among the doomed on the scaffold who were anxious to undergo this sacramental ceremony, but there was no water at command to meet the want of the occasion. It so happened, fortunately,— providentially, rather, the zealous believer would regard it,—that a savage passing by flung a stalk of green corn on the platform. It was in the morning. The distillations of the night had not wasted as yet under the temperate warmth of the hour, and from the dews that clung to the long blades of the maize the eager servant of Jesus gathered the precious drops that served his purpose, and the saving rite was accomplished. The prisoners, for the time being, however, were reprieved,—all except the natives Ahasistari, Paul, and Stephen, who, with the cruelties common in such cases, were put to death, one in each of the three towns of the tribe through which they passed. René Goupel, who, at liberty or in bonds, never failed in God's service when opportunity offered, for having attempted to make the sign of a cross on the brow of a child, was cleft through the skull with a tomahawk, near the village of Andagoran. Jogues himself, although through repeated miraculous escapes, and at the cost of cruel suffering, escaped the fate of his companions. Kept under strict surveillance as a prisoner, he was nevertheless, after awhile, allowed the freedom of the villages, where he employed himself contributing to the spiritual comfort of the Huron captives, and the instruction, where it was tolerated, of their savage masters. As the fruits of his labor during the few months of his forced sojourn among the Mohawks, he reckons in his record of the service "about seventy baptisms, besides many confessions." Having received friendly warning, at length, that the Mohawks, exasperated by a late defeat before Fort Richelieu, had determined to revenge themselves by the sacrifice of his life, he managed to effect his escape into the Dutch settlements on the Hudson.

In 1646, having in the mean time sailed for Europe, visited Rome, and been honored by Pope Innocent XI., because of the tortures he had undergone, with the title of Martyr, Jogues was appointed by the Superior to revisit the scene of his captivity and establish a mission there among the Mohawks. To cross the St. Lawrence, then, was to venture into the jaws of death. But he upon whom the agents of hell had done their cruelest already —the single living Martyr of all the dead—was not to be deterred from the mission. "*Ibo*," said he, as he wrapped his dark gown about him, kissed his crucifix, and started on his journey,—"*Ibo—et non redibo!*" He went, and he never returned.

John Lalande, a Frenchman, attended the doomed father when he started. After having proceeded some distance on their way, they encountered a band of savages, painted and clad in the colors and costume of war, by whom they were seized, bound, and conducted to Gandawague, a Mohawk village on the Caughnawaga. In a conference which was held, after their arrival there, a division arose as to the disposition that should be made of the prisoners,—some of the clans advising their release, the rest insisting upon their execution. While the council deliberated—it was in the evening—one of its members withdrew, and, under pretense of hospitality, invited the prisoners to his cabin. As they were about to enter, a savage, concealed behind the door, sprang out, and, with his tomahawk, cleft the skull of the missionary. Lalande shared the fate of his distinguished companion.

Seven years after the unhappy adventure of Jogues, John Le Moyne took up the cross, and, undismayed by the cruel fate of his predecessor, followed into the field left unoccupied by the death of the Martyr. Arrived at Onondaga, he consented, at the invitation of some of the Iroquois, backed by the entreaties of the Huron captives detained there, to open a mission at that town. This settlement was discovered to be peculiarly desirable, as it afforded a larger scope to his influence than could be commanded at any other point, in that it was discovered to be the central capital of the Long House, where the representatives of the Nations were accustomed to assemble in their annual councils, and whence, consequently, radiated, to a controlling extent, the influences, moral and political, which moulded the convictions and fashioned the character of the common population of the confederacy.

The early labors of Le Moyne were promisingly successful, especially among the Hurons, who, associating the rites of worship with the memories of the homes from which they had been torn, were all the more favorably inclined to its observances in their captivity. Nor was their example lost upon the Iroquois.

The good priest had served but a few months at his post when the news—the great news, heralded, according to the legend, by the captive Seneca woman—of the advance of the Eries was blazed abroad from fire to fire throughout the tribes of the Nation. Of the warriors who gathered at the call of the council to meet the invasion, was one, an Onondaga chief, Achiongeras, a man excellent in reputation among the captains of the clans. On the eve of his departure he called on the Black-Robe, pictured to him the perils he was about to encounter, declared that his courage must fail him if not inspired by brighter assurances for the future than the superstitions of heathenism afforded, and implored that he might be received into the confession and under the protection of the faith of the Prayer. Persuaded, after due investigation, that his convictions were genuine and sincere, Le Moyne led him to the water, and, by the mystical rite of the church, admitted him into its communion. The converted chief, with the dews of baptism yet damp on his brow, then started on his march, and, at the head of his savage legion, was soon forth from the village and away on the warpath.

The opposing forces came together. The battle waged long and fiercely, and the lines of the Iroquois were slowly but steadily giving way before the enemy, when Achiongeras, whose intrepid bearing had made him conspicuous in the fight, suddenly paused and beckoned to the braves who supported him. They gathered about him at the signal. Dropping upon his knee, the Christian chief lifted his crimsoned hands towards heaven, the group of assembled clansmen imitating the action, when with a solemn vow they unitedly plighted their faith, and that of their people, to the God of the Prayer would He vouchsafe them rescue in this crisis of their peril. The vow was honored. Animated afresh, as by a divine inspiration, the wavering band regained its footing, won back its lost advantage, and, profiting by the recovery, paused not until the strife was over, and the field triumphantly, overwhelmingly won.

Achiongeras and his companions were true to their pledge. After the return of the victorious army, a general council was called, when, by solemn decree, Christianity was established in the capital of the confederacy. The French were invited over to plant a settlement. Fathers Menard, Dablon, Broar, and Boursier, under lead of the Superior of the mission, assumed the direction of the enterprise. The party, attended by a numerous escort of savages, launched their fleet of canoes at Quebec, ascended the St. Lawrence, with the banner of the Cross waving its silken folds in the gentle May-breeze at its head, and amid the roar of cannon, and the ringing cheers of waiting multitudes, landed, after a tedious but prosperous voyage, on the shores of Onondaga, where, after consummating the trifling arrangements necessary for their own temporary shelter, they proceeded directly to the erection of a house of worship. And so arose the great central Mission of St. Mary's of Ga-nun-ta-a.

Among the branches of this chief station, established as they were in each of the tribal districts of the Ho-de-no-sau-nee, and through which the Sacred Mysteries, to the enlightenment of all, and the happy conversion of thousands, were made to reach the ears of the people, was the one organized by Father Chaumonot, at Gandagare, among the

Senecas. This worthy pioneer labored diligently at his post, and was permitted to rejoice, as one of the first fruits of his toil, in the conversion of Annontenritaoui, the head chief of his tribe. Frenin, Allouez, Raffeix, Pierron, Garnier, and others, followed soon after, all exerting themselves in the duties of their office so profitably, that when, some years after, the English asserted their claim to the region, and the Jesuits were forced to abandon the ground, they left upwards of five hundred baptized natives, as conservators of the Faith, behind them.

When the Senecas, therefore, began to occupy the lands along the western valleys left vacant by the expulsion of their enemies, although unattended by the Black-Robes, they went not out in ignorance of the saving belief of the Prayer. They carried the Cross with them, and the name of Jesus was not strange in the ears of the people whose wigwams soon dotted the valley of the Alleghany, and whose tents were pitched down by the shores of the Beautiful River. The old chief Shekellamy, of the Cayugas, father of Tah-gah-jute, renowned under the more familiar name of Logan, had knelt in confession, and taken his vows, at the altar of God. Anastasius was in the communion of the church,—he, the chieftain of Loretto, who led the Indians from the fort at De-un-da-ga,—old Fort Duquesne,—and was mainly instrumental in the defeat of Braddock on the Monongahela.

By the middle of the eighteenth century, when

the early white traders began to extend their commerce beyond the mountains, numerous settlements were found at different localities on the Ohio, composed, besides the Iroquois, but subject to them, of the Shawanese from Florida, and Delawares immigrated from Eastern Pennsylvania. The first prophet from abroad to lift up his voice in this new wilderness was Denis Baron, a Recollect, who had come to serve as chaplain to the French soldiery at the occupation of Fort Duquesne, or the "Fort of the Assumption," by which title it appears to have been dedicated on the first recurrence of the festival of that name after the arrival of the troops. The services of Father Baron were not limited to the garrison. Free intercourse was allowed with the natives, the soldiers, excepting such as were on duty, passing the greater portion of their time in and about the bark cabins which they had built for themselves outside the fortification. By this means the good priest was enabled to mingle with the savages of the neighborhood; as the result of which quite a number of conversions, not only among the Indians, but of the whites, seized in their wars and held as captives, are reported in his Register, forwarded to the Superior at Quebec. But the operations of the chaplain, and the projects which may have been entertained with regard to a special spiritual occupation of the ground, were cut short through the abandonment, by the French, of the fort in 1758, their surrender of the Ohio valley possessions in dispute, and retirement back into their own proper provinces beyond the St. Lawrence. For nearly thirty years subsequently the Faith was left without an advocate on the frontier.

The Abbé Benedict Joseph Flaget was the earliest apostle, afterwards, to unfurl the standard of the Cross in Western Pennsylvania. He spent several months, in 1792, at Pittsburg, administering to the spiritual necessities of the settlers, and of the soldiers, collected there under General Wayne, just then on the eve of his memorable march against the Indians. But he who was destined to be the Pioneer of the Faith in this newly-developing quarter of American civilization, had not yet quite appeared.

Demetrius Augustine Gallitzin, begotten in a line of noble descent, was borne at the Hague, on the 22d of December, 1770. His father was the ambassador representing Russia in Holland: his mother, Amelia, Countess of Schmettan,—a German family of high distinction. The young prince received his training under the tutelage of Voltaire, an intimate personal friend of his father's;—a training conformable, of course, to the skeptical creed of that eminent philosopher. But maturer reflection brought with it purer convictions: the heresies of deism were discarded, and the youthful pupil in unbelief became the convert of Christianity. When seventeen years of age, he connected himself with the Catholic Church. In 1792, accompanied by his tutor, the Rev. Mr. Brosius, he came to America, entered the Sulpitian Seminary at Baltimore, completed his studies at that institution, and three years afterwards was admitted into the priesthood, —the second theological student of his faith to undergo ordination in the United States. For a few years subsequently, after he had taken orders, his labors were confined to Cumberland, Hagerstown, Chambersburg, Path Valley, and other points in Pennsylvania. At length he conceived the project of penetrating farther towards the border, and choosing out a suitable locality, with a view to establishing a colony, and through this means, of giving rise to a hallowed influence whose beneficial force might be felt in the modeling of society out of the heterogeneous population newly planted in the young settlements of the West. Accordingly he selected a site, in an uninhabited waste on the Alleghany Mountains, erected a rude cabin for his own shelter, and a log chapel for the accommodation of such straggling worshipers as Providence might throw in his way. He then purchased large tracts of land, which he divided into farms, and sold at nominal rates, or gave gratuitously to settlers willing to share the chances of the future with him, and so began his work.

By his adoption of the Catholic faith the young priest had forfeited all title to his father's property. His sister, the Princess Anne Gallitzin, who, after his disfranchisement, became sole inheritress of the estate, lent a partial aid to her brother, by which he was enabled to meet, to some extent, the expenses of his enterprise; but her contributions ceased, presently, upon her marriage, and Demetrius was, thenceforward, left to his own resources. But his misfortunes were not permitted to cripple his industry. Forests were felled, lands were cleared, acres were tilled, cottages were built, and soon the mountain wilderness, stripped of its savage features, began to display the cheerier view of field upon field greenly grown, or goldenly ripened,—beautiful in promise and rich in reward,—to crown the labor of the husbandmen. Meanwhile the indefatigable missionary neglected not the more important obligations of his office. From home to home did he journey, from neighborhood to neighborhood, exercising his deeds of charity, imparting his lessons of religious instruction, until the name of Father Smith—the humble title which, in lieu of the more illustrious designation, he saw fit to assume—was known, respected, and revered in every household on the border.

Gallitzin began his mission in 1799, with, perhaps, a dozen men of his faith scattered about through the mountain, and no other sanctuary, save the little oratory of Father Flaget, in all the West, than the one of logs thirty feet long, which he himself had reared. He lived to see the village of Loretto, which he had founded, grow into a populous and flourishing town; to find the Faith, whose standard he had been the first to restore since its going down amid the ruins of Fort Duquesne, established upon a footing from which no revolution of time or circumstance was ever afterwards to displace it; to witness new chapels spring up, one by one, till every hamlet almost, dotting the lowlands down upon which he looked, had its spire; to behold his mission prevail, until the apostolic number of his original followers had increased and multiplied a thousandfold; till hospitals and houses of industry, by the liberal charities of his people, were erected; and till boarding-schools, free-schools, orphan asylums, and theological colleges were institutions common throughout the land, as were the necessities which called them into existence. He died at Loretto in 1840.

Such were the early missionaries, by whose instrumentality the light of Revelation was made to shed its first glories in the wilderness and on the border. Should it be charged, as illiberal antagonists have charged, that the labors which were spent were productive of but temporary and doubtful results, and that relapses into their original superstitions were apt to overtake the converts as soon as relieved of the protecting presence of their teachers, it ought to be borne in mind that the material to be operated upon was crude as savage imperfection could make it,—incapable of the impressions possible to a condition of higher sensibility and refinement,—and that the misfortune was not a fault inherent in the creed, or chargeable against the ministers, and their modes of its interpretation. But the imputation is not admitted by the religionists against whom it is leveled. They not only deny the apostacy alleged, but claim for their proselytes a distinguishing superiority over all the native populations, pagan or heretical, besides. If challenged to the proof, they refer to the evidence of Protestant witnesses,—men and women of popular note, and competent from personal observation to testify of the facts. They point to Bishop Fenwick, who, of later date, found a whole tribe of Passamaquoddies true to their Christian allegiance, and whom he commendingly notes as "a living monument of the apostolic labors of the Jesuits." They allude to Sir George Simpson, who relates how the Chippewas preserved their faith, unsustained by the aid of a priest, through the years of half a century. They quote from Mr. Buckingham, who, speaking of the Hurons, says: "They are faithful Catholics, and are said to fulfill their religious duties in the most exemplary manner, being much more improved by their commerce with the whites than the Indian tribes who have first come into contact with Protestants usually are." They repeat the Rev. Dr. Morse, who writes of the Indians in Western

Michigan, at *l'Arbre Croche*, "the seat for sixty years or more of a Jesuit mission," that they "are much in advance, in point of improvement, in appearance, and in manners, of all the Indians whom I visited." They cite the observation of Mrs. Jameson, who, in the way of a contrast not flattering to creedists of different denomination, speaks of the people of a tribe whom she visited, as having "heard them sing Mass with every demonstration of decency and piety;" and the corroboration of Harriet Martineau, expressed generally with regard to the nations of the Northwest, that "one thing is most visible, certain, and undeniable, that the Roman Catholic converts are in appearance, dress, intelligence, industry, and general civilization, superior to all others." But there is a more striking, because more recent, instance of the indisputable blessings accruing from the labors of the Black-Robes among the savages, to which they refer with special satisfaction, because so well attested by clouds of living witnesses. The Chopunnish, or Nez-Percés, noted, long ago, as a selfish, avaricious, miserly, root-eating tribe, inhabiting the distant regions of Oregon and Idaho, were visited many years since by the Catholic missionary, who has maintained a permanent occupation of the ground ever since,—uninterfered with, of course, in a quarter, until within a twelvemonth or so ago,* so remote and isolated from

---

* This article was written in 1868.

civilized life, by ministers of any other persuasion. This nation has been brought under the control of Christian influence,—has made rapid progress towards refinement, is active in the peaceful pursuits of industry, and, in marked contrast with surrounding tribes, stands noted for the orderly behavior, sobriety, purity, and intelligence of its people.

To whom it is due let honor be accredited,—not grudgingly and reluctantly, but with a hearty will, and abundantly. If the Jesuit, defiant of perils, seen and unseen,—perils that threatened death, and visited it, in every imaginable form of terror, and through every conceivable shape of torture,—dared to prosecute the errand appointed for him, over immeasurable leagues of dreary, desolate distance, and by pathless ways, through solitudes, vast, waste, and wild, as solitudes might only be that had been left untenanted and untraversed, save by roving beasts and crawling reptiles, since God spoke them into being; if he followed his pilgrimage patiently and hardily, in despite of summer's heat, of winter's cold, of storm, of night, through sickness as it fell, and want, and famine; and all,—Heaven's pity on him!—all *alone;* is he to be denied of his glory on the uncharitable plea that he was driven to the task under sentence of his Superior, and as constrained by the obligation of the oath of his office; or that he was tempted to the sacrifice by a mad zeal for the extension of the temporal authority of the church, and for the aggrandizement, especially, of his own ecclesiastical order? If the formulary of his profession —not his *creed*, because the creed of all Christ's followers is one—sanctions a scheme of views and practices not in accordance with the notions and customs of the sects which repudiate him, must the disciple of Loyola, therefore, be esteemed as a vessel of dishonor, and disowned as a false prophet among God's people?

Old Menard hazards his life for the love of Jesus, traveling and tarrying, as duty bids, on the water and on the land; yet, in his frail canoe, amid the tempests of the one, or under his arbor of fir-branches, exposed to the bitterest of midwinter severities, on the other, he is to be found, at the dawn and decline of each day, bent in devotion, repeating "Our Father which art in heaven," and closing the invocation with the supplicatory chant to the Virgin, "*Mater amata intemerata, Ora, ora pro nobis!*"—Is the hymn a sacrilege?

Marquette lies, throbbing his life away, on the shore of Lake Michigan. He addresses his intercessory prayer to the Mother of his Master, and then, as the last act of his life, raises the Cross to his lips and kisses it, in sweet regard for Him whose sacrifice it typifies. Was that an idolatry for the soul to shudder at?

A poor Huron captive is burning to death at the stake, when Father Jogues, himself a prisoner, under the pretended purpose of proffering the victim a taste of water to cool his parched tongue, rushes into the flames, and administers to him, covertly, the sacrament of baptism. Did the Recording Angel write down the false pretense as a sin of special enormity,—one that, measured by the standard of a strict morality, should appear in startling judgment against the offender in the last day?

He who has laid to heart, dutifully, the admonitions of inspiration, seeks not to examine too inquiringly into the faults of a brother. He remembers the lesson of the Mote and the Beam; and, above all, forgets not that the graces which constitute the glory of Christian character are Faith, Hope, and Charity, and that "the greatest of these is Charity."

THE MORAVIAN.

THE MORAVIAN.

I.

THE MORAVIANS IN EASTERN PENNSYLVANIA.

DRIVEN from his dominions by the Elector of Saxony, a community of Moravians—or, as they distinguish themselves, *Unitas Fratrum*, or *United Brethren*,—residing in Berthelsdorf, a village of Upper Lusatia, under the patronage of Count Zinzendorf, and to carry out a project which they had already contemplated, emigrated, in 1734, to America. They reached their destination, after a prosperous voyage, in the spring of the year following, settling themselves in Savannah, in the State of Georgia. The object of their undertaking was to introduce the gospel to the Indians of the New World. About five miles from Savannah, in the river of that name, is an island, which, at the time, was occupied by quite a community of Creek Indians. Among these they established themselves, opening schools for the children, and proclaiming the "Great Word," day after day, to the people. They were not allowed, however, to prosecute their labors long enough to reap any substantial reward. In consequence of a disagreement with the provincial government, growing out of a refusal to take up arms against the Spaniards in their attempts to expel the English from Georgia, the Brethren left the region, looking towards the north for the seat of a new settlement.

Induced by favorable representations, they moved into Pennsylvania, where, attracted by the inviting meadows which border its rivers, they planted the little colonies—grown into pleasant and prosperous towns since—of Bethlehem and Nazareth. These towns were made the central seat of the Brotherhood, where, dwelling together in amiable companionship, its members could carry out among themselves the usages, economical and social, as well as religious, peculiar to their creed, and whence they could, at the same time, send forth their evangelists to "testify the gospel of the grace of God" to the unenlightened natives. The resident members of the Society, towards this grand aim, were covenanted through their charities, their contributions, and by every means which arising exigencies might invite, and which it was possible to command, to lend themselves to the support of the missionaries. The missionaries, on their part, were to conform to certain rules which had been suggested by Count Zinzendorf and approved by common concurrence of the Brotherhood,—rules, by the way, very nearly of a type with those to which the Jesuits had been pledged, and conformably with which they had served in their earlier operations among the tribes. They were to submit themselves to the wise direction and guidance of God in all circumstances; to seek to preserve liberty of conscience; to avoid all religious disputes; to preach the gospel of Jesus Christ, and to endeavor as much as possible to earn their own bread. In a strange land, with the Puritan to beard them on the Border, and the Pagan to persecute them in the Wilderness, and with uncultivated wastes to serve in, where sustenance was meagre and hard to come by, the task demanded and the terms imposed were of no contemptible consideration. But they were men willing always, and bold, to meet their responsibilities.

Under the enterprise of Brother Christian Henry Rauch, a mission was opened and a community established in Shekomeko, a Mohican village, twenty-five miles east of the Hudson River and near the Connecticut border. Through his instrumentality, three of the natives, Shabash, Seim, and Kiop, were converted and baptized, under the names respectively of Abraham, Isaac, and Jacob, into the church,—the three "firstlings" of the Faith in America. Rauch was joined afterwards by Martin Mack, Gottlob Buettner, Frederick Post and others, whose common field of operations, with Shekomeko as the centre, extended from Pachgatgoch in Connecticut, to Albany, New York, on the north, and Shomokin and Wajomick on the Susquehanna, in the west, embracing various villages of the Mohican, Shawanese, and Delaware Indians. The missionaries encountered serious opposition in their work. Post, in company with David Zeisberger, made a tour through Northern New York among the Iroquois. As the Six Nations were suspected of cherishing a sympathy for the French, the object of Post and his associate's visit was set down as a political one, and on the charge that they were secretly co-operating with the confederacy to bring about an alliance with the enemy, they were arrested at Albany, brought to New York and cast into prison. Although discharged, after a confinement of six weeks, by an act of Assembly, they were prohibited from preaching, and ordered to leave the State. In Connecticut they were accused of papistical proclivities, and had to encounter such a pressure of Puritanic resistance on the ridiculous charge, that they were constrained to desist from their labors. After an existence of some four years, the mission of Shekomeko was abandoned, the few Christian Mohicans composing its congregation retiring with their teachers to the friendly shelters of the Moravians at Bethlehem. Here, a short distance from the town, for their temporary accommodation, the modest hamlet of Friedenshütten, or the Tents of Peace, was built on the Susquehanna River.

Thus far the operations of the Brethren had been moderately, but promisingly, successful. Bands of converts were to be found, here and there, throughout the entire range over which the journeyings of the missionaries had extended. To bring these scattered groups together, the more effectually thereby to extend a salutary supervision over their spiritual as well as worldly interests, lands were bought on the Mahanoy, to which they were invited, and whither they repaired. The fertile acres of the purchase were fenced off into fields for cultivation, all except a small portion, which was set apart as a seat for the dwellings of the settlers. A church was built in the heart of this reserve. Clusters of cottages were planted along the rising grounds on one side adjoining, and the homestead of the missionary, and the consecrated plot, with its narrower abodes for those who, once housed, were to know thereafter no change of habitation, on the other. And so arose, in the valley of the river, the settlement of Gnadenhütten,—the happy village of the Tents of Grace.

The converts gathered at Gnadenhütten, besides the Mohican families flitted from Shekomeko, were chiefly Delawares. With the abandonment of the superstitions of their fathers, they had quit their vagrant courses and were settled into a community soon noted for the thrift, the exemplary habits, and the well-regulated behavior of its people. With the dawn of each day, before assuming their allotted labors, and at its decline, when toils were ended, they might have been seen tracing their way to the sanctuary of the village, there to present their stated offerings of worship at its altar. Psalms of praise saluted the morning; hymns of thanksgiving ascended in the evening; voices were lifted in prayer, and lessons of instruction declared, —Christian Rauch officiating, or Martin Mack, the first commissioned to administer the Word and the Sacraments among the converts. But the peace of the settlement, propitiously as it opened, was not to remain long undisturbed.

In the active hostilities which opened in 1755 between the French and English, although they declined taking any part, the Moravians had to bear their full share of the resulting distresses. Many of the converts, too easily seduced from the paths of peace when the war-trail offered its more congenial attractions, deserted the Tents of Grace and betook them to the camps of the unbaptized insurgents, who, espousing the cause of the former of the belligerents, had taken up arms against the latter. The rising of the savages created intense alarm throughout the settlements. After the first act of barbarous warfare, which consisted in the burning of several houses not far from Shomokin, and the massacre of their inmates, the threatened population took to flight, scattering in the deeper wildernesses towards the mountains on the one hand, and with their faces seaward on the other, wherever a way of escape seemed to offer from the perils by which they were surrounded. The

Brethren in Bethlehem and Gnadenhütten alone, of all whose safety was menaced, refused to forsake their homes. "The peace of God comforted them, and preserved their hearts from fear and despair." The pagan Shawanese—much the larger portion of the tribe—employed every inducement to win over the residue of their clansmen, who still maintained a fidelity to the Moravians, but without success. Death was threatened if refusal were persisted in, but the loyal adherents were not to be moved. The mission-house on the Mahanoy was attacked and set on fire, eleven of the Brethren and Sisters perishing in the flames. The visitation was borne by the sufferers with a spirit of martyrly fortitude. Steadfastly they maintained their place, comforting and sustaining each other as they might, and looking to God as their refuge in the dark times of their affliction. "O Lord, we beseech Thee," was the burden of their daily prayer, "save Thou us, that all may know that Thou art the Lord, even Thou only."

Through four years, down to the time of the abandonment of Fort Duquesne and the retirement of the French to their own provinces, were these faithful saints forced to endure the persecutions of their relentless enemies. Meanwhile the task to which they were dedicated was not forgotten, nor the zeal diminished with which it was pursued. The Indian villages along the waters of the Delaware, the Lehigh, and the Susquehanna were visited. The missions of Friedenshütten and Tschechschequannink on the last-mentioned river were established, while ministers, such as Grube, and Mack, and Roesler, and Kiefer, were sent abroad among the settlements to declare the Word, wherever Christians were to be comforted, or heathen to hear and be reclaimed; and the work of the Lord went on and prospered in their hands. The emigration of the main body of the Delawares and Shawanese to the West, shortly before, and during the war, and the reports of the region which found their way back to Bethlehem, led the Brethren to look with special interest in that direction.

Christian Frederick Post has been mentioned in connection with the operations of the Moravians in Eastern Pennsylvania. He was a joiner by trade, but a man of more than ordinary intelligence, and, being animated with a lively religious zeal, soon abandoned his humble calling, and, qualifying himself for the office, became a minister of the Faith,—one of the most enterprising and efficient among his co-laborers of the Brotherhood. By reason of his marriage to a native, although an excellent Christian woman, he was deprived of his right to be regarded as a missionary of the Society. Yet the disfranchisement was rather technical than real, for, while not officially acknowledged, his priestly services were neither forbidden nor disowned by his associates. In 1758, by appointment of the Governor of Pennsylvania, he visited, on two occasions, the tribes settled in the Ohio Valley; the object of the undertaking being to counteract the mischievous influence of the French, and to insure, if possible, the establishment of amicable relations between that doubtful people and the English. Success attended his embassy. The savages refused to rally to their support, and the consequence was that, as General Forbes approached soon after with his army, the garrison of Fort Duquesne deserted their stronghold without the offer of a blow in its defense. Again, in 1761, Post repeated his visit; not, on this occasion, in the capacity of a political envoy, but as an ambassador of the gospel. He prosecuted his journey into the interior until he reached the wigwams of the Shawanese and Hurons on the Muskingum River.

These adventures of the distinguished Moravian were not achieved without their attending risks and trials. His route led through an unexplored wilderness. Bands of savages infested the woods, and the red stakes, used to fasten prisoners to for security during the halts of a march, found here and there driven into the ground, and the fresh scalps stretched on hoops and hung on bushes by the wayside to dry, plainly indicated that they were abroad with no innocent intention. His food consisted of such provision as the chances of each day, out of the spare resources of the forest, afforded; while as to shelter, for thirty-one nights, as the journal of one of his expeditions intimates, he lay in the woods with the heavens for his covering, and the dew settling so penetratingly on him that it "pinched close to the skin." But "the Lord preserved him through all the dangers and difficulties" of the way, and brought him, "under a thick, heavy, and dark cloud," safely to its termination. Foremost of "evangelical" apostles in those distant wilds, he nevertheless discovered that he had been anticipated, and that the tidings of the Cross were not unknown on the Muskingum, although the Jesuit fathers,—Jogues, perhaps, or Gravier, or Mermet,—to whom the enlightened were indebted for the story, were dust and ashes generations ago.

Post requested, and obtained, permission of the Indians to establish a mission among them; built a house,—the first one erected in the State of Ohio,—went back to Bethlehem for an assistant, and early in the year following returned with John Heckewelder, and commenced his religious labors at the new station. Before his plans were fairly entered upon, dissatisfactions sprang up, which were to culminate in the war of 1763; the Indians began to show violence, and the post was abandoned.

But the experiment of the Christian pioneer, if a failure in itself, was not without its beneficial results. His explorations satisfied the Brethren that an inviting field offered beyond the Alleghanies for the display of missionary enterprise. Mingos and

Shawanese, Tuscaroras and Hurons, had their villages or scattered lodges dotting the plains and water-courses from *Alleghene*—for so the *country* up towards its source, and bordering on the stream of that name, then known as the Ohio, was designated—to the levels of Sandusky, and from the Onenge River, or Venango, to the Muskingum. There, too, were to be found the towns of the emigrated Delawares,—the tribe nearest their hearts as the one among whose people they had dwelt, and out of which the principal fruits of their labor had been gathered. The remnant of that nation, still lingering in the original neighborhood, was rapidly diminishing. English settlers were intruding with fast strides on their patrimonies. The Iroquois, proud and unfeeling masters, had found it serviceable to their own aims to aid in these aggressions, which they did with a no doubtful or hesitating interference. "We conquered you," they had arrogantly said through their messenger, Paxnous, an old chief of the Shawanese, "and made women of you. Therefore we charge you to fall back immediately. Don't deliberate, but remove away, or the Great Council will come and clean your ears with a red-hot iron." The unhappy Lenni-Lenapes had not dared to dispute the order, and soon the places that knew them were to know them no more. The Moravians would not desert them. The Tents of Grace must be pitched anew—so they determined—in the far wilderness whither the exiles had wandered, and the messages of Peace must be borne to the shores of the rivers where their cabins were planted.

II.

THE "PLACE OF HOGS" ON THE UPPER ALLEGHANY.

THE morning service had been held in the chapel at Friedenshütten. The prayers of the congregation had been offered with unusual solemnity; the voices of the worshipers had mingled in hymns of adoration with more than common fervor, and with the sentence of the benediction still lingering in their ears, the Brethren were gathered in the open space that lay under the shadow of their sanctuary, to bid God-speed to one of their number about to leave them on a distant, arduous, and perilous journey. David Zeisberger had been a conspicuous actor in all the leading enterprises of the Society since the date of its organization at Bethlehem. He had penetrated the territories of the tribes of the East, even to the cabins of the Iroquois at Onondaga. He had prayed in their wigwams; he had preached in their villages. He had organized new circles of believers, gathered in to strengthen the bands of the old, or associated apart and made the centres of new settlements. Enterprising, intrepid, indefatigable, zealous,—the Paul among the Apostles of the Unity,—if the Good Cause called for extraordinary undertaking in any newly-chosen line of action, he was looked to by the congregation as the champion for the duty. When the project of a mission in the West was resolved upon, therefore, his appointment to see it carried into effect followed as a matter of course; and on the 30th of September, 1767, amid the solemn ceremonials of worship, the blessings and the sad farewells of his people, accompanied by two native converts, Anthony, and John Papunhank, he took his departure from Friedenshütten.

The familiar scenes of the Susquehanna were soon lost to the view of the Moravian, as he penetrated the forests through which his tortuous and difficult way conducted. There was no defined route to guide his progress. The paths which led through the wilds, traced there by the herds that roamed their recesses and the tawny hunters that made prey of them, were devious and uncertain. Obstacles, seemingly insurmountable, interposed to impede his advance. Rivers intercepted his course; marshes lay before him, whose miry soil at every step sank under his feet; dense thickets had to be pierced, and great plains to be traversed, thick with rank grasses that lifted their closely-clustering spears high above his head. Day after day he toiled laboriously on, to be rewarded at night with such rest as, stretched on the bare ground and wrapped in his blanket, he might best secure, under the pouring rain that fell almost incessantly during the weeks of his travel. But the indomitable missionary persevered. On the 16th of October he reached the Alleghany. The villages of Goschgoschuenk were before him; the Beautiful Valley was under his feet, and his journey was ended.

Zeisberger found the Indians at the Place of Hogs,—as the true interpretation of the name makes it, not inappropriately,—ignorant, depraved, and heathenish; utterly given over to shameful and diabolical superstitions. "Satan," he says, in his report, "has here his great power; he even seems to have established his throne in this place." The novelty of the Moravian worship, however, proved attractive, and the religious exercises held at his lodge were largely attended. The first, and, indeed, the only one of his hearers, during this preparatory visit, to become "powerfully awakened," was a blind old chief, Allemewi, of the Delawares, who from the day of his arrival had manifested a friendly interest in the missionary and in his work. Zeisberger, after a short stay, went back to Bethlehem, but, in May of the next year, returned again, bringing with him an assistant brother, Gottlob Senseman, together with three families of native converts from Friedenshütten, and, building a log cabin at the outskirts of the central village of the three which constituted the town of Goschgoschuenk, established himself in the place. Fairly domiciled in his new home, the missionary entered, without delay, on his work. Chapel services were instituted, and observed daily. "Preaching" was held at noon; morning and evening meetings were assembled, where prayers were offered, and hymns, the composition of the Brother himself, sung in their own language to his Delaware hearers. The savages, in their best of holiday finery, with their faces freshly painted in black and vermilion, and their heads garnished with fox-tails and tufts of feathers, attended in crowds and participated in the exercises with gravity and decorum. For some time these services were allowed to go on without interruption or hinderance. Interest began to awaken in the hearts of the people, and the Brethren were comforted with the prospect of profitable results soon to be realized from their efforts. But bitter disappointments were in reserve for them.

The captains of the tribe, a cabalistic order, in one sense, professing the knowledge of certain secret, supernatural arts,—arts by which the populace were persuaded that waters were poisoned and sickness engendered in the camps of their enemies, and to which the initiated were indebted for their eminent influence,—apprehensive that the conversion of any one of their class to the new doctrine would lead to a confession of the deceit by which their practices were accomplished, began, upon the first symptoms of success, to open their batteries of attack against the missionaries. Converts, it was charged, were enticed into the communion to be made slaves of, and the deceived would learn, to their grief, that baptism was the seal of perpetual bondage. The King of England, it was declared, had written letters, warning against the Brethren as emissaries of the devil, who would lead their dupes straight to hell. The inspired teachers, the sorcerers, and the medicine-men were called to the rescue.

"Come to Jesus, who bled and died for you," Zeisberger would affectionately exhort. "Call on Him for mercy, that He may deliver you from the power of Satan."

"I have been intimately acquainted with Jesus for some time," Wangomen, a defender of his faith, would rejoin; "I have enjoyed a familiar intercourse, indeed, with Him these many years, and He never told me that He had become a man, or that He had shed any of his blood."

Faith and repentance, as specifics for spiritual purification, were ridiculed as chimerical and preposterous. If the formule of the Psalmist—"Purge me with hyssop"—had been recommended, cavil might have been hushed, because the practice of their own doctors of divinity could not consistently have repudiated that herb, when themselves were accustomed to prescribe jalap and ipecacuanha for the same purpose.

The old women of the villages were incited to join in the general outcry. Because of the strange doctrines, they said, the worms were destroying the corn in the fields; the deer were retreating affrighted from the woods; the trees were refusing their fruits, and henceforth they might look for chestnuts and bilberries in vain. Orators from other towns came in, offering their eloquence on behalf of the opposition. "Cousins," said one of them, a Seneca chief of Zoneschio, "I perceive that a Black-Robe has come among you. This man will seduce you, and make you forsake your old customs and manner of living, if you attend to him. I advise you not to hear him, but to send him away. If you do not, you may find him, some day, lying dead by the wayside." The converts were called, contemptuously, *Sunday Indians*, and insulted with the degrading epithet of *Shwonnaks*, or White-folks. As of their own race, and apostates besides from the faith of their fathers, these unhappy ones were made the special objects of the malice of their enemies. The abuse with which they were visited was soon followed by violence, till at length, driven forcibly from their cabins, they were compelled to fly for protection to the lodge of the missionaries.

The blind chief, Allemewi, was the only friend the Brethren could rely on, outside of their communion. He shared with them in their care of the persecuted, and, at the same time, exerted himself to appease the excitement of the populace. But his efforts were unavailing. The lives of the ministers were threatened. It was proposed that they should be stoned, or murdered, and cast into the river. Two of the savages were covenanted to see to the execution of the design, but, perhaps restrained by superstitious dread, when the hour came to administer the stroke, their hearts failed them, and they retired abashed from the presence of their intended victims. Other conspiracies were formed to carry out the same murderous intention, so that, to guard against assassination, an armed watch had to be kept up nightly about the house of the Moravians. It was finally deemed expedient to abandon the station. Accordingly, Zeisberger and his colleague, with their handful of adherents, withdrew, retiring to the town of Lawunakhannek, some fifteen miles below, and on the opposite side of the river.

This forced desertion of Goschgoschuenk was a grand achievement for the captains, the sorcerers, and the women. Wangomen, inflated with the idea that he had been a conspicuous instrument in the affair, was particularly jubilant. As it was in the line of his profession, he took to the vacated pulpit of the chapel himself at once, but having unfortunately yielded to a besetting weakness, and giving drunken utterance to doctrine so vile and abominable as even to offend the ears of his not ever-fastidious congregation, he was dragged from his place and summarily cast out of the sanctuary. Glikkikan, captain, warrior, counselor, and speaker of Pakanke, the Delaware chief resident in Kaskaskunk, seems to have conceived that a mistake was made in the management of matters, and that the case of the missionaries might have been settled up by force of argument far more satisfactorily than by process of violence. He had finished the business for the Black-Robes in Canada in that way, and did not presume that the little man from Bethlehem was ribbed with tougher metal, that he could long resist the penetration of his logic and eloquence. He decided, even yet, to make the attempt, and invited quite a party of his townsmen to accompany him to Lawunakhannek and witness the controversy. Conscious though he was of his own power, he did not think it prudent to undervalue that of his antagonist, and prepared himself accordingly; well considering beforehand what to say, in order the more pointedly and effectually to confound the Moravian. But the counselor had undertaken more than he could manage. The evidence of the Truth, through the lips of the Brethren, fell on him with irresistible persuasion. He acknowledged the weakness of his cause, admitted its errors, and on his return to Kaskaskunk not only confessed his discomfiture, but nobly indorsed the new Faith, and urged the acceptance of the gospel on the people.

Affairs began to wear a more promising aspect. The uncomplaining temper of the missionaries, their never-failing patience under whatever visitation of wrong or violence, commanded, at length, the forbearance of the savages, and they were permitted the undisturbed enjoyment of all desirable social and religious privileges. Comfortable houses were built in lieu of the rude hunting-huts which had first afforded them shelter. A chapel was erected, graced with the extraordinary and attractive appendage of a bell, the gift of the friends at Bethlehem. Presently the cheerful evidences of well-applied industry began to appear. Grounds were cleared, gardens were planted, and fields of corn grew and ripened in the sun. Here, too, under the dews of divine influence, began to spring up the seed of a more precious sowing. The living knowledge of the Faith took root, at length, in the hearts of the people. On the 3d of December, three penitents, a father, mother, and child, were admitted, through the solemn ritual of baptism, into the church, in the presence of a large concourse of witnesses, all of whom were deeply impressed with the ceremony. The occasion was honored with the attendance of quite a company of the villagers of Goschgoschuenk, who entered into the spirit of the prevailing excitement very enthusiastically, but, perhaps, with more zeal than knowledge. So earnest were they in their ardor that they gravely proposed to lay the question before the town council, and have themselves and their fellow-citizens legislated into the communion, without delay; but the missionaries interposed, letting them know that conversion must come by the grace of God, and not by act of Assembly. But the most interesting event of this delightful season was the conversion of the generous-hearted, stanch old friend of the Moravians, blind Allemewi. "Brethren," said he, as at his own request he was carried to the lodge of the missionaries, "I can bear it no longer; I must open my mind to you. I am convinced that I am a lost sinner, and unless my heart shall soon receive comfort I must die." "Come to Jesus," was the responsive invitation; "weary and heavy-laden as you are, there you will find rest for your soul." His wife and friends tried to dissuade him, but he had resolved on his course, and on Christmas-day the believing chief was sacramentally sealed into the fellowship of the Unity. So were gilded the closing hours of a year obscured with clouds and darkness through nearly the full measure of its circle; so, though the watches were long and weary, the night of sorrows was told at last, and joy came in the morning.

While yet congratulating themselves on their successes, the Brethren were called on to undergo new tribulations. Unfriendly relations had for some time existed between the Seneca Indians and the Cherokees. Late events had not mitigated the traces of estrangement, and it scarcely needed a petty act of outrage, which was perpetrated by the latter, to bring the quarrel to a crisis, and precipitate the parties into active hostilities. Lawunakhannek lying in an exposed position between these rival tribes, the Christians were left in a predicament of great insecurity. The excitements of war, besides, not only precluded the possibility of extending the conquests of the Faith, but were a temptation too strong, oftentimes, for even the perseverance of the saints. When blue, typical of peace, was the color of the day, the gospel had its chances, but its power was paralyzed when the hatchet was red, and warriors were abroad in black and vermilion. In view of these facts, the Brethren began to discuss the expediency of continuing the mission at that place. Repeated requests to settle in their region had been made by the prominent men of the Delawares on the Big Beaver, seconded warmly by Glikkikan, the captain and controversialist of one of their villages. Next to the settlements on the Muskingum, those on the Beaver were the most populous of any within the territorial bounds of the Delaware Nation. The wider sphere of usefulness presented in this field, and the ostensible readiness of the people to receive the Truth, were additional considerations to be taken into account in the estimate of the question of duty. After due deliberation it was decided to make the change. On the 17th of April, 1770, a fleet of sixteen canoes shoved off from the river-shore; the little band of Moravian disciples were launched upon their long voyage, and the mission of Lawunakhannek was abandoned.

III.

THE "VILLAGE OF PEACE" ON THE BEAVER.

PAKANKE, the chief, had summoned his sages, and conference was held in the council-hall of the Delawares on the Big Beaver. Kaskaskunk was all astir with excitement consequent upon the arrival of the Black-Robe of Alleghene, and his band of emigrants, from Lawunakhannek. The wise men were assembled to greet the strangers with a formal reception; a civility to which they were hospitably entitled as invited guests, and which was offered with more than usual ceremony because of their distinguished quality. Zeisberger was before the Session, attended by a few deputies, to represent his people on the occasion. Speeches were made and responded to; pipes were passed in ratification of sentiments expressed, and strings of wampum interchanged as records, for future reference, of the proceedings. The invitation to establish a community in the neighborhood was then officially reiterated, and a spot of ground designated and dedicated to the missionaries for their exclusive occupation.

Entered upon their new possessions, the Christians began the work of improvement without delay, and with their accustomed vigor. Fields were cleared and planted; huts were built, hastily and rudely, for present occupation, and a house completed for purposes of worship,—all for temporary use, and constructed of bark. The usual routine of duties was at once resumed; hours of toil, of rest, and of worship succeeding each other, and commanding their appropriate observances regularly and duly. As time wore on and the more urgent demands of agriculture were satisfied, the settlers turned their attention to the improvement of their domestic accommodations. A neat and orderly array of dwellings soon offered more comfortable shelter to the families, and on the site and over the ruins of the abandoned bark cabins were planted the more permanent foundations of Languntoutenuenk, or Friedenstadt,—the Village of Peace.

Pakanke, as has been seen, had spoken his welcome. The terms of his address were liberal enough, but the spirit lacked the ring of genuine cordiality. As of the household of the Lenni-Lenape, he inclined favorably to the Red-folk of the emigration; because of the political distinction which his patronage of the Black-Robes would reflect upon his clan, he could tolerate, nay, he might congratulate himself on their presence; but the instincts of the savage Adam—the easily ascendant propensities of ab-original sin in the man—were all against the religion of their importation. When, on the 12th of June, the example of her husband wrought redeemingly, at length, on the rebellious conscience of the wife of Allemewi, and she was baptized into the communion, the chief of Kaskaskunk witnessed the novel ceremony with ill-concealed disapprobation. But when Glikkikan, his lieutenant, brought down by conviction, craved permission to transfer his lodge to Friedenstadt, that he might dwell there as one of the Congregation, Pakanke did not hesitate to avow his displeasure. "You," he exclaimed, "a brave and honored man, sitting next me in council when we spread the blanket and considered the belts of wampum, even you would go over and forsake us!" "I would go over to them," said the determined prime minister, "and with them I would live and die." Then the chief, when he found that reproach fell without effect, and that expostulation was fruitless, began to ply severer censures. The captain was charged with sorcery; he was stigmatized as a *Shwonnak*, and pointed at scornfully as a recreant to the venerable traditions of his people. Nevertheless, with a constancy more creditable to the orator than characteristic of him, he continued steadfast in his resolution. The Brethren came in, as well, for their share of the outpourings of savage wrath. Pakanke withdrew from them the protection of his countenance, impudently denying that he had ever approved of their emigration, or that they were settled on the Beaver by his authority.

At this crisis, while opposition was in a fair way to ripen soon into positive resistance, its development was unexpectedly and effectually arrested.

Col. George Croghan, delegated in 1755 by Sir Wm. Johnston to visit the West, in order to counteract the hostile operations of the French and maintain amicable relations with the Indians of the border, had, in the sagacious discharge of his mission, acquired a commanding influence among the tribes. Their own amiable character, coupled with the devotion of the Moravians to the pacific measures which it was his policy to promote, commended the Society to his favorable notice, and from the time of their first settlement on the Alleghany, shortly after which he had been visited at Fort Pitt by Zeisberger and Senseman, he had always contributed, as occasion offered, to their welfare. When information reached him of the disturbances which had been excited at Friedenstadt, he promptly interposed in their behalf. With much earnestness he exhorted the offended Kaskaskunkian to cease controversy with the Christians, assuring him that their intentions were honorable, and not by any means adverse to the interests of his people. The advice of the English commissioner caused the chief to waver in his purpose. It so happened that just then a fatal disease raged with great violence in the Delaware villages. The prevalence of this epidemic was attributed to the workings of magic, and the populace, very pliable under a panic, were easily induced to believe that the fatal visitation was chargeable to their rejection of the religion of the Black-Robes. A special meeting of the counselors of the tribe at Gekelemukpechuenk, or Still-Water, on the Muskingum, was called, and, as the result of its deliberations, an envoy was sent with a black belt of wampum of a fathom's length to Pakanke, and an order demanded for a convocation of the Council. "There is a contagion among us;" such was the purport of the message. "Many Indians die. We shall all die unless we have help. Convene a Council on this belt. Whoever does not receive this belt shall be considered as an enemy and murderer of his people, and must be treated according to his deserts." Pakanke was wise enough to accept the precaution obscurely conveyed in this communication. A prudent respect for consequences decided the course for which the advice of Col. Croghan had prepared the way. Hostilities against the Christians ceased, and peace prevailed in Friedenstadt.

The career of the community was now, for some time, one of almost uninterrupted prosperity. The possessions of the Brethren embraced several hundred acres of land, a large portion of which, lying along the rich bottoms of the Mahoning, the Shenango, and the Beaver, was brought under cultivation, yielding to its industrious owners broad and bountiful harvests. The surrounding woods abounded in game, while the rivers furnished in full supply their daintier tribute of pickerel, bass, and salmon to lend a savory variety to the tables of the households. Schools for the education of the children were established both at Friedenstadt and at Kaskaskunk. Workshops were set up, where the mechanical arts were taught and put into successful practice. The raiment in which the associates clad themselves was woven in hand-looms of their own contriving, from yarns of their own spinning. Axe, mattock, spade, plow, all the utensils used in the clearing, the field, and the garden, were wrought at their own fires and on their own anvils. Debarred of its luxuries, the substantial provisions of life were theirs in adequate plenty, and the former deprivation was more than compensated in the healthy relish with which the invigorating tasks of acquisition enabled them to enjoy the latter.

Meanwhile the spiritual interests of the mission were not neglected. The only damaging accusation which remained unsatisfied against the Christians was that their converts, by the terms of communion, were to be relieved from the payment of their proportion of the national taxes, and from rendering the customary tribute of wampum to the chiefs. To quiet the apprehensions of the parties particularly concerned, a formal declaration was issued by the Brethren, to the effect that while they would not interfere with affairs of state, nor participate in the wars that might arise, yet they were willing to bear their share of responsibility in all matters affecting the public welfare, save in any case where it was contemplated to disturb the peace of the white people or of other Indian nations. This announcement met with approval. The Cæsars of the tribe were satisfied, and the missionaries had an open field for the exercise of their labors. And now "the peace of God, brotherly love, and a desire to cleave to and love God, our Saviour, began to prevail most powerfully in the Congregation." Glikkikan was moved to tears by a discourse delivered at a daily prayer-meeting, greatly to the disgust of the heathen, who marveled that a captain so valiant and so noted should allow himself by such a display of weakness to sink so low beneath the level of professional dignity. But the captain clave to his conviction, and together with another convert, the chieftain Genaskund, was admitted shortly after into the communion. One after another, a son of Pakanke's among the rest, the unregenerate were "led to accept the gracious invitation given to all that labor and are heavy laden." Visitors were attracted from Shenenge and other distant villages to hear the wonderful tidings in the chapel of Friedenstadt. A wicked sorcerer from abroad, as he stood listening to the testimony of an Indian sister, said he had a great mind to try a few experiments of native legerdemain on her to her personal prejudice. "I do not fear his threats," said the sister; "for if my life were taken by such practices, I should but go home to my Saviour." The awakening was specially marked among the unbaptized, the catechumens, and the children; all making confession of the abominations of heathenism, and uniting in earnest entreaty to God for mercy and pardon. Another visitor, an anxious inquirer, sought to learn which was the true way to happiness. "The Quakers," said he, "maintain that their doctrine is true; the English Church asserts the same; and the Brethren say that theirs is the Word of God." The reply was,—Come to Jesus; learn to love Him, and that will show the way. Last of all, the chief of sinners, as well as of his tribe, Pakanke, that sturdy adversary of the gospel, resolved to visit Friedenstadt. He did so, tarrying there for several days. The truth took effect upon his stubborn conscience, and when he went back to Kaskaskunk it was to exhort his children to do as he had done, —go to the missionaries, listen to their words, and learn to love Jesus.

The Moravians, however, seemed to be predestined victims of misfortune. They might enjoy seasons of repose, when, exempt from molestation, they could pursue their work and worship according to ordinance, but if frustrated in one scheme of annoyance, the devil would fall back upon some new device, so that these intervals of tranquillity were seldom of long-uninterrupted continuance. For pushing enterprise the whisky-trader enjoyed a reputation second only to the trapper and the hunter, upon whose heels, as they penetrated the wilderness, he was sure to follow, close as their own hounds that were trained to the attendance. Whence his supplies of the commodity in which he dealt were procured, and by what means transported from point to point, were problems often to puzzle the curious, but so it was that seldom a tent was pitched in the forest, and never a cabin reared in the clearing, but that the keg and the cup—or the rye straw—were conspicuously at hand to indicate his presence and to advertise his profession. Zeisberger, mourning over the deplorable results of the trade in the Susquehanna settlements, flattered himself that he was beyond the range of its commercial traveler when he found himself at the head-waters of the Alleghany, where the face of a white man was so rare a sight that on his arrival a courier was dispatched to the chief of the tribe, thirty miles away, to notify him of the extraordinary visitation. But the peddler had preceded him. Petroleum at four guineas a quart was a commodity worth coveting, and the fame of the fountains at

Venango was not likely to fail of being blown abroad, and of attracting the notice of the gain-seeking adventurer. He had ferreted out the spot. The principal statesmen of that branch of the Delaware dynasty were no strangers to him, nor to his liquor. The sachems knew a keg when they saw it; the captains might have stood as tasters at the tables of the connoisseurs; and so habituated to the use of the straw were the rank and file of the people, that prohibitory legislation was found necessary for the maintenance of the public peace. Savage ingenuity was quite as expert at evasions of unpalatable laws as the wit of the keenest of pale-faced dodgers. The chiefs, however far they might extend their authority in secular affairs, dared not interfere with the commons in their religious ceremonies and observances. Under cover of this right the latter took shelter,—established the Festival of Rum, and in the celebration of it got religiously drunk, as often as they pleased, with impunity. As might be expected, this became at once the favorite red-letter day of the native calendar, and was in the full tide of popularity, greatly to his surprise, when Zeisberger first appeared at Goschgoschuenk.

The Moravians were the earliest advocates of temperance in America. While whisky was accepted as the good creature of God, and taken to, lovingly, in all circles besides, it was denounced by the Brethren as the chief of evils,—the prolific parent of vices and immoralities,—and placed under ban of the community accordingly. As censurers of his calling, and, more especially, as stumbling-blocks in the way of his custom, the missionaries were peculiarly odious in the eyes of the trader. He traduced their religion; he vilified their personal characters; he misrepresented their motives; he seconded the native sorcerers in their ridiculous, but dangerous, charges; and, to quicken at any time a spirit of mutiny against them, never hesitated at the gratuitous distribution of the crazing element in which he dealt among the disaffected. But for his agency, directly and indirectly felt, it is doubtful whether the state of affairs would have arisen which rendered necessary the abandonment of the station on the Alleghany. The same line of opposition was followed up at Friedenstadt. Liquor was freely circulated among the populace. The savages were incited to acts of lawlessness. Death to the missionaries was threatened, and, on more than one occasion, attempted. The settlement was invaded, now and again the intoxicated mob assailing the houses of the inhabitants, forcing their doors, breaking their windows, and compelling the affrighted inmates to take to the woods for safety. The continued forbearance of the Brethren only tempted to new aggressions, until, in the end, riot enjoyed unbridled license, and the Village of Peace became the scene for the sport, at pleasure, of tumult and disorder.

An additional grievance was in reserve for the community. Kaskaskunk was a village of marked importance among the Indians as a war-post, where centered all the principal war-paths from the North, and whence, by one common trail, passing through Friedenstadt, communication was had with Fort Pitt. Near to the latter-mentioned town was the Scalp Spring,—a fountain famous far and near as the place of rendezvous commonly appointed for the gathering of the clans when the red hatchet was abroad and strife was in the wind. In the spring of 1771, certain of the vindictive among the white settlers about Fort Pitt, whose taste for carnage seems to have been sharpened rather than sated by former indulgence, banded together, and, taking to the shelters along the Ohio, on the plea of revenge for past injuries, began an inhuman slaughter among the unoffending Indians inhabiting the valley. To escape the cruelties of these rude border-men, the terrified natives deserted their homes on the river, and fled for protection to the interior. Their stories told of the barbarous conduct of the pale-faces created intense excitement among the various clansmen, who determined upon swift and severe retaliation. A call to arms was proclaimed among the tribes, and soon the painted warriors began to assemble at Scalp Spring. As of kindred color with the perpetrators of their wrongs, the Brethren were included in the same doom of meditated vengeance, and it was only by reason of strict vigilance—a constant guard of competent force being maintained about their houses—that they were able to protect themselves against attempted violence. This state of affairs continuing, the missionaries became disheartened at their prospects. Without peace, that cardinal principle of their religion, of which there seemed faint promise now, they could not look for prosperity. The circumstances of their position led them to reflect gravely upon a step which, in view of other considerations, they had already contemplated with favor. The tribe of the Delaware nation settled on the Muskingum had, for some time, been insisting upon the establishment of a mission within their boundaries on that river. As a field of labor this region had been held in high estimation since its first visitation by Post. The natives professed a warm regard for the Brethren; the valleys were fertile, and the locality, so many leagues distant from the frontier, was, presumably, out of reach of the border marauder and the whisky-trader. The project was broached, and, after a full consultation of its members, ultimately resolved upon by the Congregation.

Meanwhile correspondence was held with the Brethren in Friedenshütten and Tschechschequannink, the two settlements on the Susquehanna. The predicament of these associations of native Christians was similar to that of the converts of Gnadenhütten. They had no valid title to the lands they occupied, the ownership having passed, by conveyance of their masters, the Iroquois, to the English, who in their eagerness after the bargain did not stop to inquire into the honesty of its transaction. Besides, their situation was precarious from the fact that, lying in the debatable territory dividing the contestants, they were exposed to the ravages of both parties in the skirmishes that were continually springing up between the whites and the savages. To tarry where they were, with a way of escape open, was to resist a plain indication of duty. When, therefore, the invitation from the Muskingum, which had been extended to them through their friends on the Beaver, was received, they accepted it without hesitation "as proceeding from a gracious direction of the providence of God."

And now were to sink into final extinguishment the fires on the hearths of the native converts in the valleys, where so long they had lived, and toiled, and worshiped together. Their cottages were to be forsaken, their fields abandoned, their sanctuaries left desolate; and for the protection —the forbearance, rather—which the invaders of their soil, disciples avowedly of the same faith with themselves, were not willing to lend, were they to be indebted to the charity of unbelieving barbarians.

IV.

THE JOURNEY THROUGH THE WILDERNESS.

THE sacrament of the Lord's Supper was celebrated with unusual solemnity at Friedenshütten, on the 6th of June, 1772. Nine years before, John Papunhank, the first native convert on the Susquehanna, had been baptized into the death of Jesus. This last Sabbath of the occupation of the village was to be made equally memorable by the admission of his daughter, through the same rite, into the communion of the church. By the following Friday the preparations of the people were completed, and after religious services in the chapel, where praise and thanksgiving were offered to God for past favors and blessings, and his protecting presence implored to attend them on the journey, they started upon their distant pilgrimage.

The emigrants, two hundred and forty-one in number, were divided into two companies; one, led by the Rev. John Ettwein, to proceed by land, the other, under direction of the missionary John Rothe, by water. The clothing and lighter household furniture were carried, chiefly, on pack-horses; but when these animals, with which they were inadequately provided, were fully loaded, stores of valuables remained, too precious to be left. These were gathered into bundles and borne upon the shoulders of the men and women. Among the rest thus burdened was one; a mother, who carried her crippled son, a helpless child of eight or ten years of age, in a basket strapped on her back. Seventy head of cattle brought up the rear of the procession. The more cumbrous articles of value, such as plowshares, harrow-teeth, mattocks, axes, and the like, together with pots and kettles of brass and iron for domestic uses, with others of larger capacity for sugar-making purposes, were stowed in boats, to accompany the party that was to go by water, under charge of Brother Rothe.

The navigation of the Susquehanna was difficult and dangerous. The restless current of the river, now tumbling in cascades, now tossing in wild floods along the rugged slopes of its channel, seriously interrupted their passage. To stem its tide required the steady aid of oar, and pole, and line, and to avoid the attending risks to the keels of the vessels, unceasing vigilance. Progress could be attempted only by day. At twilight the flotilla would seek the shore, where, with such shelter from the inclement weather as the chances of the scene of bivouac afforded, the weary crews would retire for rest and cover through the night. To add to their trials, the measles broke out among them; many, especially of the children, suffering severely from the malady. So they advanced until, on the 29th of June, after a voyage of nearly three weeks, they reached Great Island, in the West Branch of the Susquehanna. Here they were met by the band under conduct of Brother Ettwein, and hence the united company resumed its march by land.

The trail which they followed, scarcely distinguishable at times, led through forests that seemed interminable, through thickets that could scarcely be penetrated, and over streams that were crossed with great labor, while during the greater part of the journey the rains fell almost incessantly. Venomous reptiles infested the way. Several of the horses were lost at different times from the bite of rattlesnakes, Brother Ettwein himself narrowly escaping the same fate, having accidentally trodden upon one with fifteen rattles that lay coiled among the bushes. Much annoyance was experienced from the vicious assaults of certain small insects called Ponks, or *Living Ashes*, by the Indians. In one locality especially, known as Ponks-utency, or the Habitation of the Sand-fly, they abounded, so that the air was filled by them as with a mist. They were particularly tormenting to the horses and cattle, who, when the evening fires were lighted, would rush toward the flames and stand amid the smoke for protection against their attacks. The native legend accounting for the origin of this insect states that, once upon a time, a wicked hermit, who was a magician, made his abiding-place amid the rocks there, and spent his days in alarming, and occasionally murdering, unsuspecting travelers who happened to pass that way. A certain warrior undertook to rid the region of the mischievous recluse, sought him out, and, having dispatched him, burnt his bones and scattered their dust in the air. But though the magician was disposed of, the curse was scarcely abated, for of all the ashes sown to the wind, each separate particle became a thing of life, winged and fanged, to hover around and visit revenge, through time to come, upon the race of his destroyer. Several of the emigrants died during the journey. The crippled boy who had been carried on his mother's back, after having long borne up under the fatigue of the march, sickened at last and began to sink rapidly. Conscious that his end was at hand, the child asked to be baptized. His request was granted, and none too soon; for within a few hours subsequently his spirit was caught away, and its wasted frame committed to the mould.

Throughout their dreary pilgrimage the religious duties to which they were accustomed were never forgotten or neglected. Morning and evening their wonted social devotions were duly observed. Prayers were said, praises sung, and words of exhortation delivered with constant regularity. Nor did they fail to invite those among whom they fell along their route to participate in their services. "They had no greater satisfaction than to tell their fellow-men, from the experience of their own hearts, how happy that man is who believes in Jesus."

On the 29th of July they reached the Alleghany River. Canoes were here prepared, in which the heavier goods, together with the aged and infirm of their number, were placed for easier conveyance to their destination. Near this point they were met by Brother Heckewelder, with men and horses from the Beaver, under whose escort they proceeded now, until, on the 5th of August, they were saluted with the greetings of the Brethren at Friedenstadt.

Arrived among their friends, the emigrants tarried while a deputation, headed by Papunhank, started for Gekelemukpechuenk to complete arrangements preparatory to the general movement of the body to the Muskingum. Matters having been satisfactorily adjusted, the march was soon resumed, and continued until, in due time and without interruption, its point of destination was reached. A few months later, in April of the succeeding year, they were followed by the Congregation at Friedenstadt. Two settlements were made on the Muskingum,—Schönbrunn, the Beautiful Spring, two hundred miles from its mouth, and Gnadenhütten, composed of the Mohicans among the emigrants, ten miles lower down the river.

The communities, with accustomed energy, fell to work without delay to establish themselves comfortably in their new homes. Their villages were carefully and regularly laid out; wide streets were opened, with fences thrown across at either end, so that the cattle might be excluded and perfect cleanliness secured in these public thoroughfares. Chapels were erected,—imposing edifices in the eyes of the people, with their solid walls of square-hewn logs, their shingled roofs, their belfries, and their bells! School-houses were built. Fields, inclosed with rail fences, were made ready for the plow, and gardens, surrounded with palings, for the spade. Fruit-trees were planted, and ornamental shrubbery set out about the houses. The results of their industry were soon the wonder and admiration of their ignorant and thriftless neighbors, as the cultivated soil shot up its growth of corn, and the pasture-lands filled with increasing herds of cattle, of horses, and of hogs.

Rules were adopted by the Congregations for the maintenance among them of fitting discipline. They were to know no other God than He who created and redeemed them; to rest from all labors on Sunday, and punctually attend its stated services of worship; to honor their parents and support them in their old age; and to be obedient to their teachers, industrious, truthful, and peaceable. They were to renounce all juggles, lies, and deceits of the devil; not to use *Trchappich*, that is witchcraft, in hunting; nor to attend dances, sacrifices, or heathenish festivals. No thieves, murderers, drunkards, adulterers, or whoremongers were to be allowed fellowship with them. They were each to have but one wife, who was to be obedient to her husband, take care of the children, and be cleanly in all things. The use of rum was prohibited. They were not to run in debt, nor to purchase goods *knowing* them to be stolen; and, finally, no man inclining to go to war—which is the shedding of blood—could remain among them. These rules were regularly read before the churches at the commencement of each year, and no one refusing assent to them could be received into the brotherhood.

The labors of the missionaries were not restricted to the new Christian settlements. Zeisberger made a tour among the Shawanese, who, contrary to his expectations, bearing in mind their illiberal behavior on the other side of the mountains, received him with much kindness. At Waketameki, fifty miles below Schönbrunn, on the river, he met with a son of the old chief Paxnous, the bearer of the threatening message of the Iroquois to the Brethren at Gnadenhütten on the Mahanoy, who entertained him generously, and inclined a complaisant ear to his spiritual counsel. His recommendation secured the missionary a friendly reception from the heathen teacher of the principal town of the tribe to which he next directed his steps. A room was fitted up specially for his use, where he daily unfolded the mystery of godliness to large and attentive audiences. Nor were the words of inspiration presented in vain. "I believe," testified the teacher, touched by his eloquence, "that all you preach is truth. A year ago I became convinced that we were altogether sinful creatures, but we did not know what to do to gain eternal salvation. Now you are come, and I verily believe that God has sent you to make his word known to us."

As their reverend visitor was about leaving, the chiefs and council, through the lips of the teacher, delivered a parting message. They rejoiced that he had come among them, bringing the word of God, which they had heard with pleasure. They had convened together, and after full deliberation had passed a resolution unanimously. True, the women were not present, being engaged at the time in gathering in the crops; but that did not signify, for what the men agreed upon they would undoubtedly assent to. They had resolved to receive the word of God, and desired that a Black-Robe would come and dwell with them, and teach them how they might be saved. An official declaration of such a spirit from the council of a tribe whose sympathies had all along been regarded as irreclaimably at variance with the spirit of the gospel, particularly as interpreted by the Moravians, was as unexpected as it was gratifying to Zeisberger. His visits were repeated, and precious results might have ensued but for the public excitements which presently arose to unsettle the repose of the people, and to bar the way thus auspiciously opened for the introduction of the faith among this gentile nation.

The missionary next directed his attention to Gekelemukpechuenk, the Delaware capital on the Muskingum. His preaching there told with effective power on many of its inhabitants. Echpalawehund, an eminent chief, was among the converts. His renunciation of heathenism produced quite a stir in the town. The enemies of Christianity cried out vehemently against the act, and were for banishing the Brother, as the cause of it, from the country. Why, said they, should this pale-faced palaverer be allowed to come and unsettle the peace of the people? They had lived contentedly enough while they had clung to their inherited belief and followed the good old Indian customs, and now they were told that these customs were sinful, and that their sacrifices were an abomination in the sight of God. Were they to submit to the innovation—to allow their rites to be openly scorned, the religion of their fathers to be slandered, and their captains to be bewitched—without resistance or protest?

A council was called, which continued in session over the question for three days. The friends of the Moravians were found to outnumber their adversaries, and it was finally resolved, that while the natives of Still-Water were not willing to adopt or approve of all the usages peculiar to the Unity, they would, nevertheless, change their manner of living; prohibit drunkenness, abandon their other vices, and not allow whisky-traders, who were the authors of all wickedness, to enter their town. In proof of their sincerity in the matter involved in the last item of their resolution, they seized upon the stock of a traveling dealer who happened to be in the place, broke open the casks, and emptied their contents into the street. The work of reformation was complete—while it lasted; but such a wholesale waste of good liquor was a trial that savage virtue could not stand the test of more than once. The sacrifice was never repeated. Other traders, ignorant, or careless, of the unfortunate example of him who had fared so haplessly, entered again the forbidden limits, and the beverage soon offered as freely and was as popular as ever.

One of his old adversaries at this crisis turned up again to oppose his work and offer annoyance to Zeisberger,—Wangomen, the prophet of Goschgoschuenk. Wangomen was good on the stump,—a fluent talker, a finished hyperbolist, of bold eloquence, and apt at the tricks of his profession; but the orator had a *penchant* for liquor, and under its stimulus was, too often for his reputation, tempted in his declamation to overleap the bounds of discretion, as on this occasion. His language was lofty, his argument was bold. Was this an emergency calling for a sound defense of the religion of their ancestors? The Place of Hogs had provided them with the champion for the task. Common prophets there were, who had been near enough to heaven to hear the cocks crow, and to see the smoke of the chimneys of the celestial cabins, but he had his home in the side of the Deity, where he was accustomed to walk in and out at pleasure. What he had to say, therefore, might be regarded as authoritatively spoken. Zeisberger's God had become a man, and died. This could not be the true God, or he, the orator, would have been acquainted with the circumstance, as he had never been away from paradise long enough, at any time, not to have noticed so extended an absence. How would the Black-Robe have them seek for salvation? Faith, as a means, might do for the paleface; ipecac was the medicine for the red man. The former was too mysterious in its use to be relied on; they could have an active consciousness—one that ought to satisfy of its efficacy—in the workings of the other.

Zeisberger replied that the God whom Wangomen preached, and whose servant he was, was no other than the devil, the father of lies; that his conception of the Great Spirit was a contemptible one, and that his views of the disease of sin were as ridiculous as the nostrum proposed for its eradication.

A Mohican hearer arose to testify in the missionary's behalf. He had been afflicted to that degree that nothing could comfort him. He had no rest day or night, and, driven by distraction, had left his wigwam and taken to the woods. His friends suggested ipecac, as Wangomen had done. He had given the emetic an honest trial. It had dispossessed him of his dinner, but not of his despondency. Then, giving heed to the advice of the Black-Robe, he had lifted up his voice to the newly-revealed Divinity, imploring, "O God! who madest all things, I know not where Thou art, but I have heard that Thou dwellest in heaven: take my sorrow and grief from me!" His prayer was heard; the burden was lifted from his heart, and he was comforted. The controversy resulted in the palpable defeat of the heathen orator.

Notwithstanding the resistance of the native teachers, and the more bitter opposition of the whisky-traders, who, venturously penetrating the waste places beyond the border, had not allowed themselves to be distanced, as has been seen, by the enterprise of the Brethren, the work to which the missionaries had consecrated themselves went steadily on. Villages, near and remote, among the Shawanese as well as the Delawares, were visited; many of the prominent men, especially of the latter tribe, were converted; the gospel was preached in the Great Council of the capital; White-Eye, the historically-famous chief captain of the tribe, with his staff-officers, Netawatwees and Gelelemend, or Killbuck,—the appellation by which he is locally remembered,—became advocates of the faith; heathen usages dropped into disrepute; equal rights and privileges with those enjoyed by the rest of the people were accorded the Christians, and the missionaries were granted full liberty to exercise the functions of their office, without molestation or interference. To crown the happy achievements of this reformatory movement, the nation, by the act of council assembled at Goschachguenk, the new capital,—Gekelemukpechuenk having been abandoned (1774),—formally resolved to receive the gospel. An embassy was dispatched to Schönbrunn, bearing an address in which this determination was set forth, and praying the missionaries that they might have a new town built, "that those of their people who believed might have a place of refuge;" not a town for the aged and grown folk only, but chiefly, rather, for the young people and children; for it was their intention "that this establishment should last as long as Indians exist." A suitable spot was chosen on the east side of the Muskingum, three miles below the capital, and the new settlement of Lichtenau (1775) was established.

The mission was now in the full noon of prosperity. Although, from the unwholesome exposures attending the opening up of their settlements out of the rank wilderness, many of the faithful had sickened and died, yet, at the occupation of Lichtenau, their membership amounted to four hundred and fourteen souls. Schools, provided with books translated into the Delaware tongue, by Zeisberger, for the use of the children, were maintained in each of their towns. The public preaching of the gospel was regularly observed. The warriors of the tribes gathered in throngs at the chapels. The sick, the bedridden, women *in dolore laboris*, and travelers arrested on their way by sudden illness, begged to be carried to the missionaries, that they might be comforted in their extremity by the hopeful assurances of inspiration. The future presented a prospect luminous with promise, and the hearts of the Brethren were glad as they looked to the seemingly near fulfillment of their fondest anticipations. But these anticipations were not to be realized.

V.

TROUBLE AT WORK IN THE TENTS ON THE MUSKINGUM.

IN the month of May, 1774, a hunting-party of Indians, with their wives and children, planted their temporary lodges at the mouth of Yellow Creek, opposite Baker's Bottom, on the Ohio. A backwoodsman of the name of Greathouse visited the encampment in an ostensibly friendly manner, and invited the party to join him in a drink. They retired, for this purpose, to the cabin of an acquaintance of Greathouse's, of the name of Baker. Here they were plied with liquor until brought helplessly under its influence, when they were set upon by their host and treacherously massacred.

The sister and other relatives of Tah-ga-jute,—a Mingo, more commonly known, in connection with a famous speech of very doubtful authenticity, as Logan,—were among the victims of this outrage. Intelligence of the calamity having reached the ears of the Mingo, who, at the time, was on his way to Pittsburg to "brighten" his friendship with the officers of the garrison there, his feelings were excited to an intense degree. He had hitherto been the friend of the white man. The door of his cabin had been always open to receive him, and shelter, food, and drink freely offered for his entertainment. This act of viperous ingratitude was his reward! Stung to the quick at a requital so cruel, he discarded from his bosom the last sentiment of compassion, and pledged himself to revenge.

As the story of the massacre was carried abroad and told in the villages of the tribes, a corresponding fury inflamed the hearts of the natives. The Shawanese and Mingos organized into companies, and, making for the Virginia border, began to deal bloody retribution on the isolated white inhabitants of that newly-occupied region. The successful issue of one adventure whetted the appetite for another, and so, with fresh eagerness and increasing activity, the incursions continued.

The Delawares were strongly urged to join in the rising. Means, open and secret, were employed to force them into co-operation. Entreaty, menace, derision, were resorted to in turn, and with a decided prospect of success. The younger warriors, when their manhood was appealed to, when they were threatened to be branded as cowards and repudiated as *Shwonnaks*, became restive, and demanded of their elders that they should be permitted to take up arms. The chiefs and captains resisted the pressure as best they could, compromising the demand, which they dared not deny and would not grant, by postponing action upon it from day to day, and maintaining meanwhile a position of neutrality. This indecisive policy of the council was attributed to the influence of the missionaries, against whom the enraged insurgents began to direct their attacks. Armed bands on their way to and from the border would parade the streets of Schönbrunn and Gnadenhütten, exciting the alarm of the inhabitants by demonstrations of violence as they went, or filling them with horror at the ghastly display of the bleeding proofs of achievement on their return. Fire and slaughter were threatened against the Congregations. An army of a thousand men, it was said, was organized among the Shawanese, who were presently to march down on the Muskingum towns, and if the Christians refused to enter their ranks the lives of all were to be forfeited, and the places of their habitation made waste and desolate. Again, it was reported that the Virginians, supported by a strong body of troops, sent out by the governor of that province, were under way, and that they had signified their intention to destroy all the villages, beginning with those of the converts on the " Elk-Eye," between the river and the lakes.

By the advice of his colleagues, Brother Rothe, with his wife and two children, retiring from the scene of disturbance, withdrew to Pittsburg, and thence, shortly afterwards, to Bethlehem. The rest of the missionaries tarried resolutely at their posts. Precarious as was their predicament in the passage of these events, manifold and imminent as were the perils to which they were exposed, the Congregations were mercifully preserved the while, without the loss of a life. The rising was suppressed early in the ensuing autumn, and quiet once again restored, through the valor of the Virginia troops, in an action on, or near, the Kanawha.

Disabled by defeat, the savages retired from the contest, but not with a mind to rest tamely under the surrender. Though overcome, they were not subdued, and the terms of submission to which they ass nted, it was mentally reserved, should be respected just as far as must be, and no further. Let a fair prospect of success open anew, and they were ready to lift the hatchet and take to the warpath at a moment's warning. They had not long to wait.

Although distantly removed from the scenes of its principal military operations, the yeomanry of the border were none the less enthusiastically aroused, nor a whit more dilatory in their resolve to take up the rifle for the national defense in the great Revolutionary struggle, than, within the more immediate line of action, were the patriotic colonists inhabiting the older settlements along the sea-shore. Aware of the vast importance of the acquisition, both parties in the contest were alike anxious to command the good will—if possible, the co-operation—of the Indians, and for this purpose had their emissaries early abroad and actively at work. The result was as might have been anticipated. Cherishing the recollection of their wrongs, and eager in the hope, under the proposed alliance, of a more prosperous faring in a new attempt at retaliation, the Shawanese were won, with scarce a wooing, to the side of the British. Similar motives had their weight in bringing about a like decision on the part of the Iroquois and Hurons.

The concurrence of the Delawares was all that was needed to complete a general confederacy, and place the tribes of the wilderness, as an undivided body, in hostile attitude against the colonies. All the arts and devices which "untutored" ingenuity could invent were employed to invite—to entrap—to force them into the combination. Their patriotism was appealed to, their pride, their fiercer passions, and particularly, as the most feasible point of approach, their fears. "Keep your shoes in readiness," came a warning message from the Hurons, "to join the warriors." Following the herald that bore it arrived an embassy of twenty deputies, who, with a thrice-repeated offer of the war-belt, demanded their assistance, declaring that all the nations besides, below and beyond Lake Erie, were united as one man for the fight. Again, the action of a general council held in Detroit was published throughout their towns, where, without a dissenting voice, it had been resolved that the hatchet should fall on the head of every one who refused to take it up. No neutrals were to be tolerated. To intimidate them further, reports were circulated that a general had arrived in Pittsburg, on his way to the Muskingum, who was resolved to destroy the whole race, without quarter to any red man, friend or foe, heathen or Christian. A trio of white renegades, notorious in border history, Simon Girty, Alexander McKee, and Matthew Elliott, visited the villages, and, repeating the lying rumors which had already been put afloat, stated that it was the fixed intention of the Virginians, after having first persuaded the Indians, by false but fine-sounding representations, into a sense of security, to take advantage of their confidence and commit wholesale slaughter upon them all. The traitors then exhorted them to rise, and turn out to a man against the intruders; not to suffer them to cross the Ohio, but to fall upon them wherever they should be found, or their country would be lost to its legitimate owners forever. The statements thus propagated had their effect.

Captain Pipe, a Delaware hatchet-bearer of influence, had all along bitterly contended against the introduction of Christianity into his tribe. His wife, a prophetess of the Wangomen school, for some time shared with him in his opposition, openly protesting that the missionaries were deceivers, and that their religion was false, as she ought to know, who had been in the mansions of the Spirits and seen the strawberries and the bilberries, as large as apples and in great plenty, that flourished in the Elysian gardens; but being present, on a certain occasion, at the baptism of a child, "the Holy Ghost labored powerfully on her conscience," and she was converted. Her change of heart, instead of appeasing the malevolence of her husband, only confirmed him the more in his hostility. He conspired with the mischief-mongers of the Shawanese to breed disaffection among the young men of the nation. He obtained a supremacy over the Monseys, a discontented and troublesome tribe of his own people, a party of whom, at his instigation, visited Schönbrunn and attempted to sow the seed of dissension among its inhabitants. He visited the converts in person, and by continued endeavors tried as he could to unsettle their convictions and bring them back to their old superstitions. Unhappily, his labors were too successful. Newallike, a chief who had come from the Susquehanna to join the Brotherhood, yielding to the tempter, relapsed into heathenism, followed in his apostasy by quite a band of seceders from among the believers. So great, indeed, was the defection, and so unmistakable were the demonstrations of violence growing out of it, that Brother Heckewelder, who had charge of the Congregation, with the faithful few left of his flock, abandoned the town, after having torn down the chapel to prevent its desecration, and retired to Lichtenau.

But, adroitly as the plans of Captain Pipe were managed, the interests of peace and good order, on the other hand, were not left to languish for lack of good championship. Netawatwees, the head chief of the nation, wielded steadily the high influence at his control in that direction while he lived, and it was while on a mission, in pursuance of the same policy, to Tamanend (Col. George Morgan, the excellent Indian agent), at Pittsburg, that he unfortunately died. The vacancy which he left in the council of his people, however, was equally well supplied, at least, by Coquehagechton, or White-Eye, the chief of the captains, than whom there was not a man among the rulers of the Lenni-Lenape of more commanding authority. Indeed, it was to his interference, pressed with uncompromising determination, that the Christians were indebted for the restoration of the favor of the head chief, which at one time, through the machinations of their enemies, he had been induced to withdraw. At the present crisis White-Eye not only declared against intermeddling at all, as a nation, in the quarrels prevailing, but insisted that the Christian Indians and their teachers, against whom the ill will of the war-party was especially directed, should be guaranteed full safety and protection. While he was willing to bear the opprobrium of being considered weak-kneed as regarded troublous complications outside, he at the same time let it be clearly understood that he would not be slow to draw his knife in defense of the just privileges of his people, without regard to creed, among themselves. Rivalry, as a consequence, grew hot and high between the contending parties.

Wars are always popular—in their kindling process; during the period of new buttons and fresh paint, of foils and blank cartridges, and while the rule of misrule is tolerated (the better to entice recruits) at mustering-stations, along thoroughfares, and in camps. The savage, neither more nor less human, or inhuman, than his pale-faced brother, is captivated as readily by the pomp and circumstance of military preparation as the most exemplary Christian that ever put on cockade, or paraded a highway, or drained a tankard, on the eve of a crusade. Captain Pipe, hence, as the leading spirit of the belligerent interest, was the popular favorite; but White-Eye possessed the counter-advantage of an all-prevailing influence among the men of chosen character who directed the counsels and shaped the policy of the tribes.

The arrival of Girty was a godsend to Pipe. His declarations as to the hostile intentions of the Virginians were taken as confirmatory of what had been urged all along by the captain, but which, from a well-known proclivity of the witness, had been received with some degree of allowance, and, to that extent, failed in the desired effect. The people were exasperated, and grew clamorous for war. Guerrilla bands were organized; plundering excursions undertaken; retreats of hunters, and trappers, and traders sought out, despoiled, and devastated; and death by rifle-shot and blow of tomahawk dealt upon more than one among the surprised border-men.

Affairs were on the verge of irretrievable disorder, when White-Eye called a general council of the nation. The wise men of the tribes assembled, and before them the chief of the captains arose, and pleaded eloquently in the behalf of peace. His hearers would not be entirely persuaded. Finding that, for the present, nothing better could be accomplished, he earnestly advised against undue haste; urging, before resolving on a final decision, for a delay of ten days, that so much time at least might be allowed for further information—from Tamanend at Pittsburg, possibly; at all events, from some source more worthy of confidence than Girty or either of his fellows.

The captain charged, in reply, that White-Eye was in secret league with the Virginians, and that it was in the interest of these his friends—enabling them thereby the less hurriedly and more effectually to complete their plans—that the postponement of action was proposed. He closed his speech with the offer of a resolution to the effect "that every man should be declared an enemy to the nation who should throw an obstacle in the way that might tend to prevent the taking up arms immediately."

So pointed an impeachment of his loyalty—for it was evidently aimed at him—provoked an impassioned rejoinder from White-Eye. "If you mean to go out in earnest," said he, "you shall not go without me. I have advocated peace measures to save the nation from destruction; but if you believe me wrong, and are determined to give more credit to vagabond fugitives, whom you know to be such, then your decision is mine; I shall be with you—not like the bear-hunter," with a scornful glance at Captain Pipe, "who sets the dogs on the animal to be beaten about with his paws, while he keeps at a safe distance. No; I will myself lead you on,—place me in the front,—and be the first to fall in the fight. You have only to determine on what *you* will do," he concluded. "My mind is made up not to survive my nation; for I would not spend the remainder of a miserable life in bewailing the total destruction of a brave people who deserve a better fate."

The orator gained his point; Pipe's resolution failed; the ten days' delay was granted. And now the opposing parties, in tremulous suspense, as inconsistent rumor from time to time gave tongue to dubious tidings, awaited the issue of the truce. Again and again the sun rose and set; again and again morning brightened into noon, noon deepened into dark; night and light followed in their order, until the skies of the east were goldening in the dawn of the ninth day, and still no message from Tamanend,—no assurances, for better or for worse, from their white friends at Pittsburg. The war-faction was jubilant. The encampments in the neighborhood of the towns grew hideous with the noise of revelry; the rattle of drums and the storm of voices mingled discordantly in the chant of their battle-songs. The Feast of Dogs—a repast sacred to the savage Mars, and only partaken of on the eve of a campaign—was prepared. The heads of the warriors were shaved afresh, their faces besmeared with red and black, their scalp-locks anointed with tallow and tipped with the white plumage from the crest of the eagle, while all about the dusky masses thronged and pressed and roared, active in the busy, boisterous engagements of ready-making for the war-path.

It so happened that the Brethren at Bethlehem, anxious about the missionaries, from whom for several months they had received no intelligence, had commissioned two of their number—Heckewelder, with them on a visit, and John Shabosh—to proceed, if possible, to the Muskingum, but, at all events, as far as Pittsburg, ascertain their situation, and, as circumstances indicated the need, to provide for their relief. Arriving at Pittsburg, they were first informed of the critical state of affairs in the Indian country; how that Girty had fled there, and was striving by false representations to incite the savages to insurrection, and how Colonel Morgan, and the officers with him, had tried to send messages of peace to the Delawares, but ineffectually, the runners whom they would have employed declining the service, through fear of roving gangs of insurgents that infested the wilderness. Heckewelder was advised against pursuing his journey; but in view of the consequence of his mission,—deemed all the more important because of the very reasons pressed against its prosecution,—he decided, with his colleague, upon the venture.

At eleven o'clock at night on the third day after bidding adieu to their friends at Pittsburg, mercifully conducted by the hand of Providence through the perilous exigencies of the way, the reverend envoys reached Gnadenhütten in safety. Being informed of the proceedings of council, and that to-morrow only intervened before the final day of the term of suspension agreed upon, after a brief rest they arose at three o'clock next morning, mounted fresh horses, swam the Muskingum, and, pushing speedily forward, in the course of a few hours halted within view of Goschachguenk.

Great was the chagrin, not to say mortification, of Captain Pipe at this inopportune arrival. He could readily calculate, without waiting for its development, upon the result,—defeat to his plans, demolishment to his expectations, shame and calamity to himself. The reaction would be sudden and not agreeable to contemplate when the warriors found that they had been duped by his representations; that their revelries were premature, their recourse to paint and tallow precipitate, and their immolation of victims a superfluous waste of dogs; in short, that they had made themselves ridiculous.

The people soon gathered about the missionaries, anxious to hear what they might have to say. Heckewelder, after White-Eye had notified him of the charges made by Pipe, invited a meeting of the council, and briefly laid before them the news of which he was the messenger. He told them of the achievements of the colonial troops; of the surrender of General Burgoyne; of the despondency of the British; of the confidence of Congress in the success of the Revolution; and, as more nearly affecting the interests of his hearers, of the most friendly assurances which, on behalf of the American people, he was delegated to deliver by Tamanend. White-Eye followed the missionary in a speech of some length, and with the effect that might have been expected from so popular and eloquent an orator. Pipe attempted no reply, but quietly withdrew from the assembly, and presently from the town. His scheme had miscarried. To prevent an attempt at its repetition elsewhere, the chief captain prepared a message, which was dispatched, by runners, to the Shawanese villages on the Scioto: — "Grandchildren! Ye Shawanese! Some days ago a flock of birds, that had come on from the east, lit at Goschachguenk, imposing a song of theirs upon us, which song had wellnigh proved our ruin! Should these birds, which on leaving us took their flight towards Scioto, endeavor to impose a song on you likewise, do not listen to them, for they lie!"

For a season following the failure of this insurrectionary experiment, the peace of the settlements remained undisturbed. Gnadenhütten and Schönbrunn, abandoned during the troublous time, were reoccupied. The new town of Salem, five miles below Gnadenhütten, was built (1780). Many of the converts who had been carried away by the defection at Schönbrunn repented of their apostasy and were restored to the communion. The missionaries and teachers, conspicuous among whom was Glikkikan, the convert of Kaskaskunk, diligently and profitably strove in their labors of love among the unbelievers. Numbers were awakened, "overpowered by the grace of God," and made subjects of baptism. White-Eye was brought under conviction, but excused himself from joining the church, on the ground that the act would be inconsistent with his profession. When he could cease to be a politician he would be a Christian. He proposed to disembarrass himself of the hinderance by retiring from public service as soon as possible; but the praiseworthy intention failed in the postponement. Shortly after, on the march with General McIntosh's army to erect a fort at Tuscarawas for the protection of the peaceable Indians, he was seized with the smallpox and died. His death was an irreparable loss to the Moravians, and a calamitous one, as events determined, to the nation whose affairs, amid its turmoils, he had administered with so much prudence and sagacity.

VI.

CAPTAIN PIPE PLANS NEW MISCHIEF, AND WHAT CAME OF HIS SCHEMES.

WITH the ever-lively recollection to stimulate him of his mortifying discomfiture in council by White-Eye, the intelligence of the death of that renowned chief no sooner reached the ears of Captain Pipe than, relieved by the circumstance of the fears which, in spite of the opposite promptings of a more intense but irresolute sense of wounded pride, had held him back, he set himself with ready alacrity to redeem his fame, recover his influence, and restore into pattern again the broken threads of the old conspiracy. "Behold!" he exclaimed, exultantly, as he reappeared in the circles from which he had been ejected; "Coquehagechton is gone! The Great Spirit has put him out of the way that the nation may be saved!"

Gelelemend, or Killbuck, who with two colleagues, upon the decease of White-Eye, was placed at the head of public affairs, to serve during the minority of the legitimate heir to the head-chiefship, although a man of irreproachable worth, was far from equal to the responsibilities of his new position. He was not to be deceived by the rhetoric, nor tempted by the corrupt approaches, of the insurrectionary leader, but he had not the courage to face him on the challenge and meet menace with defiance. Under pressure of that argument he yielded, deserting his people, and retiring with his colleagues upon the protection of the white friends at Pittsburg. But one obstacle remained as an interference to the complete accomplishment of the captain's designs. If the missionaries could be induced to follow the example of Gelelemend, then the field would be left open, and little doubt remained but that, aided by his staff of counselors, Girty, Elliott, and McKee, and supported by his cut-throat body-guard of Monseys, he could force the neutral party to terms, and have the Delawares, as a nation, committed to the war. The missionaries, however, had made up their minds to stay by their Congregations, and were not to be persuaded or intimidated. Attempts were made upon their lives. Senseman was attacked, but fortunately rescued by the timely arrival of two of his neighbors, while out gathering greens, one day, in a field near Schönbrunn. Edwards and Young narrowly escaped being shot while planting potatoes at Gnadenhütten; while Heckewelder was waylaid on different occasions, and only preserved by special interposition of Providence.

Finding his efforts ineffectual to either win over the converts or compel the voluntary withdrawal of their teachers, Pipe resolved upon a new course of procedure. He visited the English governor, Arend Schuyler de Peyster, at Detroit, and in an interview with him represented the Christians as partisans in the American cause, who were acting as spies, and through their missionaries carrying on a secret correspondence with the enemy, to the serious detriment of the English interest. He then suggested that an order should be issued for their removal from the Muskingum to some quarter farther north, more nearly within scope of loyal oversight, and beyond convenient reach of communication with the Yankees. The governor approved of the proposition, and sent a commissioner to Niagara to lay the matter before a council of the Iroquois, then and there in session, and to secure their agency in its execution. The Iroquois were willing that the refractory Congregations "should be made soup of," and so resolved, but devolved the brewing of the broth on their neighbors the Chippewas and Ottowas. These tribes declined the task. The half-king of the Hurons was then appealed to, and, from motives of compassion, as he declared,—"to save the believing Indians from total destruction,"—accepted the service.

The force organized for the enterprise assembled at Sandusky, where they were joined by Pipe and his party. A war-feast was held preparatory to action, a roasted ox forming the repast; and when the revelries appropriate to the occasion were ended, ammunition was served out to the men by Elliott, and the band, divided into companies, began its march.

In the afternoon of August the 10th (1781), the force, numbering one hundred and forty, but soon recruited to over three hundred men, with Pipe and the half-king at its head, and bearing the British flag, was seen, to the consternation of its inhabitants, approaching the town of Salem. A message was sent, conveying assurances of safety, and requesting the Christians to appoint a place convenient to the three settlements where a conference could be held. Gnadenhütten was designated, on an accommodating plateau, in the vicinity of which, on the day following, the half-king ordered the pitching of his tents. The formal interview between the parties took place on the 20th. The half-king delivered the opening speech of the occasion:

"Cousins! Ye believing Indians in Gnadenhütten, Schönbrunn, and Salem! I am much concerned on your account, perceiving that you live in a very dangerous spot. Two powerful, angry, and merciless Gods stand ready, opening their jaws wide against each other: you are sitting down between both, and are thus in danger of being devoured and ground to powder by the teeth of either one or the other, or of both. It is therefore not advisable for you to stay here any longer. Consider your young people, your wives and your children, and preserve their lives, for here they must all perish. I therefore take you by the hand, lift you up, and place you in, or near, my dwelling, where you will be safe and dwell in peace. Do not stand looking at your plantations and houses, but arise and follow me! Take also your teachers with you, and worship God in the place to which I shall lead you, as you have been accustomed to do. You shall likewise find provisions, and our father beyond the lake [the governor at Detroit] will care for you. This is my message, and I am come hither purposely to deliver it."

The orator, having ended, presented a string of wampum as a minute of the delivery. The missionaries requested twenty-four hours for reflection, and, having considered the proposition, offered, next day, their reply:

"Uncle! Ye captains of the Delawares and Monseys, our friends and countrymen! Ye Shawanese, our nephews, and all ye other people here assembled! We have heard your words, but have not yet seen the danger so great that we might not stay here. We keep peace with all men, and have nothing to do with the war, nor do we wish or desire anything but to be permitted to enjoy peace and rest. You see yourselves that we cannot rise immediately and go with you, for we are heavy, and time is required to prepare for it. But we will keep and consider your words, and let you, Uncle, know our answer next winter after harvest. Upon this you may rely."

The reply was not at all satisfactory to Captain Pipe, who insisted with the half-king that he should cease further attempts at persuasion and resort to compulsory measures. A council of war was called. As the result of its deliberations, the direct question was put to the Christians: "Will you go with us, or not?" They repeated the answer they had already given, and added that they intended to abide by it.

A few days afterwards, Zeisberger, Senseman, and Heckewelder were walking together through one of their gardens, along a way that led to the burying-ground of the town, when a party of Wyandots, who were concealed behind a fence, sprang up, seized upon them, and dragged them as prisoners into the camp, where they were met with derisive greetings, and hailed with the chant of the death-song. They were then brought before the half-king and his chiefs, when the proposition was again made,—" Would they go to Sandusky, encourage their converts to go along, and not attempt to run away from their escort on the route?" With no alternative at choice, they promised, and were set at liberty.

Short space was granted in which to make preparation for the journey, but such arrangements as could be effected were undertaken without delay. Under cover of the night, the implements of labor most valuable to them—plow-irons, harrow-teeth, hoes, saws, and culinary-ware—were carried secretly to the woods and buried. Having thus disposed of the articles most valuable to them, but not conveniently portable, they loaded their canoes with provisions, and packed their horses with such lighter goods as were indispensable, especially for the comfort of the women and children, on the way. On the morning of the 11th of September the flitting Congregations turned their backs upon the Muskingum villages,—Gnadenhütten, Schönbrunn, and Salem,—endeared to them by so many blessed associations, and began their weary march to the far-away scene allotted for their abode on the marshy lowlands of the lake-shore. Quite all the possessions which they had accumulated by years of patient industry and thrift—the greater portion of their cattle, their herds of swine, their broad acres of maize, ripe but ungathered in the fields of the valleys which they had brought under culture, the gardens with their yield of fruits and vegetables, and, equally regretted, and more in the end to be deplored, because never recovered, books and manuscripts of the missionaries—were left behind at the mercy of the ruthless horde of plunderers, who, ere the exiles were fairly out of view, had begun their work of destruction, tearing down the fences of the inclosures, and turning their horses in upon the corn.

On the 11th of October they reached the Sandusky. Their first care was to erect cabins for their protection through the winter, a bitter foretaste of which they already experienced in the chilling blasts that swept the naked wastes in midst of which lay their appointed quarters. These shelters, because of the scarcity of timber, and the distance across the marshes from which the nearest available supplies had to be brought, were very small, poorly heated, from lack of space for fireplaces, and entirely without flooring, the water flooding the interior as the recurring thaws of the season cracked the frozen soil and opened up sluices under the foundation-logs of the walls for the inundation. As the weeks glided by, their limited stores of provision became exhausted. The few cows which they had been allowed to bring with them, without food, failed to yield milk, and began to die of hunger. To support life, recourse was had to the carcasses of the starved cattle, or to roots and berries, gathered, all shriveled as they were, from the bushes, or painfully dug out of the hard ground. It was a time of terrible trial to the poor Moravians. The strong among them found their energies rapidly giving way; famished children wept and prayed and raved for bread; while nursing mothers, scarce able to maintain a wretched being of their own, could afford no nourishment for the helpless starvelings at their bosoms, lying there wailing and dying in their arms. It became painfully evident that immediate action must be taken for the relief of the suffering community. A general consultation was held, the result of which was the appointment of a deputation consisting of about one hundred and fifty men, women, and children, to return to the Muskingum and procure supplies out of what might remain of the unharvested crops on the abandoned plantations of that river. The party was organized, and, after an affectionate interchange of adieus with the friends that were to remain behind, started upon its errand.

Meanwhile, upon a citation from De Peyster, Zeisberger, Senseman, Heckewelder, and Edwards, led by the half-king,—Girty, who was to have assisted him, being fortunately absent, with a band of Wyandots, on a raid along the Ohio bottoms,—had repaired to Detroit. The commandant received them kindly, lodged them and provided for their wants with praiseworthy liberality. On the appearance of their accuser, Captain Pipe, they were summoned before De Peyster for examination. The captain failing in his anticipated proofs of the treasonable correspondence complained of, and, in fact, after some hesitation, making a complete retraction of his charges, public declaration was made of their innocence, and the missionaries were not only set at liberty, but commended for their fearless devotion to the noble and disinterested work to which they had dedicated their lives.

Sad as was the trial of separation that day when the relief-party, appointed to go to the old settlements for food, started on their journey, it was not what it would have been could a suspicion have arisen of the consequences—merely as a possible contingency—that were to follow the enterprise. Prowling bands of savages on the one hand, and gangs of rude border-men on the other, were known to be abroad, but it was not anticipated that they would be encountered in any force, or, if they should be, that violence was necessarily to be apprehended from either. Their friendly understanding with the American officers at Pittsburg had not been disturbed, and it was hardly to be looked for that the heathen clans—mostly tribesmen of their own—would deal more cruelly with them, at worst, than they had already done,—the risk of which, to that extent, they were willing, for the end in view, to hazard. Proper caution, nevertheless, was to be observed, and they decided, upon reaching the Muskingum, not to visit the towns, but to encamp in the woods. They were making their arrangements accordingly, when two or three of their fellow-communionists, happening in upon them from Pittsburg, gave such assurances of non-interference from that quarter, that, for the greater convenience of their business, they concluded to change their plans and occupy the villages.

For several weeks, toiling night and day, they pursued their labors, plucking the ears from the stalks, stripping off the husks, and carrying great loads of the corn away to carefully-prepared hiding-places in the woods; whence, from time to time, and with ease and dispatch, future supplies might be obtained, as the wants of the Congregation demanded. One evening, when their task was nearly completed, four Sandusky warriors appeared among them on their way back from an expedition down among the white settlements on the Ohio. They had captured a woman and a child in the valley, while wandering, so they said, both of whom they had killed and impaled on the river-shore. The victims, it was added, would be discovered,—without doubt were already discovered,—pursuit would certainly follow, and unless the Brethren, who, if not set down as its actual perpetrators, would be charged with having connived at the deed, made instant retreat towards the lake, they would, in all likelihood, be overtaken and murdered. Relying upon their well-known reputation as a society religiously averse to bloodshed, and satisfied, against whatever treacherous suggestion, with the pledges of friendship so recently renewed at Pittsburg, they declined, after consultation, to act upon the advice of the warriors.

By this time, however, they had laid up as large a stock of provision as was desired, and notice was accordingly served throughout the villages for all to put themselves in readiness for returning to Sandusky. On the day previous to the one fixed for their departure, Jacob, one of the converts, stood on the river-bank, a short distance from Gnadenhütten, and, while engaged in tying a cornsack, saw a body of from one to two hundred white men approaching the town. He was on the point of saluting the company, when to his consternation a shot was fired from its ranks at one of the Christian Indians, who, at the moment, was crossing the river in a canoe. The shot seemed to tell with mortal effect, the man dropping from his seat at the discharge, into the bottom of his vessel. Jacob fled affrighted, but, instead of escaping to one or other of the villages and giving the alarm, he ran to the woods, where he lay hidden for twenty-four hours. There was no other witness of the occurrence, the rest of the Brethren being scattered, beyond view, here and there in the cornfields.

The company of border-men continued their march, without any further act of hostility, until they had approached the fields where the Indians were at work. On meeting with them they manifested great cordiality; expressing themselves as entertaining an ardent sympathy for the Brotherhood; referring to their handsome chapel in rather extravagant terms of admiration, and discoursing, with a zeal that was very captivating, as indicative of a highly-sanctified temper of heart, upon religious topics. They then declared the object of their visit. They were there "as friends and brothers, who had purposely come out to relieve them from the distresses brought on by the enemy on account of their being friends to the American people," and formally proposed to conduct them to Pittsburg, where their wants would all be satisfied. The Christians, unsuspicious of evil, reciprocated their greetings with unaffected warmth, and expressed a cheerful willingness to follow them as proposed. "God has ordained it," they exclaimed, in their gratitude, "that relief should reach us, and that we should not perish in the barrens of Sandusky."

Having all gathered in at Gnadenhütten, word was sent to Salem of the arrival of the whites—quite a detachment of the latter accompanying the messengers appointed to convey the intelligence—and of their charitable intentions, inviting the Brethren there to come over and join in the proposed movement. They gladly acquiesced in the arrangement. The simple preparations necessary

—or possible—were soon made. Out of consideration for their greater comfort in journeying, urged tenderly, but so tenaciously as to have justified a suspicion of some unfair intention, if the honest Moravians had been given to doubting, the whites proposed, and were permitted, to take in charge all their guns, axes, and knives, with the promise that they should be restored upon their arrival at Pittsburg.

The party reached Gnadenhütten. Assembled all in the village, a change, marvelous as sudden, took place in the conduct of the border-men. No longer needed now in the further prosecution of their plans, disguise was cast aside, and the deceivers presented themselves in their genuine character. They charged upon the Moravians, insolently and unblushingly, although they knew the allegation to be false, that they were not what they claimed to be; that their professions were hypocritical, their practices dishonest; that their horses had been stolen from the white settlers, as was indicated by the letters—for what knowledge had they of letters?—with which they were branded; that their axes, stamped with white men's names, had been procured in the same way, as were also their wooden bowls, their spoons, their teakettles, pots, cups, and other utensils of the sort; in short, that they were warriors and enemies, and that they must make up their minds to meet the treatment due them as such.

In vain the unhappy creatures whom they had entrapped protested their innocence. They could account for the lawful and honest acquisition of every article of property in their possession. The irons for the brands were made by the smiths on their own order, to mark their own horses for identification among themselves. With their habits refined under training of the missionaries, and enabled thereto out of the abundance rewarding their industry, they were qualified to live, and did live, like Christian people, and had long owned, and had in use, the cooking and other domestic implements peculiar to civilized life. That they were not heathen Indians, or of those that were at strife with the Americans, might be seen from the fact that they did not appear in the savage costume; nor were their faces painted, nor did they wear the feathers, nor the scalp-locks, which distinguished the warriors. Some few of the bordermen were inclined to deal leniently with them, and indeed refused to participate in the after-proceedings, but the majority were not to be moved. Their fate was sealed.

Two adjoining buildings were selected as places of confinement, into one of which the men were thrust, and the women and children into the other. A council of the whites was hastily held, after which the formal announcement was made to the prisoners that they must die. With folded hands, imploring piteously, they prayed for life. The ears of their captors were deaf to entreaty, and if they yielded so far, at length, as to postpone the execution of their resolve until next day, it is more than likely that the respite was granted, not from motives of compassion, but that, like tigers, they might enjoy the tortures of their prey, and from their agonies derive a keener relish for to-morrow's feast of blood. Convinced at length that the consciences with which they had to do were proof against appeal, they ceased the effort. "We can call God to witness," said they, "that we are perfectly innocent; yet we are prepared and willing to suffer death."

No symptom of weakness betrayed itself thereafter. They had made their plea, earnestly but not cravenly, as true men may. It had failed. They accepted the failure, and with unfaltering composure awaited what was to come. Heroism had never a nobler illustration than was exemplified in their cases at that most trying crisis. All through the night devotional services were kept up; words of exhortation were interchanged, mutual confessions made, and prayers and praises offered at the throne of Grace. "I have been an untoward child," said Brother Abraham, "and have grieved the Lord by my disobedience, not walking as I ought to have done, yet will I cleave to my Saviour with my last breath. I know assuredly that He will forgive me all my sins and not cast me out." While still religiously engaged, singing together a hymn at the moment, the impatient ruffians who had voluntarily assumed the task, entered the rooms, and, harshly interrupting the proceedings, asked the prisoners if they were ready. They had committed their immortal souls to God, they said, and were ready. One of the border-men took hold of a cooper's mallet that lay on the floor, observing, as he did so, "How exactly this will answer for the purpose!" and with a heavily-wielded blow at the head of Brother Abraham brought him to the floor. Plying the weapon right and left, he did not pause until fourteen of the Christians were prostrate, struggling in the agonies of death. He then delivered the mallet to one of his fellows, remarking, "My arm fails me! Go you on in the same way!" And so, while a victim remained, the work of butchery continued.

Sixty-two men and women and thirty-four children were stricken down, scalped, and left crushed and bleeding on the floors of these slaughter-pens. Two only escaped; one, who by adroit management had extricated himself from the cords with which he had been bound, crawled through a window and secreted himself in the cellar of the house in which the Sisters were confined, their blood streaming down upon him through the seams in the floor as he crouched there; and another, who, felled, scalped, and left for dead like the rest, had nevertheless revived afterwards; betraying the fact, however, by no sign, but lying where he had fallen among the slain, without motion or groan, although suffering indescribable torture. In this predicament he lingered while the light lasted, and as long as there was danger of discovery. Under cover of the darkness both managed to retreat undetected from the building and gain the woods, whence, as the night deepened, they resumed their flight, and after a painful journey succeeded, at length, in reaching Sandusky in safety. But ere yet beyond view of the village, as they were able to relate to the horrified Congregation on the lake-shore, they had seen the torches applied to the slaughter-pens; they had seen the flames leap up and reach and spread, until the buildings were all enveloped in the blaze; and, in the glare of the fire, they had witnessed the dark forms of the border-men group and mingle, and in grim pantomime make display of their exultation at sight of this closing act of the hideous tragedy. Among the victims of the massacre was Glikkikan, the Delaware captain, who from the date of his conversion had continued, through all its vicissitudes of fortune, with the Congregation, loyal to the Faith, and true in his attachment to the missionaries.

Early in the morning of the day following the fatal one at Gnadenhütten, the band of assassins mounted their horses and started for Schönbrunn, to enact similar violence against the Christians who had taken shelter in that settlement. Fortunately, two Brethren from that locality, walking towards Gnadenhütten, encountered accidentally the dead body of one of their number, a young convert called Joseph Shabosh, who had been secretly murdered, like the boatman, while out alone, and about a mile apart from the rest of his people. Noticing the tracks of shod hoofs in the soil, they suspected danger, hastened back and alarmed their neighbors. When the border-men reached the village they found it deserted; and although the Indians who had fled were retired so short a distance up the river that they could see the movements of their pursuers, they remained undiscovered. After robbing the houses and stables of whatever properties of value they could lay hands upon, the plunderers, without choosing to resume pursuit, turned about and took up their route for home. Arrived at Pittsburg, the effects which they had stolen were offered for sale at public auction; on which occasion the scalps taken were brought out and proudly exposed, as trophies of heroic achievement, before the gaze of admiring bidders and beholders.

To COLONEL DAVID WILLIAMSON belongs the distinction of having led, as ruffian-in-chief, in this memorable adventure. If he is to be accredited with the account of the expedition, as published at the time in the *Pennsylvania Gazette*, wherein it is said, "We arrived at the town (Gnadenhütten) in the night, undiscovered; attacked the Indians in their cabins, and so completely surprised them that we killed and scalped upwards of ninety, but a few making their escape,—and returned to the Ohio without the loss of a man," then was he contemptible as a mendacious braggart. "Did you not hail and welcome the believing Indians," was the more truthful charge uttered against him and his gang by the savages, alluding to this occasion, shortly after, "as friends? You assured them of your friendship. You told them that they need not fear any harm from you. Did they run from you when they saw you coming? Did they fire a single shot at you? No. We warriors warned them to beware of you and your pretended friendship; but they would not believe, and for this they paid with their lives." If when, two months afterwards, a second expedition was undertaken to finish the work at Sandusky so prosperously begun on the Muskingum, and when in turn the border-men were surprised, the projector of the movement was the first man to take advantage of chance, desert his comrades and seek safety in flight; and if in that same adventure the more honorable but less fortunate Colonel Crawford, who would not abandon his followers, was captured, most cruelly tortured, and murdered, in retaliation for the crime in which he had not participated, then was the denunciation of the civilized world well bestowed, and the judgment of the savages well awarded, when they pronounced the leader in both enterprises a black-hearted assassin, a betrayer, and a coward.

VII.

THE DISPERSION OF THE CONGREGATION; ITS RESTORATION, AND ITS RETURN TO THE MUSKINGUM.

THE condition of the Brethren on the Sandusky was melancholy in the extreme. Their place of habitation amid the soggy flats of that half-deluged region was inhospitable, comfortless, and of such dismal associations that they would not give it name, but left it as a blot or a blank to fill its place in the record of their wanderings. The lands around them were rich enough in the production of rank and unwholesome vegetation, such as found indigenous growth in the contaminate soil; but no effort of industry could overcome their stubborn resistance to every attempt at better culture. The winter climate was cruel beyond endurance. In months of milder temperature the air was charged with pestilence. Men pined miserably from disease and want. Fevers racked their bodies. The proper prey of vultures—cattle fallen dead by the wayside, of famine—was a last resort for sustenance, upon which they fed hungrily. Persecutions assailed them from every quarter. They found themselves betrayed by friends in whom they had trusted; and the hands which they had clasped in pledge of that confidence, lifted treacherously against them, were red with the blood of their martyred kindred. They were despised and rejected of the tribes of their own race; and how could they hope, and for what could they hope, from the people that recognized Pipe as a partisan, and Girty and McKee and Elliott as allies? Their missionaries, towards whom, in the cares of life, they had been used to look for guidance and support, had been forced away and kept in banishment. God seemed to have forgotten to be merciful; to have disowned their devotion, mocked at their calamities, and given them over utterly to helpless, hopeless abandonment.

Some of the better qualified by grace and faith among the converts, who had been accustomed to serve as assistants to the missionaries, maintained the forms of worship in the community, the exercises peculiar to which were for some time marked by affecting displays of interest; but the artful conspirators who had successfully engineered the removal of the shepherds were not to be easily foiled in their experiments upon the flock. They poisoned the ears of the people with baneful accusations against their white leaders. The Muskingum massacre, they alleged, was planned with their knowledge; else why, instead of waiting with their followers to share the disaster that was to happen, had they allowed themselves to be carried off to a place of safety beyond the water? Murmurs of discontent at length began to prevail. Here and there a disciple of weak faith gave way. Soon backsliders made open confession of relapse, and boldly advocated apostasy to the rest. To complete the array of adversities hemming the unfortunates about, and closing in upon them irresistibly, the arm of civil authority was interposed. The half-king of the Hurons, " so incessantly tormented by his evil conscience that he could not rest as long as any Christian Indians were in his neighborhood to remind him of his treacherous and cruel behavior," commanded them peremptorily to disband and leave the country. The order was not to be disputed. Heavy at heart for the separations that were to take place, but without a sigh of regret at parting from the huts of logs and bark in which a wretched tarrying of six months had been endured, and that were never sanctified by a single endearing home association, on an April day (1782) they gathered up the ragged remains of their possessions, took their various courses and wandered off, some to the country of the Shawanese, and some to the Miami River. And so the community was broken in pieces; and so the nameless settlement on the Sandusky was abandoned forever.

The missionaries had scarcely retired from Detroit, after their acquittal in the trial to which reference has been made, when, upon additional charges preferred by the same parties, they were again brought before the commandant. On this occasion, however, they were not subjected to even the form of an examination. The commandant was satisfied of their innocence, and assured them that it was only with a view to their welfare that he had ordered their appearance at Detroit, being convinced, from reliable information, that if they remained at Sandusky it would be at the imminent hazard of their lives. He gave them permission to tarry under his protection at Detroit, or return to Bethlehem, as they chose. Duty and affection forbade their assent to either arrangement. It would be inhuman, it would be unchristian, in the hour of trial to forsake their scattered flock entirely. Their first wish was to establish a settlement in some new and safe locality, where they could gather around them their dispersed people, contribute to their comfort, and preserve them in the faith of the gospel. Learning their project, De Peyster approved of it, and, exerting his influence with the Chippewas, secured a grant from that tribe of a portion of their territory on the Huron River, thirty miles above Detroit, for their use. The missionaries took possession of the little domain, measured off fields, laid out gardens, built cabins of bark, and sent messages to the wandered exiles of the Congregation, inviting them to repair to the NEW-GNADENHÜTTEN reared for their reception. Abraham, the old Mohican captain and early convert, was one of the first to respond. Others followed, and soon again others, singly and in families, until quite a community was gathered in, and the new village began to wear an inhabited air and assume something of that homelike aspect which had so endeared their former settlements to the hearts of the Christians.

Before winter set in, the temporary bark huts were torn away and comfortable log cabins put up in their stead. The ground was cleared of underwood, in readiness for the plow and spade, when the coming of seed-time should call for their employment. Colonel De Peyster generously furnished supplies of garden and farming tools, a boat, a pair of cows, and some horses; his wife, at the same time, offering, as her contribution, an assortment of seeds, roots, and plants. To meet the wants of the people through the winter, hunting and trapping were resorted to; what flesh they had to spare, together with the hides and furs of the captured game, being taken to Detroit and there exchanged for meal and wearing-apparel. The women, and men inexpert at the use of the rifle or the snare, remained at home, improving their leisure in the manufacture of canoes, baskets, bowls, ladles, and brooms, or, further on in the season, tapping the maples in the neighboring groves and distilling their juices into sugar. With these articles quite a traffic was carried on with the white population in and about the British fort.

Thus the first winter, and so year after year, passed by. Busy hands did what was possible to improve the lands, and make more and more comfortable the dwellings and neat and ornamental the thoroughfares. The rough features of the native wilds of the vicinity were made smooth; meadows lay green and smiling on the water-shores where thickets of stunted oak-saplings, densely grown, had flourished; and cattle browsed on open ranges —pastures teeming with verdure—where, in the copses, foxes erewhile had made their hiding-places, and the deer had taken for refuge when pursued by the hunter.

The religion of the Moravian meant work as well as worship. While demanding strictly its tithes of devotional offering, it exacted no less rigidly its equal measure of muscular tribute. A system of belief thus severe in its requirements was as little to the relish of the savage as—could it be less than? —it would have been to the mass of paler-complexioned and more orthodox creedists. It called for long years of patient labor among the folk of their chosen nation, to win over to the Unity the converts of which its small flock was composed. The flesh more powerfully than the devil was up in arms against the attempted innovation. Under God, Zeisberger and his colleagues, with the Delawares to deal with, were more than a match for their antagonists, and out of that people were able to attract followers, and hold them fast and faithful, through whatever vicissitude of trial, to the new profession. But the Lenni-Lenapes were a race among whom virtue was not altogether effete, nor life in its diviner instincts without an aspiration. The Chippewas, on the other hand, were a miserably degraded tribe,—sunk so low as over the purely animal scarcely to have maintained a rational level in the scale of being. Indolent knaves were they, who derived their chief subsistence from hunting and fishing, or, when these resources failed, who found a satisfactory substitute in frogs, dogs, muskrats, and dead horses. Wedded to their groveling ways, they saw nothing to captivate them in the toilsome pursuits and compulsory observances of the Christians.

The missionaries labored long to educate these savages to a loftier conception of life and its duties, but their efforts were futile. Between societies whose materials were of such incongruous composition, there could exist no common element of attraction. They might exercise a mutual forbearance for awhile; but that virtue is of a precarious temper, and, if it does not ripen ere long into a feeling of more generous cast, is apt to degenerate into a sentiment of aversion. Four years of residence were spent at the settlement on the Huron. In the beginning the heathen had received the Congregation of exiles kindly. The novelty of the Christian usages having worn off, indifference followed, then distrust, then dissatisfaction. Complaints began to be made. Their hospitality was being unreasonably taxed. They wanted their own lands for their own purposes. The country thereabouts constituted their choicest hunting-grounds. The Moravians were clearing out their woods, killing their game, and soon, unless rid of their guests, they would be left destitute. Moreover, the causes no longer existed which had induced the offer of accommodation to the Society. The war had ended; peace was restored, and they were at liberty to go where they would, with none to molest them or make them afraid.

Although their occupation of New-Gnadenhütten had been one of uninterrupted repose; although Providence, rewarding their toils, had given them to enjoy plentifully of the means promotive of ease and comfort, yet the attachments of the Brethren to the place were not so many, nor so strong, but that they could be broken without insupportable regret. There were no endearing associations connected with the spot. The marked events of their experience—their struggles, their successes, their joys, and their griefs—all dated back in the past, and were linked with other scenes and other times. Lichtenau and Salem, the Beautiful Spring and the Tents of Grace, were the Zion to which their thoughts reverted. There had they witnessed their triumphs and been used to join their thousand voices in glad psalms of rejoicing. There had they suffered together when overtaken by calamity, and there the bones of their dead lay buried.

The missionaries had been defeated in the grand project which they had undertaken. On the eve of success, when their chapels were filled with attentive hearers; when chieftains, warriors, and counselors thronged with the multitude to listen to the messages of inspiration; and when the belief, which they had labored for forty years to establish as the national faith of the Delawares, seemed about to displace the ancient superstition, they found their plans thwarted, their work wrecked, their brotherhood banished, broken and scattered, and the expectations upon which they had reckoned so fondly blighted forever. In the choice of this their latest tarrying-place they had scarcely looked for more than to gather in, and maintain in the Unity, such scattered remnants as they might of their dispersed people. This done, they could entertain no dearer desire than, when the door of deliverance opened, to take up again their pilgrimage, retrace the ways of their wandering, and, as the day of their prosperity declined, to spend serenely its closing hours amid the scenes where they had enjoyed the full lustre of its noon, on the old familiar shores of the Muskingum.

When, therefore, the Chippewas intimated a desire for their removal, the Congregation, ministers and members, assented to the suggestion without a complaint. On the 20th of April, 1786, they assembled for the last time in their chapel; presented their oblation of prayer and praise, thanking the Lord for his mercies and commending themselves to his protection; then, embarking in their canoes, twenty-two in number, they bade adieu to the friends collected to witness their departure, shoved the vessels from the shore, and were gone.

It does not fall within the design of this sketch to follow further in detail the progress of the wanderers; to describe the alarms that caused a delay of a year at Pilgerruh,—the Pilgrims' Rest; to speak of the longer sojourn at Pettquotting, where Gillelemend, or Killbuck, embraced the gospel and was baptized; nor of their return to Michigan, and of their temporary settlement at Fairfield. The opportunity to carry out their cherished intention occurred at length, and on the 4th of October, 1798, seventeen years after their expulsion, the Congregation of exiles were back again on the banks of the Elk-Eye. They found their lands overgrown with tall, coarse grass, and infested with serpents. Briers and bushes, the harbor of wild beasts, thicketed the site of Gnadenhütten; all traces of which were lost except the ruins of a house or two, and, there where the slaughter-pens had stood, a heap of ashes, with here and there a bone not altogether consumed, indicating with melancholy certainty the scene of that awful visitation, never to be forgotten, of violence and fire, of treachery and assassination.

With the retirement of the Brethren from New-Gnadenhütten the mission in the wilderness may be said to have terminated. The new settlement of Goshen, erected eight miles from the spot where

Gnadenhütten had stood, on the Muskingum, was planted at a time when the region round about was rapidly filling up with white settlers. Axes were laid at the roots of the trees; clearings were made; the scared game was deserting the woods; squatters, tomahawk in hand to notch the corner hickories, were marking off their claims; log cabins were springing up, and the valley of the Muskingum was within the line of the border. The resistance of the savage to the encroachments of the pioneer only lacked the spasmodic attempt made shortly after by Tecumseh, to be abandoned in despair. Their disintegration and dispersion soon followed. With the tide of emigration flocked in other interpreters of inspiration,—stout defenders of the Faith, but whose zeal in the service never led them to tempt the perils and privations of a life beyond the advance posts of civilization. A new theatre for denominational rivalry—a supplementary stage for church extension—was found. The old field of Christian occupation, as among the Gentiles, was lost. The work of the Moravian was ended.

THE METHODIST.

(183)

THE METHODIST.

I.

THE METHODIST PREACHER OF THE BORDER—NASCITUR, NON FIT.

AS with the Jesuit began, so with the Moravian ended the missionary enterprises of the wilderness. While the Indian tribes peopled the land, and, as national communities, claimed and held the exclusive ownership of the soil; while a trespass upon their domain, or an offense against their customs, involved the risk of calamitous consequences; and while to be among them was to be shut out, utterly, from all fellowship with civilized society, the follower of Loyola and the disciple of Huss were permitted to enjoy undisputed possession of the field. "Evangelical" competitors stood aloof. It was their business to keep pace with the progress of light; not to invade the kingdom of darkness. Their boldest advances never reached beyond the clearings. Did Brainerd "undertake the arduous work of a missionary to wild barbarians"? The work was a few months' toil at the Forks of the Delaware, and the wild barbarians were Irishmen as well as aborigines. John Stewart, the mulatto Methodist exhorter, in 1816, "located" temporarily among a band of Hurons at Sandusky, but it was thirteen years after Ohio had been admitted as a State into the Union. Isaac McCoy, a very worthy Baptist divine, established the Carey Mission among the Pottawottamies on the St. Joseph's River, in Michigan, but it was in 1822, when the Territory had already been represented for three years in Congress. Indeed, even though a self-denying spirit equal to the undertaking had not been wanting, more adventurous enterprise could scarcely have been expected, when the esteem is considered in which the savages were held by the sects of the day. They were imps of hell's begetting, whom it was religious duty to exterminate,— the predestined victims of perdition, whom it was contempt of God's decrees to try to bring under sanctifying influence, — Hittites and Girgashites possessing the land, whom it was the bounden duty of the Lord's elect, rather, to smite and utterly destroy, to make no covenant with, and in whose favor to show no mercy: all consistently with the gospel according to Moses. Entertaining such views of the present *status* and future prospects of the race, to have attempted their reformation would have been more than a work of supererogation: it would have been to dispute the designs of Providence, to squander the time of his servants, and rashly and imprudently to expose the safety of their persons. They declined the venture. As others of their own people led, they might dare to follow, but discreetly, within bounds, and never beyond where the surveyor and the squatter, at least, had been before, to prepare the way and make straight the paths for the succession.

The cession to the British, by the Iroquois, of the country south of the Alleghany and Ohio Rivers, in 1768, opened up the extensive regions of that portion of Pennsylvania drained by the Monongahela, Western Virginia, and Kentucky to the occupation of the whites. Explorers penetrated the wilderness, speedily followed by traders, who commenced a lucrative business in furs and skins with the Indians. These, in their turn, were succeeded by adventurers of more reputable vocation; men who, with their rifles on their shoulders and their dogs at their heels, preferred to win by skill and daring the valuable spoils which had been the objects of barter to their predecessors. The favorable report given upon their return, of the countries which they visited, aroused attention. Listeners to their narratives, told in social circles or at domestic firesides,—especially the young who had yet their fortunes to carve out, and who wanted neither the vigor nor the will to do it,—were easily tempted to make trial on their own account; and so, from the old settlements of Eastern Virginia and North Carolina, started that tide of emigration which was soon to make populous all the new border, from the valley of the Monongahela to the far hunting-grounds of the Cherokees on the Kentucky. Permanent settlers occupied the lands. Surveys were made, cabins were built, acres were cleared, the soil was tilled, farm was added to farm, villages sprang up, and all abroad the inflowing populations were spreading, mooring, improving, and multiplying. As the process of importation went on, speculators joined in it, helping to swell the moving current—and add to the list of their destined victims. Extensive tracts were bought, or laid claim to, by these professional sharpers, which were sold in parcels to newly-arriving emigrants, who seldom paused to inquire into the validity of titles, and were made the subjects of gross imposition. They frequently paid the price of their purchases two or three times over, to find that even then their claims were utterly invalid. The country beyond the Ohio attracted their attention. Its lands were not in the market, and therefore lay out of the reach of the avaricious operator. The shores wore a fruitful and inviting aspect. Easily induced to run the risk of annoyance from the savages, the settlers, many of them, resolved upon a change, and, crossing the river, began to take possession of the new territory, establishing their settlements in the regions watered by the Muskingum, the Scioto, and the Miami.

But the provinces of the lower coast were not to enjoy a monopoly of the new field of occupation.

Massachusetts, some twenty years subsequently to the movement of her more enterprising sisters, put in her claim. A party of emigrants under the auspices of the "Ohio Company" crossed the mountains, reached the Youghiogheny, built a vessel, which, in honor of the memorable craft that had borne their fathers on a still more daring voyage, they called the "Mayflower," and, pursuing the remainder of their journey by water, tarried not until they had attained their point of destination, at the mouth of the Muskingum. The tract included in the grant of the company covered a large portion of the eastern section of what was afterwards the State of Ohio, and was not of the choicest part of its territory; but the "Huckleberry Knobs" were a vast improvement on the sterile patches of New England, and the new-comers were delighted with the change. Glowing accounts were sent back of the country. It was a land flowing, literally, with milk and honey. Its meadows, without cultivation, were equal to the support of millions of cattle, winter and summer. Sicily could not afford finer wheat-lands. There were bogs producing cranberries enough to supply tarts for all New England; while the legs of the horses roving the plains were dyed to the knees with the juice of the wild strawberry. Fresh recruits poured rapidly and continuously in. Marietta sprang at once into importance as a town. The neighboring country filled up,—the axe laying bare new openings for homesteads farther and farther back into the woods. School-houses were built, teachers employed, and, in a short time, all the machinery by which well-regulated Yankee communities at home are governed, set swimmingly in motion.

Thus were the nearer quarters of the Northwest Territory invaded at the south and at the east, and thus were brought together in the same Commonwealth two various classes, which were ultimately to blend together, and out of their united thrift and enterprise to build up one of the most prosperous and populous republics in the whole of the confederate group.

As between these classes, there were striking points of contrast. The Down-Easter, in his transplantation, lost none of his distinguishing characteristics. He was his identical self on the border as in the Bay State. His institutions he had brought with him as part and parcel of the miscellaneous stock of "notions" that constituted his baggage,—his Bible and his ballot-box, his spelling- and his statute-book (is it superfluous to add, his jack-knife and his dialect?),—all that could be made available "to secure civil rights, establish law and order, introduce a pure religion, and provide for universal education." True to the habits in which he had been trained: of thinking,—and he was shrewd at it; of doing,—and he never wearied of it; of appearing,—and, down to his cloth, its cut and its brass buttons, he never varied in it,—he underwent no change; dealing with his neighbor, serving God—and himself—as he had always done, as his fathers before him had done, and as his children after him would continue to do.

Not so with the Virginian. Cut loose from his anchorage on the Chesapeake, he left all behind him, as he went on his wanderings, save a stout heart throbbing for adventure, and a stanch arm nerved to achieve it. The old ways of life, the influences of home and of society, except as they may have operated to induce a general tendency of character, were discarded and abandoned. He threw them off, as unsuited to the uses and the fashions of the woods. Accoutred in his hunting-shirt of linsey-woolsey, his buckskin breeches, fox-skin cap, and easily-fitting moccasins, and with his rifle, his pouch, and the knife at his belt as his only *impedimenta*, he launched out, freighted to his full desire, upon his voyage. At his journey's end he could find him the means to satisfy his wants as their cravings demanded. Hungry, the forest abounded with every variety of game from which to choose his fare. Overtaken by nightfall, and anxious for repose after the toils of a day, the shadow of a rock, a shelter of boughs thrown loosely together, or a bed of leaves with the broad oak-branches overhead for cover, lent ample accommodation for his comfort. In unrestricted freedom he roamed the forest, knowing no law save the law of right between man and man, which he was scrupulous to respect himself, and for which, in his own behalf, he would have contended to the death. Uneducated, and without opportunity of instruction other than such as his own experience offered, the sciences of the schools were sealed mysteries to him, but his understanding was not wanting in the "gifts"—well cultivated—that suited much better the exigencies of his case. He had his religion. If, in the practical working, it partook of the severe type of the older dispensation, when retaliation was a virtue, and "a tooth for a tooth" an accepted maxim among the faithful, it was because the flesh is weak, and temptation, with treachery and cruelty to contend against, is strong; and because man, until sanctified by the purer influences of the gospel, is of the earth, earthy,—frail, fallible, and inflammable.

The example of the adventurer was not lost upon the squatter, nor that of the squatter upon the settlers; so that when, in a short time, the region was filled with a more numerous population, its constituents came in for a share of the inheritance; the original leaven in the little was still perceptible in the lump. In selecting lands for improvement, the party intending to "locate" would choose out of the unoccupied woods a desirable spot, with his tomahawk hack off a chip from the corner trees of his claim, and thus, without any of the formal processes by which properties customarily fall into ownership, would take possession and proceed to business. This novel style of *indenture* answered every purpose, and was respected, between neighbor and neighbor, as inviolably as though executed in parchment and sanctioned by affixture of wax and seal, after the more legitimate fashion. First having gave first right,—a right which, if possibly any may have lacked the conscience, certainly none had the hardihood to dispute. As the people multiplied, and customs more in accordance with civilized practice began to prevail, they were submitted to as unavoidable necessities of the new situation; but in no case were they allowed to the interference with ownerships, whether in properties or privileges, acquired under the former usages. The compass and the chain might mark out the boundaries of new claims, but never cross the lines already defined by the tomahawk. A title with a deed was good, certainly, but equally so was one without it,—probably better, as there was plausible argument to offer, in time, when so many were defrauded through the double-dealing of the land-trader.

So with regard to the civil regulations of the day. The borderer, although content to be a *nomos* unto himself, was not averse to the introduction of "professional" law, and was content to abide by its decrees; provided, always, that they were in accordance with his own individual notions of justice. He would not divest himself of the right to hang a highwayman or a horse-thief on the nearest tree, in order that punishment (with the intervening possibility of a flaw in the writ— or the jail, to favor an escape) might be brought about, more formally, through the verdict of a jury and the sentence of a court. Neither would he brook interference if, when wronged by the savage, he chose, at his own time and in his own way, to recover full satisfaction for the injury; and Mingo and Delaware could well attest how severe was the wrath of the *Long-Knife*,—as by way of distinction the Virginian was called,—and how terrible his revenge, when recompense was due for provocation.

With the Ohio Company it was part of their scheme of colonization to send out with the emigrants men qualified to discharge the various ministries of responsibility in the settlement. Marietta was to be kept under guardianship until she became of age. For the management of her schools teachers were provided. She had a superintendent to regulate her public affairs. Magistrates were appointed to administer justice; physicians to wait upon the sick; while to look after her spiritual interests the services were engaged of the Rev. Daniel Story, the "first regularly ordained Congregational minister" in the Northwest Territory (1788).

The Virginians, on the other hand, could not— indeed, did not care to—look for men to fill their offices. As a want was felt and an opening for supply advertised itself, the candidate for the position, one of themselves, and not from solicitation, but on his own motion and at his own venture, put in an appearance. The country was not exempt from diseases. The Esculapian aspirant saw that infirmities might be put to profit; noticed symptoms; made himself acquainted with the remedies in vogue among Indians and old women; gathered in supplies of pink-root, sarsaparilla, ginseng, jalap, and ipecac; offered his services, and medicine became a profession. Education was not in eminent favor along the frontier. Boone, and Stewart, and Finley, and Holden were not remembered as having been patrons of learning; and if they, the illustrious in border history, were content to dispense with letters, might not their successors be satisfied? But there began to be those of more liberal views, who were not disinclined to admit the advantages of instruction: the Master was found to take advantage of the concession, and schools were started, backed by sufficient support to keep them in living condition for two or three months, in the wintertime, out of the twelve.

People who have once enjoyed the opportunities of Christian worship are seldom entirely weaned from their attachment to its observances. The dwellers on the frontier, partly through choice, but mainly from necessity, may have neglected the duties to which they had formerly been accustomed, but their respect for the word, its ordinances, and its ministers, had never failed. The pioneer may have left his Bible back among the forsaken properties of home, but the lessons gathered from its pages were not forgotten. As the floating elements of which it was composed settled down, and society began to assume orderly shape, the church was felt to be a prime desideratum. But how was its establishment to be brought about? Domestic missionary societies were not in existence. Laborers, except of unevangelical order, would not volunteer without hire; and silver and gold had they none to offer. As in the case of the other professions, if they were to be served they must serve themselves. Out of their own Galilee must arise their own prophets. There were men among them willing for the office; but to be fitted for it, according to orthodox rule, would require years of preparatory training in schools far removed and difficult of access.

But a new order of the priesthood had lately arisen. Rev. John Wesley, of the Church of England, impressed with the conviction that he was divinely appointed for some extraordinary work, carried his enthusiasm so far as to run into certain irregularities, on account of which he was debarred the privilege of the pulpit. Not to be silenced, he invited hearers, and in the open air at Moorfields addressed the multitude. So great was the success of the experiment that he was induced to persevere in it, making frequent journeys abroad through the country, and preaching daily in the streets, fields, and cemeteries, before large and admiring assemblies. Although he himself maintained to the end his connection with the Episcopal Church, his labors resulted in the establishment of a separate ecclesiastical organization, which spread rapidly at home, and in due time extended beyond the ocean. To look after the spiritual interests of the classes which were formed in different localities, "leaders" were appointed from among the laity, who were authorized to exercise all the ordinary functions of the preacher. A "call" to that post, without regard to intellectual fitness, was the single qualification required. It was the style of institution that suited the wants of the frontier precisely. The young forester, abandoning his axe and rifle at the cabin door as the disciples their nets by the sea, took up his easy license and started abroad, the duly commissioned standard-bearer of the Faith. Its solitary places awakened at the sound of his voice crying in the wilderness. His labors prospered, his circuits widened, and soon, throughout the length and the breadth of the land, the Methodist was known, famously and familiarly, as, *par éminence*, the Minister of the West,—the Black-Rob of the Border.

II.

THE ARREST, AWAKENING, CONVICTION, CONVERSION, AND THE CALL OF THE PREACHER.

A GLANCE at his earlier life, his adventures, and his experiences, will be appropriate as serving to illustrate the character of the Methodist preacher of the border. Abundant facilities for this purpose are offered in the autobiographies which he has contributed for the popular edification and entertainment. Their details present him in the various circumstances and vicissitudes of his career: as a thoughtless worldling, wedded to unhallowed pursuits and amusements; as a voluptuary, tempted and fallen into sin; as an alarmed offender led to penitence; and as the humbled creature of conviction made the hopeful subject of conversion. The portrayal is thorough and complete.

He is generally born of poor but respectable parents. More or less religious influence has been brought to bear upon him in his childhood; usually — although his father has not always proved delinquent—through the instrumentality of his mother; herself an old Virginia Presbyterian most likely, unless, under the eloquence of Whitefield, made a convert to the creed of the Moorfields reformer. His Christian education, like his secular, however, has been, at best, a limited one, not often extending beyond a knowledge of the Lord's Prayer, the Ten Commandments, and a lesson or two out of the Mother's Catechism. Yet is he not unaccustomed to the forms of religious observance. He has seen church service, has knelt at evening worship in the family, and been used to the "Now I lay me down to sleep" of his own private devotions. Thus far experience has gone; giving its dash of color to his life, its faint outline of impression to his character, to die out utterly, or attain a ripe finish of shape and complexion, as future contingencies may determine,—thus far, and no farther.

In his youth we find him, if not born on Western soil, drifted thither with the tide of emigration, one of a still unbroken household group, gone in quest of better faring to the border. The old home-altar is re-established, and its ceremonies attempted anew, but the experiment staggers; with the public administration of the ordinances neglected, example decays at the fireside; the zeal of the votary languishes, and anon the form even of the simple domestic ritual drops into desuetude. The reins of discipline relax; the disembarrassed boy, eager to profit by the release, throws himself with entire abandonment, like an impatient hound freed from his leash, or a colt from its tether, into whatever scheme of pleasure first offers or best attracts. He has an ear for music,—an eye for motion; a fiddle and a ball-room, the "Arkansas Traveler," and a Virginia hoe-down, are irresistible allurements. He hears,—sees,—engages a partner for the next set, and the text of the Ten Commandments begins to fade; when he most needs to remember, he first forgets his "Lead us not into temptation." Or he has a taste for play, —enters the card-room, soon learns to hold his hand, and pockets his hazards, too; has his steady hours at the table, and is presently the devoted servant of seven-up, old sledge, and poker. Or the easily besetting sin of the love of horse-flesh overreaches him, and he takes to the race-course, backs his charger, leaps to the contest, and over a broader way and with other goal and guerdon ahead than he entered for, rides to win—and to lose. Fairly enlisted in the devil's service, his progress does not halt. He scoffs at morality; he swears; he drinks; he frolics; he fights, and is soon proficient in all the gentlemanly vices of the backwoods.

It is entertaining to notice with what a flavor of fondness the reverend autobiographer looks back from his later lenten standpoint and lingers over this wild, licentious carnival-period in his life! how his appetite seems to whet, and his chaps to melt, at the mere recollection of the savory flesh-pots of the demoralized, discarded, dear old Egypt! Nor is he, indeed, ever entirely liberated from the tyranny of the passions to which he then succumbed. Jacob Young, the reverend, had always a fancier's eye for a steed, and boasts of the fine Arabian horse on which he threaded the morasses and swam the streams in his circuit-ridings. His original relish for the ring which Peter the Sinner had cultivated was not totally lost to Peter the Saint, in Cartwright's conversion; and the gusto is eminently professional with which he tells, through all the particulars, of a personal rencounter with a certain disturber of the peace at a camp-meeting, in which, after a solid round or two, he came off victorious; and how, on another occasion, he took an attitude and pluckily called out, "Don't you attempt to strike me," to a certain Major L., who had "clinched his fists" with that ostensible purpose in view, "for if you do, and the devil gets out of you into me, I shall give you the worst whipping you ever got in all your life."

But the carnal diversions of society by free indulgence lose, at length, their attraction, and then the satiate profligate, perhaps, takes a fancy, like Finley, for roving,—straps his blanket on his back, shoulders his rifle, and is off for the woods. The life has its trials, but is one of ever-varying adventure, the excitements of which afford abundant recompense for whatever of danger or discomfort may attend its pursuit. It is not necessarily a wicked one. To shoot a bear, and make a breakfast next morning on the rare delicacy of his paw, baked slowly overnight in the hot ashes of the camp-fire; to bag a wild turkey and dine upon it at mid-day; or to dispatch, by good luck, a buffalo and partake of his tongue with one's tea (whatever the decoction may be) in the evening; to bring down a raccoon or a wild-cat, and, in a strait, make a meal upon either, when roasts that might be preferable are not procurable; or to make merchandise of the hides and furs of all of them,—ought scarcely to occasion pangs of remorse, and, indeed, do not; but the Sabbath has been desecrated,—the crack of the rifle has disturbed its hallowed rest, and the inheritance of a guilty, self-accusing conscience, which shall find a discovery one day, is entailed upon the profaner.

As poison is administered to purge from poison, so the very excess of indulgence often leads to the correction of the habit. The sports to which the young devotee is addicted have found him, season in and season out, a faithful patron. The appointed time has always seen him at the appointed place. He has sustained his part well,—taken to it heartily, enjoyed it lustily, and left it at last without a feeling of disquietude, unless it might be one of regret that the hours of delight should have proved so evanescent. And yet once, in the order of Providence, it happens, after a run of luck high in his favor at the card-table, perhaps, or at the close of a more than ordinarily brilliant scene of festivity, as on his favorite racer he rides towards home in the night, he is suddenly arrested on the way by the miraculous shining of a great light, such as challenged the awe of Saul of Tarsus on his way to Damascus. The sight staggers him. He begins to reflect. He feels guilty and condemned. Of a sudden the blood rushes to his head. His heart palpitates. In a few minutes he turns blind. An awful impression rests on his mind that death has come, and that he is unprepared to die, when much alarmed he lifts his voice to heaven and asks God to have mercy on him. Reaching home, he retires to bed, but finds little rest, and rises in the morning feeling wretched beyond expression. He tries to read the Testament, requests his father to sell his race-horse for him, and hands over his pack of cards to his mother, who throws them into the fire.

It is the dawn of a new and momentous era in his life. *Conviction* has overtaken him. Like an attack of the bowel-complaint or the measles, and with symptoms as clearly marked through the various stages of progress, it lays hold of him, vexes him, and brings him down. He complains of broken sleep; of a fevered, irregular pulse; loss of appetite; dismal apprehensions; ghastly visions and nightmares. To shake off the disease he resorts to remedies,— the accustomed ones, first, of a glass of whisky, or a turn on the turf, or a set-to at seven-up. These only aggravate the trouble, and are dismissed for other and better expedients. Retiring to a solitary grove, he spends hours in meditation, moaning like a dove that has lost his mate, and crying like the crane in the desert; but his distress does not abate. Returning to society again, a sympathizing sister, likely, suggests singing and prayer, which, when had, afford some relief. An effect of this treatment is weeping, and a plentiful flow of tears is comforting. Dreams are found to be refreshing; active exercise in the open air serves a good purpose, and repeating the narrative of his experience in the presence of attentive listeners at the prayer-meeting is peculiarly soothing.

At length, after a longer or shorter siege of trial, his griefs suddenly disappear. A flash of light, "shining from the south part of heaven," gleams in upon his soul: he is translated into the kingdom, —born into a new sphere of glorious existence, and finds peace—ecstatic peace—in believing. As he imagines; but prematurely, as it turns out, for anon he discovers that the deliverance upon which he has congratulated himself is a delusion,—the translation a mistake,—the new birth a miscarriage. A lapse from grace, either to magnify the virtue, or to exemplify a dogma, would seem to be an absolute necessity as a precedent to its perfect attainment; and he lapses. Still, though fallen, he is not lost.

A second awakening takes place, attended by similar phenomena with the first, and working towards the same salutary end; but the progress is blocked by serious obstacles which were not encountered before. Then, oppressed with a sense of sinfulness, and anxious only on the score of forgiveness, he had addressed himself accordingly; content to implore, "God be merciful to me, a sinner!" and satisfied, as the ground of his hope in Jesus, with a faith whose only and all-sufficient article was the unwritten one—inexpressible, but fathomable easily and infallible — of the poor woman of Capernaum,—a lifted finger, and a touch of the hem of his garment. But his theological studies—for he has read, since conviction, the New Testament to some extent—have made him an "inquirer" in a new sense. Now, he cannot accept grace unless he understands precisely how he gets it, on what terms, at whose cost, and whether he holds it inalienably, or at the option, liable to be revoked, of the donor. He hesitates to reach at the purifying garment until he masters the mystery of its manufacture; how it is woven, after what pattern, and of what thread,—particularly the hem of it. The church (as comprehended in his notion of that institution) has become his object of interest instead of Christ. He must find a way to follow the Way already provided. To win the crown he must run the gauntlet of the creeds. Of Presbyterian parentage, quite likely, he has naturally a preference for that persuasion. "If I could only convince myself that Calvinism is true," he says, "I would be satisfied." But he trips at the horrid idea of the doctrine of Particular

Election and Reprobation, and stumbles against numerous other heresies, until finally he sees, "as clearly as that two and two make four, that if the Bible is true the Old Confession is false." The converse of the proposition holds good, of course; and, as he does not care yet to relinquish the Bible, further passage by the Westminster route is given up, and search made for another. He is attracted by the New Lights; but "when he hears their doctrine on the Supreme Divinity of Jesus Christ, he will not go with them," impressed as he is "with a clear and powerful demonstration of the truth, that if Christ is not God He is powerless to save." He tries the Shaking Quakers; but their worship is so ridiculous that the bare thought of following up on that line is preposterous. The Seceders invite attention; but the professors of that school are too scandalously immoral, being addicted to intoxication, and having scarcely the form of godliness about them. Communion with such a circle is out of the question. Then he tries to carve out a way of his own, along which to travel to heaven alone; but, as one astray in the wilderness, without star or compass to guide him, is apt to wander back circuitously to his starting-point, he shortly finds himself bringing up at the old booth on the race-course, and that scheme is abandoned.

At this juncture it so happens that a challenge salutes the inquirer from a new quarter entirely.

Wesleyanism, surely established now in the East, has reached the West. Brother Hickman, on a tour of observation (1776), and Lewis Lunford, the Patrick Henry of the pulpit (1779),—first of their sect to penetrate the wilderness,—are assembling the backwoodsmen in the cabins, barns, or open woods, and addressing them with an eloquence which is irresistible and convincing. He joins the throng in attendance at their meetings,—hears, is enraptured, and exults at the thought that at last he has hit upon the manifest highway to glory. He first appears at these assemblages, which are kept up daily, and is thoroughly awakened, perhaps on a Monday. On Tuesday he is brought under profound conviction, and is so distressingly affected that when he flees to the woods for relief "he does not dare to take his gun with him, for fear he should, in the hour of the power of darkness, commit suicide." The dawn of Wednesday finds him praying and wrestling, which exercise, with fasting and humiliation, is maintained through the day and all the night following. On Thursday he is about to resume his devotions, when suddenly, at say twenty-two minutes before six in the morning, "the light pours upon him in such a manner, and in such a measure," that he falls to the earth, shouting and praising God, so as to be heard over the neighborhood, and is converted. He has entered the second time into the womb, and is born again.

In the working out of the reformatory process which the "seeker" undergoes, each new phase of development is signalized by its attending supernatural manifestation. God specially interposes and is present in every act of his grace, not spiritually and metaphorically, but really and sensibly; as does, and is also, on the other hand, the Prince of Darkness, when alarmed for his interests at the detected disloyalty of a subject. At his awakening, sudden blindness (each step in the proceeding is always noted as "sudden,"—"instant,"—"like an electric flash") seizes the sinner. Under conviction, he hears a voice speaking out of heaven in syllables of censure or of admonition, and quotes its utterance; or a celestial messenger visits and counsels him in vision, while he sleeps; or the devil meets him in a cavern in the woods, whither he has retired to pray, in such unquestionable guise, and with so unmistakable an intent "to seize and drag him down to hell, soul and body," that he starts to his feet affrighted, takes to his heels, and runs, full speed, to his mother, knitting at home in her cabin, for protection. Conversion comes, attended with a literal display of light ineffable and full of glory: the subject of it distinctly hears a voice announce, "Thy sins are all forgiven thee!"— gives attention with ear and eye, and really witnesses the mountains and the hills break forth into singing, and all the trees of the fields clap their hands, in irrepressible ecstasy at the event.

After conversion comes the Call. The "convict" spends an hour following the crisis of his rescue, in a delirium of rapture, catching, peradventure, his wife in his arms, running round the house, and shouting, "Salvation! salvation!" so that his neighbors think him drunk or crazy. While thus exercised, a voice falls "like a falling star" from heaven, saying, "Go, preach my gospel!" upon which he immediately responds, "Yes, Lord, if thou wilt go with me." Forthwith, not tarrying to confer with flesh and blood, but hurrying out as fast as he can to the nearest cabin, he calls its inmates together and begins to proclaim a risen Saviour who has power on earth to forgive sins. Or perchance he may hesitate at the divinely indicated line of duty; he may, with modest emphasis, deny his fitness for the priestly office,—may withdraw to the woods and tell his Maker that if it is pressed to the alternative that he must preach the gospel or go to hell, he must go to hell, for he has not the least qualification for the work. As results of this resistance to the designs of Providence, he loses all comfort, becomes gloomy and despondent, and from a state of robust health is reduced almost to a walking skeleton. But the invisible, mighty pressure continues. There is no mistaking, nor indeed any thought of questioning, its source. At length he ceases to oppose,—with becoming humility acquiesces in the appointment, —puts on the harness, and, to his speedy convalescence, and the healthy restoration of his dwindled flesh and depressed spirits, enters the lists and takes the field. Saul of Tarsus at sunrise is Paul the Apostle at noon, and appoints to meet and address his impenitent friends at Mars' Hill by early candle-light in the evening.

III.

THE PREACHER IN THE PULPIT.

THE idea of "preparation" for the ministry was one that never found favor for a moment in the Methodist mind. Learning was regarded as not only unnecessary, but actually objectionable, in the Black-Robe; who was presumed to be chosen of God as his officer, either by act of foreordination, opposed though such a view was to a favorite denominational tenet, or by special election, just as he was; and for whom, in such a case, to try to improve upon his qualifications, would be to doubt the wisdom and defeat an evident design of the Almighty. The blind, notwithstanding the proverb, were the true leaders of the blind. Rev. Jacob Young, at one time, thought to try the experiment of a literary, scientific, and theological course, but soon found that it would not work. God, in token of disapproval, hid his countenance from him; the Bible became a sealed book; he lost his comfort, was attacked with a violent fever, and severe pain in his head, and only got well when he abandoned letters and fell back on inspiration. One of his cotemporaries testifies that he would rather have the gift of a devil-dislodging power than all the college lore or biblical-institute knowledge that could be obtained from mortal man; and gives it as his opinion that the best course of preparation for the pulpit is to take your sinner, shake him awhile over hell, then knock the scales from his eyes, and, without any previous theological training, send him out straightway to preach Jesus and the Resurrection. A writer, while he records it, boasts of the fact that, among the thousands of traveling and local preachers in his church, there were not more than fifty that had anything more than a common English education, and scores of them not that; and that not one of them was ever trained in a theological school, yet hundreds of them had more seals to their ministry than all the sapient, downy D.D.'s in modern times, presiding in the various institutions throughout the land. These plainly-spoken views were not entertained by the commoners merely of the profession, but had the concurrence of the chief dignitaries as well,—Bishop Asbury among the rest.

The study of men was recommended as the solely profitable one; that of books, condemned as superfluous. Christ had no literary college or university, no theological school or biblical institute, to train his disciples in. On the contrary, He showed his contempt for all such establishments by selecting his followers from the lowest and least-enlightened classes of society. True, the Black-Robe of the better-informed minority, as we have seen, was not utterly and absolutely unskilled in letters. With the print in clear, round type, under a favorable light, and with careful attention, having previously conned the lesson, he could read a chapter tolerably intelligibly from the New Testament, or the lines of a stanza from the hymn-book. As a somewhat common, although not invariable, rule, he could also write. On one recorded occasion he was requested by a lady, under whose roof he was tarrying for a night, while on the tour of his circuit, to act as her amanuensis in a trifling matter of correspondence. Blushingly, and with unfeigned diffidence, he assumed the task, and it is with a pardonable air of proud satisfaction that he relates to the narrator of the incident the success—rather, it would seem, to the surprise of both parties—attending the experiment. The Presbyterian preacher who had served the apprenticeship required by the school to which he belonged,—who was manufactured like a head of lettuce in a hot-house,—and who was wont to sermonize from manuscripts, was an object of mingled pity and disdain. His messages, like cold meats, carved no matter how neatly, were stale, flat, and unpalatable, which the border sinner might taste once in awhile, perhaps, but, used to hot and savory indulgences, could never be tempted to accept as a standing diet. The Methodist would set the world on fire while the Presbyterian — formal, precise, and measured as to his deliveries—was lighting his matches.

Sir Geoffrey Hudson could wield a sword and join as valiantly as Prince Rupert in a sally against the train-bands of London, and with as full a trust in the efficiency of the blade he flourished, although there were but twenty inches of him, all told, to show in comparison with the full stature of his illustrious fellow-martialist. The Methodist Black-Robe was not of inferior virtue to the pygmy knight in one striking particular at least. Reposing a confidence in his own power of achievement that was never shaken by disaster, he not only felt himself the peer of any ecclesiastical Rupert, the princeliest that ever handled spiritual iron, but would volunteer a charge, unsupported and alone, against all the train-bands of Christendom combined. There was no question within the range of theological inquiry which he did not hold himself ready, at a moment's notice, to solve to the entire satisfaction of any audience. He understood all mysteries and all knowledge : points of doctrine, made the lifetime subjects of investigation by less enlightened students of the word, and perhaps not clearly settled then, he was ready to pronounce upon off-hand, and with an air of decision that would have done credit to an Ecumenical Council.

It was difficult, if not impossible, to match him at a controversy. He could settle the business of a Calvinistic professor on the subject of Election, handsomely and conclusively, at a single tilt, and within the space of two minutes. "A few questions," says Finley, "would invariably silence him." The Baptist he found rather a tough customer, but in ordinary cases he could floor his antagonist of that cloth in half a dozen rounds at furthest. He could ring the changes on *Bapto* with a facility that was marvelous in the ears of the multitude, who were not always aware of the extent of his acquirements, and who did not know that from his one acquaintance with the original texts in both cases he might, with the same skill precisely, have gone into the discussion of a disputed hieroglyph on an Egyptian obelisk.

In the matter of pronunciation he was somewhat irregular, not conforming exactly to the rules in request among acknowledged authorities. His accents, dropped pretty much at random, were apt to fall where they were not designed to fit; his vowels were not invariably true to their colors; not a few of the consonants used to double duty would strike out in one capacity when they should have served in another; while syllables, especially the inferior ones of the heavier combinations, were sadly slighted, and, indeed, sometimes ignored altogether. Words were liable to similar discourtesy, being frequently introduced, under perverted names, into strange company, and made not only to suffer themselves, on the suspicion of false pretense, by the association, but now and then to implicate their new neighbors as conniving at the imposition. As for language, his vocabulary was not very extensive, but its resources were sufficiently abundant for his purpose. What he knew, he knew all the more intimately for not knowing more. The telling, trenchant, hell-fire-and-damnation dialect of the turf, the bar, and the ball-room he had carried over with him in his "brimstone wallet," as he facetiously terms it, at his conversion, and since kept in readiness to shake over the heads of insulting and profane sinners among his hearers.

In the pulpit the Methodist Black-Robe was in his element. The unembarrassed step with which he mounted the platform; his seemingly half-unconsciousness of the act, as with a glance of customary —so he would have it appear—rather than curious observation he lifted his eyes and swept the space filled by his hearers, as a chess-player does his board, ere the game quite opens, to see that the pieces are complete and properly adjusted in their places; the showy carelessness with which he extracted his folios from his person—it was his boast that he carried all his library, Testament, hymn-book, and "Discipline" composing the catalogue, in his pocket—and laid them down, with much deliberation, volume by volume, on the desk; and the gratifying complacency with which, flourishing his handkerchief, he proceeded to clear his throat, and his nose, violently, of such imaginary or real obstruction to clear speech as might lodge, or be supposed to lodge, in either,—all were admirably calculated, and intended, as so many advertisements to the people that, in the speaker about to address them, they beheld the right man in the right place, and no mistake,—one who was perfectly at home in it, and thorough master of the situation.

His sermons were originals; not borrowed or copied from the standard styles of the time, but fashioned after a pattern peculiarly their own. In their composition he did not allow himself to be hampered by the restrictions ordinarily regarded as indispensable to excellence in the art. He did not adhere with undeviating fidelity to the straight-forward pursuit of an argument, preferring to loiter by the way, as attractive fancies now and again sprang in his path to invite to dalliance; or, tempted by a suggestion,—butterfly-like darted up to divert him,—to follow the lure in its excursive flight, to the relinquishment of the line of his main purpose altogether. His texts—or mottoes, to speak more accurately, because they rather indicated than really formed his subjects of declamation—were selections from the Scriptures of such passages or phrases as might be introduced with effect to swell a sentence or round a period,—

which, with wonderful facility, he could contrive to do, let the tone of the topic vary as it might, —"*for he played on a harp of a thousand strings!*"

His treatment of a subject varied according to the circumstances attending its delivery. The several styles from which he had to choose were "the argumentative, the dogmatic, the *postulary*, the persuasive, the punitive, the combative, the logical, and the poetic." As affording a broader field for the exercise of his talents, and as, indeed, capable, in his hands, of embodying all the effective force without the heaviness of the others, the "poetic" stood in chief favor. The preliminary details of his discourses were managed with a tone and action remarkable for moderation, and the steady, stately tenor of their rendering. Here it was he exhibited himself in his more solid, "argumentative" mood; seizing the occasion, as the most opportune, for a specimen-display of his qualities in reserve, and to furnish a hint of the wind and bottom to be depended upon when, presently, both should be put to the trial. So, on the turf in his sporting-days, he may have walked his courser round and about the starting-post, to show his parts, set forth his points, and prove his training, before the eyes of admiring beholders, ere opening upon the proper career, where the glory came in, for which he was entered. But no sooner was this ceremony ended and the moment for "business" arrived, than a striking change became apparent. The face of the orator flushed, his eye brightened like the eyelids of the morning, the sonorous voice for which he was famous let out its power, and " his gestures grew animated as the waftures of a fiery torch." Poetry, madly broke loose, took to wild flight, and, cleaving space, went whirling through the distances without regard to laws of limitation : ascending up to heaven, descending into hell, taking the wings of the morning and speeding to the uttermost parts of the sea; plucking bright honors from the moon, sun, stars, weaving to itself garlands from the lightning's wings, toying with tempests, and grasping infernal thunder, black fire, and horror from the nether abysses.

This particular style, however, was not sustained uninterruptedly through the performance, but was relieved at appropriate intervals by such intercalary passages of pleasantry, sarcasm, ridicule, or rebuke, as ordinarily, having a direct personal application, could not fail to elicit interest and keep wide awake the attention of an audience. Some indiscreet or disorderly sinner would violate a custom, or otherwise offend against decorum, during service. The preacher, perhaps in the midst of one of his sublimest soarings, would pause, point a lifted finger at the offender,—whose misdemeanor may have been, suppose, that he had appropriated accommodation to himself, and made a conspicuous show of it, among the females on their exclusive side of the house,—let his voice drop from its strained pitch in alt, to the deep baritone level most effective for conveyance of reproof, and, after stating in measured terms his charge, to identify the culprit beyond mistake, would say, " I mean that young man there, standing on the seats of the ladies, with a ruffled shirt on, and I doubt not that the ruffled shirt was borrowed." In such-like quaint and pleasing episodes the orator could indulge at his pleasure, and with none the less freedom, that under protection of his cloth he knew he was safely sheltered against retaliation. And yet it sometimes happened, as with the Rev. C. in the instance quoted, that the party denounced would kick against the grievance. With a respect for propriety which the clerical brother might have imitated to advantage, the ruffled shirt waited until the congregation was dismissed, and then quietly informed the divine that he proposed to whip him. C. accepted the challenge, suggesting that they should retire to the woods " to fight it out." A fence lay in their way; jumping over it, C. sprained his ankle, and put his hand to his side. " Damn you," said he of the ruffles, suspicious of concealed weapons, " you're feeling for a dirk, are you?" " *Yes*," replied the reverend,—which was not strictly true, and indeed, although C., in the narration, would make it appear as an innocent bit of facetiousness, in the fact was manifestly intended to deceive and intimidate,—" yes, and I will give you the benefit of all I have," charging at once on the enemy's works as he said it. The ruffled shirt, unarmed as he was, made a leap and put the fence between himself and his opponent. A party of "rowdies," friends and backers of the priestly pugilist, joined in; the offender was surrounded, bound with hickory-bark to a pole, taken to a pond not far from the camp-ground, and "ducked nearly to death." Mr. C., meanwhile, stood by and consented, like Paul on a somewhat similar occasion,—although that was before the apostle's conversion. He refers to the whole transaction as one of a highly amusing character.

Comprehensively, the wit of the preacher may be described as of that purely Shakspearean order which, in a different sphere, and more recently, has given his classical reputation to a conspicuous fancier of the immortal text, and who stands connected, in the popular mind, with associations of the tented arena, motley tights and tan-bark. In this connection, by the way, and as a coincidence perhaps deserving notice, a characteristic fact is on record, which, as it has been made, personally, matter of special parade, each in his own ring, by both circuit- and circus-rider, should be mentioned; namely, that while one, as a strong feature for his bills, has made a boast of his "one-horse show," so has the other, with an equal flourish on the autobiographical page, of his "one-man congregation." Scrupulous moralists and men of fastidious taste might take exception, now and then, to the sayings of such Christian orators as the "Pulpit-Thumper," the "Bull-Dog," the "New Market Devil," and the "Sinai Thunderer" in their humorous moods,—when "Mather in his best comedy" and "Sheridan in his funniest farce" showed not half their mirth-provoking power,— and yet why should they, when prime ministers of the communion, grave and reverend annalists of the times, have not hesitated to excuse and to approve? Under which canvas could it have been that Mr. Merryman called out, "Pray on, Brother Walker, and if he [an obstreperous interferer] cuts up any capers, I'll down him and hold him till you're done, *for the kingdom of heaven suffereth violence, and the violent take it by force*"? Is it hippodrome or house-of-God vernacularism that the performer employs when he exclaims, "Watch and pray, friends; don't let the devil get among you on the sly, before candle-light"? Which humorist was it that relates how on a certain occasion, in a dispute with one of his own cloth, he "blowed this proselyting, sheep-stealing preacher to *Never*, where another Baptist preacher that he once heard of, would have gone if he had jumped off"?

The prayer of the service was of like composition, both in matter and manner, with the sermon. It was entered upon calmly, and with some regard to order in the conception and delivery. The voice, keyed to a natural tone, syllabled itself articulately and deliberately, moving not unstatelily as to the Dorian mood of flutes and soft recorders; while the action was just and in appropriate harmony with the speech. But, as the petitioner proceeded, the sober method soon, and by rapid development, began to manifest symptoms of derangement. Accelerating in pace and strengthening in power, his utterance ran the ascending intervals of the scale, until the height was won and the intensity reached, beyond which the capacities of the organ, in spite of superhuman effort, could not attain. To sustain the lofty elevation imposed a hard strain upon his energies, but the ordeal was gallantly met, and pluckily endured, although the severity of the labor told with torturing effect upon the machinery of the man. The veins upon his neck and forehead stood out full and round, like cords; great drops of sweat hung on his brow; the red tinging his cheeks darkened to purple; his lips grew livid; the motion of his jaws churned the secretions of their engendering, and the foam as it accumulated oozed clammily out at the corners of his mouth, thence darting in spumy flecks away upon the current of his breath over the heads of the people, or settling back, checked ever and anon by long-drawn inspirations sharply hissing through the half-closed teeth, into its proper reservoir.

At such a pitch of soaring, while lungs and muscles failed not, it was possible to keep sound and fury afloat,—but not with other ballast than the proverb allows them. The atmosphere was too thin for reason to breathe in. Up in a balloon, the scared sense lost its sanity and went a-raving. All was disorder, all confusion. Still, through the turmoil and the tangle, the busy tongue tripped on; saying the more, more vehemently, the less it had to say; quoting and misquoting scraps of Scripture; addressing the Almighty by his most awful titles in rounds of endless repetition; vociferous with exclamations; full of strange oh's; and all with such an accompaniment of yells, and shrieks, and groans, and " windy suspirations of forced breath," and clapping of hands, and shouts of glory, as, almost excusably, to tempt the uninitiated to suspect of the Deity appealed to, that "either He was talking, or He was pursuing, or He was in a journey, or peradventure He slept and must be awakened."

For the few minutes customarily allotted to this exercise, and until near its close, the style intense was kept in play, all the while, with unflagging activity. Suddenly, then, as by some trick of magic, arrested in mid-career, it paused. The rigor and tension of the countenance relaxed; the veiny currents resumed their natural flow, the cheeks and lips their wonted color. The storm was over, —ceased on the instant; and out of the great calm that ensued, fallen at a drop to the gentle tone and attunement of its opening, briefly the voice gave the rounding clause to its orison, and the prayer was ended.

The singing of the service was, perhaps, its most attractive feature. The hymns before sermon were generally selections from the book, read out couplet by couplet, for the accommodation of the congregation, among whom copies of the text, and—not to put the case too pointedly—spectacles, were much wanting. The preacher acted as his own clerk and chorister, choosing for his "tune" Dundee's wild, warbling strain, or plaintive Martyrs, or some other of the standard chants common to all the various denominations of the border. These compositions were of too staid a character to elicit that degree of enthusiasm to which the Methodist mind was partial, but, nevertheless, were rendered with no little spirit. The voices all, male and female, sang in unison. Music had not risen to the dignity of a profession in the wilderness as yet, and it was not to be expected that its rules were to govern strictly in the performances. Time, as an element in the movement, was regulated by chance, and chance by the loudest pair of lungs. As Stentor led the way, the inferior organs followed, catching, by quick imitation, his style, and conforming to his paces with a remarkable felicity of adaptation.

But the hymns of the people—the characteristic ones which reached to the heart and provoked the liveliest response—were those of native invention, not put down in the book, and therefore, vastly to the popular preference, not necessitating the services of the prompter at the desk. The composition of these hymns was peculiar. They were characterized by extreme simplicity,—not always accurate, by any means, in their rhythmical arrangement, but perhaps—for even faults will have their fascination—borrowing a feature of attraction from that very fact. As to their probable origin,— if, in the pursuit of his solitary route, the circuit-rider should at any time have had his attention arrested, while passing near some corn-field in a clearing, by a sound of voices singing, in plaintive remembrance of former times and scenes, to the play of hoes among the growing stalks,—

> "Whar, oh, whar is my good ole fader,
> Whar, oh, whar is my good ole fader,
> Whar, oh, whar is my good ole fader?
>   'Way down in de Car'lina State.
>   By-an'-by we do hope to meet 'im,
>   By-an'-by we do hope to meet 'im,
>   By-an'-by we do hope to meet 'im,
>   'Way down in de Car'lina State,"—

nothing could be more natural than that, struck alike by the pleasing mood of the melody and the simple art of the stanzas, he should have thought of the fine adaptability of both, with certain easy and obvious modifications of sentiment in the latter, for devotional purposes. His next appointment sees the experiment made. It proves a success; and the secular ditty, converted so as to read,

"Where, oh, where, now, is good old Isaac," or "Jacob," or "Elijah," or "the Hebrew Children," or any other saintly nominee, with the refrain spiritualized into, "Away down in the Promised Land," has its new, gospel destiny,—and will keep it, to animate the ardor and gladden the hearts of worshipers, for many and many a year to come.

Upon such terms of construction it was not difficult to frame verses. Melodies, as involving the exercise of invention, were the main want,—a want, however, conveniently satisfied, when it was discovered that a change of art was as possible as a change of heart, and that profane music could be brought under sanctifying influence as well as ungodly minds. Soon, therefore, this source of supply laid under contribution, quite a collection of airs was amassed; sufficient to keep up the due proportion of praise through the closing devotional services, let the interest of the occasion protract them as it might. Of these melodies, some continue, not unworthily, to hold a place, even as yet, in the local popular favor. If discarded almost entirely from the camp, for instance, that plaintive air is not a forgotten thing of beauty in the cottages that dot the scenes of its ancient popularity, which there are those who will readily recall in association with the lines,—

"There is rest for the weary,
There is rest for the weary,
There is rest for the weary,
And we'll rest there too;

> On the other side of Jordan,
> In the sweet fields of Eden,
> Where the tree of life is blooming,
> And we'll rest there too."

Others there are which are almost lost, lingering only in the recollection of the few here and there of a fast-wasting generation who, as children, sat and in still wonder listened and learned, as, at the gatherings in the groves, their fathers and mothers sang them long ago,—like this, caught one day, and made a note of, as it fell quaveringly from the lips—not reluctant to gratify a curious hearer—of one of their number:

Ye sis-ters in the Lord, Come rise and go with me, And leave this sin-ful world, And all things be-low; Come learn to watch and pray, As ye journey on the way, And you'll soon climb the banks of Cal-va-ry.

This hymn was particularly designed for the altar, or "Glory Pen," and could be continued *ad libi-*

tum by the simple substitution of "brothers," or "fathers," or "mothers," or what not, for "sisters" in the first line. While it was being sung, the custom was for the preachers and leaders to move freely about within the inclosure, exchanging greetings among themselves and shaking hands with the "mourners."

The music, that is the own peculiar music of the Methodist, was always spirited. Sentiment was not fastidious as to its style of conveyance, save in this respect only,—it never chose a slow coach. Grave or light, sombre or joyous, the airy-paced vehicle was the one for its burden. The "minor" airs in use to a limited extent, such as the one usually sung to "When I can read my title clear," with the accompanying chorus of "Oh, the Lamb, the loving Lamb, the Lamb of Calvary," etc., formed no exception to the rule. Expression depended upon degrees of intensity—the *piano* and the *forte*—rather than upon variety in mode, for effect. The worshiping assembly was a great organ, as it were, many-piped, yet with but one stop,—the swell besides, and the bellows. Nevertheless the instrument was capable of wonderful diversity in its emotional range and force. Whoever may have had the opportunity of hearing, long ago, the famous old revival hymn, will well remember with what a dread-inspiring power the opening verse (and others succeeding of like doleful tenor) fell upon his ears:

"Oh, there will be mourning, mourning, mourning, mourning,
Oh, there will be mourning at the judgment-seat of Christ!
Brothers and sisters there will part, [twice repeated,]
    Will part to meet no more!"

and how sudden and complete,—how thrilling and rapturous, the changed experience, as the chorus of voices, true still to time and tune, but bursting into a tone of vehement intensity like that which gives noise to the huzza of an army at the moment of victory, rung to the significance of the closing stanza:

"Oh, there will be shouting, shouting, shouting, shouting,
Oh, there will be shouting at the judgment-seat of Christ!
Saints and angels there will meet, [repeated as before,]
    Will meet to part no m re!"

The closing refrain of one or another of the hymns of this class brought the worship to an end. The preacher arose in his place, lifted his hands, pronounced the benediction, and his duties were done. Soberly the people deserted their seats, and calmly, as though the storm through which they were just passed had never been, withdrew from the house and retired to their homes.

IV.

IN THE SADDLE AND ON THE CIRCUIT.

THE Methodist Black-Robe had his local fields of labor, but the sphere more peculiarly professional to him was of wider embrace, reaching in grand range over miles of territory, from station to station in which he journeyed, making his stages and his stoppages according to schedule previously timed, and completing the round in a month or months, to resume and pursue it over and over again as often as was practicable during the term of his appointment. The newer circuits—those extending into the thinly populated districts of the remoter frontier, where the preacher ran the risk of passing a night once in awhile without the shelter of a roof—constituted the "Missionary" ground of the church. Ample arrangements were made, in such a case, for the comfortable protection of the "itinerant" against the roughnesses and privations to which he might be exposed by the way. Besides the Arab steed for his own riding, of which he was justly proud, he started out provided with a pack-horse to carry the few stores that were needed for his frugal sustenance, at such times as he might be compelled to camp it and do his own cooking on the route. These stores consisted of ground coffee, parched corn run through a mill and mixed with sugar, beef-tongues, cold meats, and sea-biscuits; a coffee-pot, britannia tumblers and spoons, steel knives, wooden forks, and, to complete the whole, a water-proof linen tent, large enough, if necessary, to accommodate nine men conveniently. But the missionary had counted the cost of his office before assuming its responsibilities, so that, although he may have had reason to groan under crosses, to lament over hard lodging, and to complain of picnic provender, yet did he find grace sufficient to meet each tribulation as it came, and bravely to worry it through.

Once he was under the necessity of spending a night in the log cabin of a backwoodsman on the far border. His experience on the occasion is circumstantially sketched, by his own hand, in illustration of the dire extremities to which the pioneer preachers were driven, now and then, in the prosecution of their work. There was no floor in the house, the bare ground, leveled off and smoothed down, being made to answer instead. Hickory poles were laid across at the angles of the roof where it rested upon the walls, to serve as joists, which with an over-spread of clapboards formed the upper floor. The house had neither bedstead, chair, nor table. To supply the want of the first-mentioned article of furniture, for his own and his wife's accommodation, forked sticks had been driven into the ground at one corner of the cabin as supports for poles, across which clapboards were laid, and these "covered with some bedding, such as it was." The little negro boy of the establishment slept, wrapt in a deer-skin, on the ground. So did the missionary, between two blankets, with his saddle-bags for a pillow. "Surrounded by these gloomy circumstances," he "felt rather melancholy," and his mind began to run back to former days of "ease and plenty" (he had been raised, according to a previous chapter of his autobiography, in a "log cabin," with "no floor" to it, and the "wolves howling around it at night"); but when he thought within himself that he was better off than his Saviour was, for He "had not where to lay his head," he became more contented, and had a tolerably comfortable night of it. He made his breakfast, on a board bench, of corn-bread and milk,—no spoons. One can scarcely refrain from wondering, with some view as to whom the sympathy should apply, if so miserable was the experience to the preacher for a night, what must it have been to the parishioner as the habit, without change or relief, of his life?

In his more customary ridings, however, the itinerant was not liable to risks of inconvenience, nor under the necessity of providing against the contingencies of a ground-floor, corn-bread and milk, and—no spoons. A pair of saddle-bags, packed with his little all requisite of linen and library, was his only equipage. Good houses, public and private, were not so few or far between along the way but that the hospitalities of one or the other could be claimed, at noontide for dinner, or for bed and board, wherever overtaken by its approach, at night. Householder and hostler, saint and son of Belial, with the courtesy characteristic of all classes alike, received him at his coming, and civilly entertained him; even the publican rarely demanding, and less often receiving, a fee for the accommodation. The attention which was at first viewed rather in the light of a charity by the host, soon came to be regarded as a due by the customer, who, in the end, established a habit of claiming what he desired with an independence that was imposing to behold. Was not the laborer worthy of his hire?

And it was paid liberally. In the private establishment its choicest resources were offered for his distinguished delectation. Closet and pantry were distrained of their rarest delicacies, and the poultry-yard of its fattest broodlings, to furnish a palatable variety for his table. The air and the exercise of the road were favorable to digestion; they stimulated healthily the inner man of the reverend traveler, and bred an appetite the consumptive capacity of which got to be so generally understood and appreciated as to become proverbial. He relished a turkey, and yet objected to it (or his own people have persistently slandered him) that while it was, perhaps, a little too much, as a roast, for one, it was certainly not enough for two. At the inn, where discrimination among guests, eating unavoidably at the same board, could not well be made, he had to forego the privilege of preferred meats, and fare like the rest of its patrons; but a "square meal" could always be depended upon; for there was no stint of provision ever to complain of as tables stood among the taverns of those times.

His personal wants having been satisfied, the foremost business afterwards of the Black-Robe was to make the accident of his presence an agreeable and professionally profitable one to his entertainer. Perhaps his host of the private lodge was a hunter, the warm side of whose heart he intuitively knew was to be approached through his rifle, like the Arkansas squatter's, of legendary renown, through his fiddle. To prove his skill at the craft, he would propose a mark and a crack at a hundred yards, beat the woodman, of course, over and over again, and then, commending the gun and complimenting the owner, would follow up the last fire with a few practical observations on the subject of religion. If the hunter's sound conversion did not occur on the spot, another round of shot, had next "riding" of the circuit, was never known to fail.

Nor did he any the less dutifully neglect his mission at the tavern. Whatever the chances or the circumstances attending his stay, in season or out of season, he would find, or make, an opportunity for discovering himself in his ministerial character. Probably, on entering the house of an evening, he would find the young people of the neighborhood assembled, a fiddler at play, and couples arranging themselves for a dance. A "beautiful, ruddy young lady" would walk very gracefully up to him, dropping a handsome courtesy, and pleasantly, with winning smiles, invite him out to the floor. He would rise "as gracefully as he could," move to the beautiful lady's left side, and grasp her right hand with his, while with her left wrist she would lean on his arm. In this manner they would walk to their position. The whole company would seem pleased "at this act of politeness in the beautiful young lady shown to the stranger." The negro fiddler would begin to put his fiddle in the best order. The preacher would then tell the fiddler to hold a minute, and would go on to say that for several years he had not undertaken any matter of importance without first asking the blessing of God upon it, and he now desired to ask the blessing of God on the beautiful young lady and the company who had shown so much politeness to a stranger. Here he would grasp the beautiful young lady's hand and say, "Let us all kneel down and pray;" and then instantly drop on his knees and commence praying with all the power of "soul and body" that he could command. The beautiful young lady would try to get loose from him, but he would hold her tight. The company would look curious. The fiddler would run for the kitchen, exclaiming, "Lord a marcy, what de matter? What dat mean?" The prayer would be followed by singing, the singing by exhortation, and the whole, kept up for hours, would result in the "powerful conversion" of the beautiful young lady and fourteen others,—all before breakfast-time next morning.

But the circuit-rider did not confine himself to occasional opportunities, such as these, for doing good. Indeed, they were merely incidental to the main business; sowing seed by the wayside, as it were, on the tramp between fields surveyed and located for particular tilling. His regular stations were chosen at convenient intervals along the route, ordinarily an easy day's journey apart, so that not unfrequently every evening of the week had its appointment for preaching. He was not particular in his choice of accommodation for this purpose. The best that offered was thankfully taken and put to use,—private dwellings, barrooms, tavern-porches, court-houses, barns, sheds, wagons even, and as a yet other alternative, the woods out-of-doors; any spot, anywhere; for the Black-Robe felt that when duty called he must obey at all hazards. "As the gospel was to be preached to every creature, his mission extended to every place this side of hell." Happily for the cause, Providence so ordered it that the least hospitable shift should prove the most desirable. Under the trees became the favorite assembly-room. The people were attracted to it at first by the novelty of the thing; then because of the excellent adaptation, as they soon found, of the forest, with its grand appointments,—its arches and columns, its naves and transepts, and its dim religious light, so impressive of effect,—for a sanctuary. True, the choice might seem to imply that the prejudice was not well founded which, with the ceremonies of the Catholic Church, had led the dissenter to abjure its cathedrals, and to reckon respect for the Beautiful as among the deadly heresies; but one was the handicraft of the Master Architect,— the other was apprentice-work; the original, as of God, might be admirable, but did it follow that the imitation, of carnal device, was not damnable?

As these open-air gatherings were seen to be popular; as hearers in still multiplying numbers continued to flock in, and as sinners began to show lively signs of awakening, it was thought expedient, the better to afford space for conversion to work its perfect work, that the meetings should be *protracted* beyond the limit of a single night. Hence arose that institution peculiar to the sect and to the section,—the CAMP-MEETING.

This spiritual saturnalia, occurring statedly and running through a week or a fortnight, was called (in its grand annual observance, for it also had its "quarterly") late in the summer-time, or early in the autumn, after the harvests had been gathered and before the setting-in of seed-time, the season for out-of-doors at this period being propitious, and the agricultural population then enjoying their chief term of leisure. For the scene of its orgies, a space large enough for the purpose was selected from some romantic nook of woods, thinned, if necessary, of its trees and cleared of whatever *débris* might encumber the ground. Around this area the believers pitched their tents,—of canvas it might be or of bark, or having their wagons backed into place in lieu of either, the whole sometimes fenced about with a barricade of bushes, to keep out the allies of their adversary the devil. At each corner of the inclosure a sort of rude altar built of logs, unless the large stump of a tree might be had as a substitute, was erected, upon which fires were kindled to illumine the darkness and keep off the mosquitoes. Lamps also were hung out at the tent-fronts and suspended from the branches of the trees. A platform was built at one side of the area, with a plank placed bench-high along its rear for a seat, and another elevated at the front, designed to serve as a breastwork for the preacher and a place of deposit for his "library." Under the platform a plot of ground was railed in for the exclusive use of mourners, and was known as the Altar, or Glory Pen. Back of this, seats—boards, that is, resting at either end on billets of wood or stones—were ranged for the accommodation of all who chose to occupy them during service. Rules for the preservation of order in the camp were posted up conspicuously in the immediate neighborhood, as well as on the fences and trees along the different roads leading to the ground, in case of a violation of which the executive committee was never wanting—the Black-Robe himself its most efficient member—to see to the sufficient chastisement of the aggressor.

Outside the tents the woods were filled round and about, wherever vacant space could be found, with wagons, carts, bales of hay, broken boxes, and other promiscuous litter, only room enough being reserved besides—not taking into account the ways opened, and with diligent care kept open, for access to, and egress from, the camp—for the accommodation of the horses of attendants; with here and there, in by-places, a booth, a bar between two trees, and a bush-tent. The borderman had his ruling passions: he loved his liquor; he was choice in his breed of colts, and—alas! men are weak, and women are willing, and both will err, in the bush as well as on Broadway. Within this precinct, of purer promise surely, the vender of beverages had fixed his place, and whisky was dispensed to those that thirsted among the congregation, freely and openly: here, too, was quartered the proprietor—with his property—of that elegant, full-blooded, eight-year-old Arabian, whose portrait and pedigree, in printer's ink, confronted the gaze on every walk and at every turn, publicly placarded on the same oak or hickory, likely, with the Rules of the Meeting, and whose rampant self, jauntily bedecked with ribbons and rosettes, and tightly postured with belt and bridle, was daily led out before interested groups of beholders, for parade, and other purposes ; and here the unreclaimed Magdalen made her haunt, in the twilight, and in the evening, and in the black and dark night, mingling among the strollers of the hour, displaying her charms, and with fair speech and flattering lips tempting whom she might, and, under the very nose of the executive committee, leading her captive down to the chamber of death.

Meetings in the camp were held morning, afternoon, and night, to which the people were summoned with the blowing of a trumpet, or rather of a tin horn. The daylight sessions were, comparatively speaking, tame affairs. Grace, as it was found among the tents, did not seem to flourish in the sun. Like the sorrowful tree of the Indian isle, it bloomed only in the night, too delicate and phantomy to abide the test of a more searching exposure. The opening exercises were undemonstrative. With the advancing hour interest heightened—the fervors of devotion, like the glow of the fireflies, showing brighter and brighter as thickened the dark—until, night fairly set in, illumination was at its height and enthusiasm at its liveliest.

To hasten this moment of blissful realization was the foremost aim, always, of the exhorter. His plans (for he had his plans) were all laid with a view to it.

"Brother," he would say, aside, to his assisting preacher, "have you any faith?"

"Some," the assistant would respond.

"And so have I; a little. Now, I am to preach first. If I strike fire, I will immediately call for mourners, and you must go in and exhort in every direction, and I will manage the altar. But if I fail to strike fire, you must preach; and if you strike fire, call the mourners and manage the altar. I meanwhile will go through the congregation and exhort with all the power God gives me."

Doing his part in carrying out the scheme, the first brother (who doesn't relate the circumstance) might fall short, except perhaps in producing a few promising sparks, but the second (who tells the story) is more successful,—strikes fire that catches, flames, blazes, spreads, and wraps the camp in a general conflagration. His eloquence is irresistible. Careless hearers become attentive and concerned; sinners, conscience-smitten, grow pale and tremulous with terror; sons of Belial fall to the ground in an agony of awakening; and even the Baptists, who would seem to be the most incorrigible among the unrighteous, are startled by conviction, and begin to cry out, "Oh, pray for us, or we are lost and damned forever!"

The work, once under headway, advances with astonishing progress. If the spiritual frame were liable to like infirmities with the physical, the inference would seem natural and reasonable that some colicky distemper of soul had suddenly broken out, racking the patient with ache and pang and spasm, and that, after all, the conclusions of Wangomen the Delaware were not wholly whimsical, nor jalap and ipecac to be despised as a physic for the disorder. Men—steady veterans of the border, who had wrestled with bears in their day, and could have bearded lions in their dens without an emotion—are seized with the weakness and quake and quail under its influence. Example breeds example: victim after victim is attacked, and the distemper becomes general and rages uncontrolledly. Bodies writhe and strive as in the throes of convulsion; arms fling wildly in the air; down on his knees the infected subject falls in attitude of prayer, his head forced back upon its column of support, until the tight cordage of the neck seems ready to crack under the strain; faces, picturing, in sharp relief, each one its own peculiar presentment of the passion at play within, look fixedly up and staringly, through dry, hot, bloodshot eyes, towards heaven; hair, tossed and tangled, stands all affright on end, or, broken loose from its folds, on the part of the women, streams in disheveled tresses to the earth, and is trampled, trailing in the dust, under feet of the shifting multitude.

Convicts foam at the mouth, gnash their teeth, and gasp like drowning or dying ones for breath; or with less frenzied demonstration, swaying their bodies to and fro the while, now wring their hands, now clap them,—clap them with a will, the sharp concussion producing reports like pistol-shots. Sighs and sobs distress the air. Groanings and moanings, wails, and shrieks, and howls, and shouts of anguish, fear, despair, exultation, bursting full vent from a hundred—a thousand—thrice a thousand throats, rise, and rolling in tumultuous tide, away and away, flood the solitudes with a torrent of uproar. The horses at their troughs in the woods pause over their oats, and, pricking their ears, stand still-bound in listening wonder; the trader in Bourbon, confounded, suspends his traffic; while they of the Scarlet Letter, the fair unfortunate, shuddering as they hear, to shun the notice which they just now courted, steal shrinkingly aside and hide them in the dark.

Meanwhile the preacher, having wrought his material up to the proper pitch of frenzy, changes his base of operations from the pulpit to the Glory Pen, crowded now to its utmost capacity with seekers and mourners. He is still in the fireworks line, but, instead of throwing his matches promiscuously at the heads of hearers, as from his former position, he singles out his subjects and applies to each one separately his own particular lucifer. There is a distiller of the name of H——, say, in the crowd,—a green-timbered fellow, coarse in the fibre and full of the sap of sin, whom he takes hold of. He is an uninflammable customer, hard to heat, but finally warms by friction, ignites, and is brought under in a blaze of blue light. The exhorter announces the victory with a shout, "Glory to God! H—— is down! H—— is down! Glory to God!" A Frenchman who had fought under Napoleon, next operated upon, perhaps, takes spark more promptly, and exclaiming, as he surrenders, true to his soldierly training, "*Vive l'Empereur Jésus!*" is off like a rocket,—"a case of conversion so clear and powerful that infidelity itself is abashed and confounded." A practical joker of the Belial family, who has come with a batch of frogs strung together to slip over the head of the exhorter while stooping and praying for the mourners, is then encountered, maybe; finds to his astonishment that he is made a Chinese cracker of, and explodes ere well aware of it, while waiting an opportunity for his proposed diversion. Among the women success is easier than with the men, and more certain: they seldom miss fire, but, kindling readily, flare up and go off gloriously, coruscating in well-sustained style, like Roman candles. It is a singular circumstance, which lookers-on are not slow to notice, that the cases calling for much the greater share of attention are from among the ladies; that the handsomest girls are always the wickedest; have to be approached the nearest;

need the closest exhorting; must be entreated the most lovingly, and are the most apt to give way physically; to faint—and to fall as seems inevitable generally, except as the ministerial arm with round embrace interposes to prevent the catastrophe. Bishop Asbury expresses his fear somewhere "that the women and the devil will get all his preachers."

When not engaged in what may be styled confidential conferences, or private ministries exercised in exclusive behalf of individuals, the preacher moves about, picking a passage with careful steps, among the mourners, and casts his exhortations, as he goes, in sententious discharges, right and left among them. "Don't be composed," he says to one of the kneelers, who scarcely seems to need the admonition,—" don't be composed, but pray on, brother; pray on; there's no composure in hell or damnation." Another is blandly smiled upon, and encouraged with gratifying assurances that he is clearly on the highway to glory, the convincing evidence of which is, that bobbing up and down on his knees, and going through the motions of washing his hands in the air, he gives shout to the original, expressive, and highly devotional sentiment of "Hell! hell! hell! hell!" The "fine, beautiful" daughter of a father almost irredeemably lost, as she is taught to believe, in Presbyterianism, is assured, when she affectionately suggests him as a subject of exhortation, that his case, though critical in the extreme, is not absolutely hopeless,—the vilest Calvinist may return: "Pray on," he says, "and the work will be done. It is not the old big devil that is in your father, but a little, weakly, sickly devil, and it won't be a hard job to cast him out. If God takes hold of your father and shakes him over hell a little while, and he smells brimstone right strong, if there was a ship-load of these little, sickly devils in him, they would be driven out just as easy as a tornado would drive a regiment of mosquitoes from a stagnant pond." "Sister," he inquires, cheerfully, of a young woman, "have you found your ransom yet?" The sister is surprised to learn that her engagement with Mr. Ransom, which she had supposed to be entirely a secret between that gentleman and herself, is known to the itinerant, but does not deny the situation, and blushingly responds that she is looking for him back next Friday evening. "And Brother G——," he goes on to query of a next "exercised" subject, "how do you feel in the spirit to-night?" "Bully!" says Brother G——.

To heat the blood of his subjects up to the grace-enabling mark—173° of the spiritual Fahrenheit—was what the profane would call the "dodge" always of the exhorter. He seemed to act upon the presumption that souls feverishly sin-sick must be made flightily worse before there was any hope of their growing better; like the physician who made it his standing rule of practice, in all cases, to first throw his patients into convulsions: there he had them where he wanted them exactly, for that was his specialty,—he was "* * * * on fits."

Midnight usually brought the performances to an end. The last hymn was sung, the last prayer said; the multitudinous noise of worship rolling off in one stormy, final discharge, swept in fast-bearing reverberations afar, lessening as it sped, fainting, fading, dying,—dead in the distance; quiet ruled in the camp, save as disturbed by the occasional burst of a sob, or groan, or shout of "Glory!" from some not entirely-subsided enthusiast; lights were extinguished; worshipers retired to their tents. The curtain had dropped on the closing scene, and the drama was ended.

Journeying thus from post to post, the itinerant pursued his mission, erecting new stations, planting new societies, creating new classes, and enlarging generally the borders of the Methodist Zion. Repeated riding of his circuit made its course a familiar one. His own presence, and that of his horse, became accustomed ones to the people. He formed acquaintance with man, woman, and child at every cabin. He won upon their confidence by conforming to their ways and participating in their social usages,—ready ever for any reasonable frolic: to take a hand at a husking, lend a lift at a raising, be about at a log-rolling, stir his turn at an apple-butter boiling, or handle a cleaver at sausage-chopping on a butchering-day. Nor would he frown upon the harmless enjoyments of the young men and maidens at their festivities of a winter evening; as, indeed, why should he? for "Peeling the willow" was not proscribed by the Book of Discipline, nor promiscuous kissing in "Come, Philander, let's be marching," nor "holding" in "Tired of my company," nor "bundling" as an institution by itself. By secular conformities and indulgences such as these, the preacher established himself in the popular liking. For patronage bestowed, he enjoyed it, reciprocally, at his own *soirées;* and improved it,—with what result, arithmetically considered, was made largely to figure on the records of the next annual conference, where it stands yet in authentic confirmation of the marvelous doings of those Pentecostal days.

V.

THE CANE-RIDGE REVIVAL.

CAMP-MEETINGS had their origin, as described, in the year 1800. The first experiments met with such extraordinary success that they were rapidly followed up by others, and with a continually growing patronage, so that attendants, counted in the beginning by scores, multiplied into fifties, from fifties increased into hundreds, and presently were reckoned by thousands. The first of the more imposing series that figure so prominently on the autobiographical page, happened at Cabin Creek, Kentucky, in the spring of 1801. This was succeeded, with brief intervals of time and accommodating ones of distance, by others at Concord, Point Pleasant, and Indian Creek. But the illustrious one, where occurred the famous Cumberland Revival, and which the few, the very few gray-bearded fathers still living who were witnesses of it, always refer to with proudest satisfaction, took place in August, and was held at Cane Ridge.

The Rev. Robert W. Finley, a Presbyterian minister originally from Pennsylvania, had removed to Kentucky, and, in 1790, fixed his residence in Bourbon County, where, clearing a spot out of the canebrakes, which grew all over the broad acres there for miles, he built a log cabin, opened a farm, and erected a church. The scene of the great revival in question lay within the lines of his parish. The miraculous manifestations, as they were regarded, of the divine presence at the previous meetings, had long been the topic of talk abroad, and the settlers, all on the tiptoe of expectation, were ready to take advantage of the leisure which the season offered, attend at the appointed place, and put to the proof of their own eyes' witness the marvels of which they had been told. Multitudes that might not be numbered began to assemble. From the remotest corners of the border, thirty, forty, fifty miles away, they gathered in. All day long, and through the night, crowds were to be seen pressing eagerly, earnestly on, their faces set Zionward, in wagons, on sleds, afoot, "upon horses, and in chariots, and in litters, and upon mules, and upon swift beasts." Roads, lanes, trails, all passable ways of approach, swarmed with train following train of pilgrims; the tramp of their progress uprooting the sod, which hoof and wheel, till then, of customary travel had scarcely scarred, and grinding the clodded surface of the soil to powder. Whole communities, including not merely the men, women, and children, but slaves and dogs even, gathered in companies and joined the general procession, leaving only an obliging neighbor, here and there, to keep watch in the depopulated settlements during their absence. When all were congregated, it is estimated that there were from twenty to twenty-five thousand people on the ground. The usual accommodations in the way of huts and tents were erected on the premises, together with a large shed capable of affording shelter, in case of unfavorable weather, to five thousand persons. Shanties were constructed for use of such as chose to turn an honest penny by offering entertainment, at so much a head, to casual visitors; and booths "for them that sold doves," each with its counter or table, knocked rudely but substantially together, of boards, whereupon were arranged platters, spoons, knives and forks, unctuous from much handling, and supply-dishes, which, replenished whenever emptied with steaming meats and vegetables, proved temptingly provocative of appetite, and seldom grew cold for want of consumers.

Outside the *sanctum* of the encampment, but closely crowding on it, were pitched the tents of the unbelievers—a promiscuous class—consisting largely of horse-thieves, gamblers, blasphemers, drunkards, adulterers, and "partakers in all manner of wickedness." Associated with the vicious and lawless, but not, as yet, utterly contaminated by the contact, were to be found the classes addicted to simply mischievous exploits, and technically known as the careless,—" men of awful depravity, that would sport while the very fires of perdition were kindling around them." A favorite amusement with these sons of Belial was to play practical jokes on the preachers and mourners. They were also given to cropping the manes and shaving the tails of horses; to tarring the seats and taking linchpins out of wagons; to detaching girths from saddles, and pilfering halters, whips, and bridles.

Of such huge and heterogeneous composition as was the meeting,—without power, and, indeed, without the disposition, to enforce order; where rather, on the contrary, lawlessness seemed to be the accepted law of the hour,—it is in no wise surprising that "nothing was exhibited to the spectator but a scene of confusion, such as scarcely could be put into human language." As many as seven preachers, out of some thirty or forty present, were to be heard declaiming at the same time; one posted on the platform, another mounted in a wagon, others pulpited on stumps, and still others perched on the trunks of fallen trees. The noise of their eloquence "was like the roar of Niagara."

Sermon, or exhortation, prepared the way for the more striking proceedings. At its close the pent up enthusiasm of the audience began to discharge. A universal cry for mercy arose. As hearts were hopeful or despondent, their corresponding demonstrations followed. The terror-stricken and despairing maddened the air with ravings of anguish. Those whose eyes caught glimpses of the dawn of redemption were in raptures of ecstasy. Every variety of emotion, in every form of expression, found vent at the same time. Sharply piercing up through the heavy under-swell of sound that rolled and roared, and without break or pause kept steadily surging on, wild exclamations in horrible commingling were to be heard,—shrieks of "hell! hell-fire! damnation!" blending with screams of "glory! glory to God! hallelujah!" The people had come prepared for the infection, expecting it, with their hearts set on it, their nerves strung for it; and they caught it readily. As with a battalion in a battlefield or a bevy of misses in a boarding-school but an example is needed to bring about a general prevalence of panic or hysterics, so a first outbreak of disorder was all that was wanting—all that was waited for—to involve the whole camp in derangement. Each following moment added fresh impulse and new variety to the excitement. Sinners were arrested,—became wrestling Jacobs,—prevailed, and were happy,—all ere the echoes, order by order, had well died away of the vociferations which indicated the various stages of the proceeding. Penitents, passing at a step from darkness into light, became "experienced." The exhorted at one moment were the exhorters at the next, flying to their unregenerate friends and entreating them with powerful persuasion and tears of compassion to fly to Christ for mercy. Some, under conviction and impelled by terror, tore themselves from the embraces of anxious relatives and struggled hard to escape from the ground. Others wept and groaned, and piteously appealed to Heaven for consolation; while others still fell to the earth and swooned away, "till every appearance of life was gone, and the extremities of the body assumed the coldness of death."

A boy, ten years of age, who for some time had stood as a listener near a platform occupied by one of the declaimers, felt himself suddenly possessed of "very strong impressions." Starting from his place, he hurried a short distance apart, mounted a log, and, lifting up his voice in a most affecting manner, began to prophesy before the congregation. "On the last day of the feast," he exclaimed, "Jesus stood and cried, If any man thirst, let him come unto me and drink." The people turned at the sound of his voice, and, attracted by the novelty of the incident, gathered in a great crowd about the juvenile orator. He was evidently an acute observer, had watched the arts of his clerical elders, and copied them well. Amid profuse tears he directed his appeal to sinners; pictured, in a professional way that indicated a remarkable memory, the terrible destiny reserved for the unrighteous, and then, by way of enticing contrast, the golden rewards that awaited the penitent in the Beautiful Land reserved for their inheritance. His audience pressed closer and closer about him, until soon his voice was smothered and his person lost sight of amid the throng. He was on the point, apparently, of being completely extinguished, when two strong men of the inner circle, seizing him in their arms, lifted him up above the heads of the rest, and held him there, while for nearly an hour he exhorted "with that convincing eloquence that could be inspired only from heaven." When exhausted, at last, of strength and of language, he took out his handkerchief, and, letting it fall from his hand, brought his remarks to a close by a happy practical application of the device: "Thus, O sinner," said he, "will you drop into hell unless you forsake your sins and turn to God!" With the descent of the handkerchief, descended the power of God upon the assembly. Sinners fell as men slain in mighty battle. Cries for mercy rent the heavens, "and the work spread in a manner which human language cannot describe."

The *falling* feature was the striking one of the Cane-Ridge meeting. It had been witnessed before, but not, till then, to any remarkable extent. The manifestations attending it were peculiar and really surprising, although not unaccountable. The subject, after having, under the stimulating influence of the unaccustomed atmosphere of the camp, been medicined up to a fitting state of susceptibility, found himself, suddenly and without the slightest premonition, beset with a nervous affection, the action of which was, out of the order of all precedent, capricious and uncontrollable. Certain members of the body would cease in their office, as though numbed by paralysis, while others, as if to compensate for the delinquency, would run into extravagant excesses of action. Legs would fail and sink helplessly under their proper burden, while arms would flourish wildly against the will and with unnatural energy. Some among the seized were struck dumb; others preserved control of their voices, but used them in a very ridiculous manner, laughing, barking like dogs, howling like wolves, bellowing, bleating, and caterwauling; at the same time leaping and dancing like dervishes or rolling on the ground and wriggling like Obi-men at a pow-wow. Frequently cases happened where all the symptoms attending dissolution appeared. The pulse gradually faded, the **breath came and went in sobs and gasps, with longer and longer** intervals of suspended respiration, until it **ceased** altogether, and the body lay as dead, still, staring, **and** cold, for hours. While the catalepsy lasted, the **patient retained full possession of his consciousness, nor, through it all, was there** (although the authorities here are somewhat **contradictory**) the slightest experience of physical discomfort.

The *jerks*, as the phenomenon got to be popularly called, were not confined to the camp-inclosure exclusively, neither were their attacks limited to seekers and mourners. The thoughtless and careless among sinners outside were visited as well, one and another being brought down "suddenly, as if struck by lightning." Professed infidels and scoffers were leveled, with the language of blasphemy on their lips. Ladies were attacked at breakfast over their toast and tea. Tossing their cups and saucers to the ceiling, they would dash from the table in great haste, "their long suits of braided hair hanging down their backs at times cracking like a whip." A converted dancing-master, witnessing the behavior of the possessed, declared that the devil was at the bottom of it, and he was determined "to preach it out of the

Methodist Church." He ran to a stand, took his text, and tried it; but, before fairly aware of it, his subject got the better of him, and he was himself helplessly under its influence. His tongue became entangled in its thread of discourse. Falling into a silly repetition of "Ah, yes!—Oh, no!"—terms thrust irrelevantly into his harangue, and on which he stumbled,—the jingle of the syllables, iterated over and over again, became forcibly suggestive of music and motion. Only the hint was needed to call into action the old professional habit, and the dancing-master, himself again, armed in imagination with the implements of his art, was instantly absorbed in the execution of a jig, fingers and elbow furiously at play, while toe and heel tapped, sounding time to the dumb performance, on the bare boards of the floor. He had overestimated his strength: still, vanquished, ingloriously vanquished as he was, "his proud heart would not submit. He gave up the circuit and retired, and his sun went down under a cloud."

A certain young man, "tall" and terrible,—an Arba among the Anakim of the outer precinct,—who sat mounted on a fine, large white horse, forming one of a party of scoffers near by, being instigated by the prime Planner of all Mischief, put spurs to his steed, and, breaking from his comrades, dashed at full gallop through the line of tents into the inclosure and among the worshipers, uttering horrible imprecations as he made the charge. Still plunging on, he forced his way, until, coming abreast of a kneeling band of seekers, his course was arrested. The mysterious Agency of the Air, the Angel of Conviction, waiting its opportunity, had met it then and there: instantly, as though an arrow sped from its bow had pierced his heart, the reins dropped from his grasp, he reeled in his saddle, and tumbled lifeless to the ground; the religious multitude testifying their exultation at the *coup de grâce* in bursts of applause addressed to the Deity, and with songs of praise and shouts of hallelujah! For thirty hours the young man lay apparently dead. Symptoms of returning animation then began to appear, rapidly eventuating, through a series of convulsions attended by fearful groans, in complete recovery. But that was not all. His newly-aroused self was no longer the Heaven-defiant self of the past. Out of that Lethean sleep he awoke a new being. "The fiendlike scowl that had overspread his features gave way to a happy smile, and, springing to his feet, the accents of anguish were changed into the loud and joyous shouts of praise."

One Dr. P. and an interesting young lady of Lexington, both "inexperienced," visited the camp from motives of curiosity, mutually agreeing beforehand that, if either of them should happen to be jerked, the other would stand by and have a care over the victim until he or she, as the case might be, recovered from the attack. The lady, in all her pride, as the narrative relates, was soon prostrated. The physician laid his finger on her wrist, found her pulse gone, became agitated, turned pale, and, staggering a step or two, sunk down, inanimate as she, in the dust beside her. After remaining for some time in this state, they both obtained pardon and peace, and went home rejoicing. Persons were seized on the road going to, and returning from, the camp; at taverns where they halted as they went, frequently in the act of taking the favorite tonic of the day, at the bar, by way of prevention; at their plows in the field, at their drudgeries in the kitchen, and at their family and closet devotions. Sinners wondered at it, affected to laugh at it, feared it, were fascinated by it, flocked to the scene—the central scene—of its operations, and straightway were down under the invisible stroke of its dealing. Like bullocks under blow of the axe in a slaughter-pen when executioners are busiest in packing-time, they dropped, —hundreds upon hundreds, nay, thousands, falling of a night. Intense excitement, accompanied with fearful forebodings of calamity, prevailed among the people. Many thought, with the dancing-master, that Satan with his imps had been let loose, and suffered, for a purpose, to enter into the hearts of men, as they were of old into the swine, what time the herd ran violently down a steep place into the sea and perished in the waters. Some imagined that because the land abounded in wickedness, a visitation of divine judgment was decreed against the nation; while others, filled with alarm, supposed that the Day of Wrath was at hand, and that the elements were about to melt with fervent heat, and the earth to be consumed.

To quiet the apprehensions of the timid and to silence the misgivings of the skeptical, certain of the wise among the churchmen applied themselves to the task of a rational solution of the mystery. The work was satisfactorily achieved; the narrative of it, as historically transmitted to posterity, running substantially thus:—

It is well known that the Baptists embrace in their communion a large proportion of the population of Kentucky, and that they rigidly adhere to the doctrines of unconditional election and reprobation, as well as to the pernicious heresy of the final and unconditional perseverance of the saints. It is equally well known that the same mischievous dogmas are held and taught by the Presbyterians. Indeed, so generally have these errors been preached by these denominations that no one entertaining genuine scriptural views has heretofore been found fearless and independent enough to call them in question. The consequence is that they have taken deeper and deeper root, and continued to spread, until it may be said that the doctrines of Calvin have filled the whole country. Under the prevalence of such teachings, supported as they are by polemical divines, whose religion consists almost entirely in a most dogged and pertinacious adherence to the creeds and confessions of faith handed down from orthodox Puritan fathers, it is not surprising that professors of religion have fallen insensibly into Antinomianism. The inconsistencies of Calvin have become the subject of the sarcastic sneers of infidels, and the inability of his followers to reconcile their doctrines "with the justice of God and the present order of things" is making fearful inroads on the faith, and strengthening the hands of the wicked. The friends of the truth have been few, comparatively uninfluential, and exposed to much persecution. At this juncture it has pleased the Lord to look down upon the people of this Western country. Man's extremity is God's opportunity, and these wonderful manifestations which are witnessed are assuredly of Heaven, given in evidence, so startling as not to be mistaken, that the Almighty means to sweep away Baptist-ism, and Presbyterianism, and every other refuge of lies; to confound infidelity and vice, "and bring numbers beyond calculation under the influence of experimental religion and practical piety."

No exact record of the saving results of the Cane-Ridge meeting has been preserved; but if an estimate may be inferred from the statement of one of the chroniclers, that he saw as many as "at least five hundred swept down in a moment," the cases of conversion must have been exceedingly numerous. But the revival bore other fruits, which were more decided in character, more lasting, and much less gratifying. While the orthodox laborers were planting the seed, and from the budding prospects of the field were rejoicing in the hope of an abundant harvest, the enemy came in and began to sow tares broadcast among the grain. Gross errors and heresies sprang up and spread among the faithful. The belief fundamental to Methodism, that Heaven made choice of its gospelers by special election, and that the gift of preaching came by inspiration,—that its exhorters, in other words, like the anointed of old, were "holy men of God, who spake as they were moved by the Holy Spirit,"—was one which was well calculated to tempt the enthusiast, especially under extraordinary excitements, widely and wildly astray. What were Books of Discipline, what were creeds concocted at conferences and promulgated by human authorities, to him,— what would they have been to Isaiah, or to Paul, or to Wesley, singled out, himself and all alike, as prophets of the Lord,—that the supremely illuminated and impliedly infallible judgment of either should be hemmed in by their limitations or embarrassed by their restraints? The result may be anticipated. Old confessions were repudiated; the Bible was pronounced the only rule of faith; each man became his own interpreter, no two interpreting alike; and soon the region swarmed with saintly adventurers, who scoured the country, scattering wide the brands of schism and making grievous havoc among the churches.

Enticed by the example of half a dozen illiterate Presbyterians who had been irregularly admitted into the ministerial office, and who had likewise become tainted with the prevailing distemper, a party of separatists, under the lead of James O'Kelly, a disappointed candidate for a Methodist bishopric, banded together, forming a society and designating themselves as *New-Lights*, or *Christians*. Their specialty was a creed denunciatory of creeds; their confession was a protest against confessions, and their church an organized body formed to resist organizations. They repudiated the doctrines of the Trinity, of total depravity, and of the atonement. Governor Garrard, of Kentucky, fell into the heresy, and made himself somewhat famous in the composition of a tract on one of the topics— that touching the question of Christ's divinity— in controversy. Others of the sloughers-off attached themselves to the Quakers, a company of whom from the State of New York had recently planted a settlement in the region. Elder Holmes, a sort of Peter the Hermit, conceived the notion that the restoration was at hand, gathered around him a group of followers, and started off for the prairies in search of the Holy Land. For many days he wandered about, reaching at last an island in the Mississippi River, where, to the interruption of his enterprise and the sad disappointment of his attendants, he sickened and died. Elder Farnum became the founder of the model institution of the *Screaming Children;* and brother Abel Sargent, the Halcyon Preacher and Millennial Messenger, who lived on very intimate terms with the angels, and received his dispatches statedly, like any other foreign ambassador, from heaven, appeared as a second Messiah, perambulating the wilderness with his twelve disciples,—all women,—and proclaiming his revelations. He denied that there was a devil, a hell, or a future judgment. On a " banter" of one of his apostles, he undertook a forty days' fast, in imitation of the memorable one in the Wilderness. He persevered in the experiment, actually abstaining all the while from food, for sixteen days, when, still persisting, he died from starvation. A certain zealot of the name of Kidwell also began to prophesy, affirming that men were never excluded from heaven because of crime; that God would not retaliate wrong for wrong; that expiation in the flesh follows for offenses of the flesh, and that out of the body is neither sin nor punishment,—the souls of all, awarded the one destiny, sharing alike in the delights of Paradise. The measure of success attending the labors of these reformers has not been recorded.

The "Falling Exercise" continued for some time to prevail as a " manifestation " in the churches, but not with the " power and demonstration " that gave it its marked distinction on this occasion. The cases of "arrest," however, as faith in its efficacy as a converting instrumentality began to waver, became fewer and fewer, ceasing eventually altogether. Near about the same time, indeed, it broke out again, but in a different settlement of the border then, and among the congregations of a different people. As among Methodists, its epidemical career was limited to the one season and the one spot,—in its traditional association with which the "Cane-Ridge" has become famous first among camp-meetings, and the "Cumberland" of towering renown among revivals.

VI.

MENTIONABLE MEN AMONG THE PREACHERS OF THE BORDER.

WHEN the material is considered of which the Methodist ministry in border-days was composed, it could scarcely be expected that any of the order should have attained to such a degree of eminence as would challenge specially the notice of after-times. Two hundred and eighty preachers, through the first sixteen years' existence of the church on the frontier, constituted the clerical (itinerant) force of the service. They were all uneducated, save in the simplest rudiments of common-school learning; or, as one of their number who has written a book is pleased to express it, "there was not a single literary man among them." Minds gotten up after that sort of fashioning are not of the stamp to make a mark that is likely to prove permanently prominent.

But there were those who in their day and generation had a distinction, and who in the circuits over which they traveled were famous. Good fighting-properties — and propensities — were respected in the church as well as out of it; and the Black-Robe who, boldly offering or accepting defiance, stood always ready, under provocation, to whip or be whipped, was noted and petted among believers quite as much as could have been Crib or Molyneaux among bruisers. John Ray has an honorable mention in history because of his "great muscular power and natural courage," an illustration of which has been particularly set forth in an anecdote. Himself and a party of other itinerants in the course of their journeying were approaching a toll-gate which, near where the road branched, had recently been moved from its position on one of the forks to the main stem, in order to command passage and control fare from travelers along both routes, when the right of the keeper to demand toll was called in question. John Ray disputed it roundly, and declared that if the rest would agree he would carry them through without cost. One of his companions expressed a desire to know how he would do it. "I will ride up to the gate," said he, "and command the keeper to open it." "But suppose he declines?" it was suggested. "Why, I will break the gate down," said John Ray, "and let him do his worst." To avoid the fray which he knew must ensue, one of the more peaceably disposed, who luckily happened to be the pursebearer of the party, trotted on in advance and settled with the toll-man, although "there was a great deal of clamoring behind him," and the " company looked sour and showed some dissatisfaction." John was deprived of the opportunity of shewing his muscle on the occasion, but not of demonstrating to the satisfaction of his fellow-itinerants that he was entirely willing—in fact, that he would be rather glad of a chance—to put it to the proof.

Peter Cartwright stands high on the record as a sharer in his honors with the redoubtable Ray: hence was he fancifully known as the "Bull-dog" among the saints, as well as among the sinners, of his time. At a camp-meeting attended by a larger number than usual of "rabble and rowdies," all drunk, and armed with dirks, clubs, knives, and horse-whips, two finely-dressed fellows marched into the congregation with their hats on, and rose up and stood in the midst of the ladies and began to laugh and talk. They were ordered to desist, but declined, couching their refusal in terms which out of the pulpit were considered profane, if not blasphemous. Peter immediately stepped down from the platform, walked up to one of the invaders, dodged a blow from a loaded whip aimed at his head, closed in on his man, and brought him to the ground. A drunken magistrate interfered, and ordered the reverend combatant to let his prisoner loose or "he would knock him down." Cartwright invited him, very coolly, to "crack away." The officer took him at his word, and aimed a blow which might have damaged his profile, except that it was scientifically parried by the preacher, who, taking advantage of the unguarded instant, jumped in, and, seizing the coat-collar of his antagonist with one hand and his hair with the other, "fetched him a sudden jerk forward," floored him, and leaped on his prostrate body. The ringleader of the rioters then stepped forward and made three passes at Peter, who, exhibiting much skill, not only warded off the thrusts, but, watching his chance, delivered a right-hander fair "on the burr of the ear" in return, "which dropped him to the earth." The friends of order then rushing to the rescue, the mob was soon dispersed. When the fight was ended, Cartwright resumed his place at the sacred desk, and, taking for a text the appropriate passage, "The gates of hell shall not prevail," preached a sermon with such "power and demonstration" that three hundred hearers fell like dead men in battle, and two hundred professed religion and were added to the church.

To excel in the art lachrymose, or be able at will to command the shedding of tears, was esteemed a rare accomplishment. Ralph Lotspiech, with no other possibly discoverable virtue to distinguish him, was nevertheless a man of mark because of his proficiency in this particular; and so, as the *Weeping Prophet*,—a Niobe in broadcloth,—he has been calendared with the illustrious and lives among the immortal of the period.

Miracles, not at all uncommon among Methodists, were sometimes a means of celebrity. Brother Joseph Dickson, a great hunter and trapper of the border, having provided himself with the necessary outfit, took passage in a "dug-out" and started off on a voyage to the wild Indian country on the Missouri. Two winters were spent in this remote and unfriendly region. To protect himself against the bitter cold of the climate, he made an excavation in a steep hill-side, where he managed to lodge with tolerable comfort. The glare of the light from the snow, however, affected his eyes to such an extent that ultimately, towards the close of the second winter, he became blind. Reduced to this helpless and hopeless condition, and with death apparently certain before him, he began to realize how great a sinner, and how utterly unprepared for the future, he was. He knelt and prayed, and solemnly vowed to God that, if he were spared and delivered, his life should thenceforth be devoted to His service. All of a sudden there was a strong impression made on his mind that if he would take the inside bark of a tree that grew near by his cave, and beat it up soft and fine, soak it in water, and apply it as a wash, his vision would be restored. He tried the treatment at night, and awoke in the morning to find the inflammation gone and his eyes made whole again. He then "felt that God had forgiven his sins, and that he ought to praise and give glory to His name." As in further evidence of the special interposition of Providence in his case, it is stated that, spring soon opening, he had "astonishing good luck" at trapping, securing a great amount of the best furs, which he afterwards sold in St. Louis for several thousand dollars. He then returned home, "took preaching into his cabin," joined the church, became a leader and steward, and acquired a renown at once, particularly as a successful agent in the collection of funds for the support of the gospel.

Others, again, were famed as dreamers of dreams and seers of visions; their power and scope of clairvoyance scarcely up to the old prophetic standard, perhaps, but among believers none the less credible or creditable on that account. John Stewart, the Mulatto of Marietta, to whom allusion has already been made, slept, and, sleeping, dreamed that he was about to commence a religious meeting. While seated awaiting the hour appointed for the opening of service, an Indian man and woman, "clothed in particular garments," entered the house "in a peculiar manner," saluted him, shook hands with him, and "seemed to manifest peculiar earnestness and interest in regard to his message." It was mysteriously made to appear to John that they invited him "to go and preach for their people," living somewhere, not definitely set forth, "*northwest* of Marietta." The dream impressed him powerfully. He tried to argue the force of it away; but it clung to him night and day. Doubting the call plunged him into a state of mental misery; the favorable consideration of it brought "great peace and joy of mind." He retired to the woods and fields, day after day, to pray, and at each visit regularly saw the Indian and the squaw, always seeming to come from the *northwest* and renewing their invitation "to come and preach for them." The mental anguish resulting from the difficulty of deciding the question of duty so agitated his body that he was thrown into a severe fit of sickness. When brought to his bed, he finally resolved that as soon as he could "pay some debts which he had contracted before he had experienced religion," he would recognize the call as of Providence, and go. His health and strength were immediately restored. Being enabled to effect a settlement of the pecuniary claims against him, he prepared himself for his missionary enterprise, followed up the *north-*

west course, according to direction, and in due time reached a small settlement of half-breed Wyandots on the Upper Sandusky, where among the first to accost him on his arrival he recognized instantly, in living identity, the Indian and squaw of his vision,—a manifest confirmation of the divinity of the dream.

The Rev. Jonathan Stamper had also his revelations. Once upon a time, in a "remarkable dream," he had an interview with the spirit of the Rev. John P. Finley, one of his best friends in life, and for whom he mourned in death as a dear brother departed; and the burden of the vision was as follows:

In his slumbers Stamper thought that he went to the house of Finley, who welcomed him at the door with his usual urbanity, expressed much gratification at the visit, took him in, and sat down with him, side by side, at the fire. Jonathan, although he said nothing, felt an anxiety, as was natural, to learn something respecting the world of spirits. The shade of the departed, divining the desire, said,—

"Brother, you are filled with curiosity."

"Yes," Jonathan replied; "my mind has taken a very curious turn."

"Well," continued the shadow, "ask any question you see proper, and I will satisfy you, so far as I can, consistently with the laws of the country where I live."

"Brother," Jonathan then began to interrogate, "are you happy?"

"Happy as heaven can make me," was the response.

"When you died, did you enter immediately into heaven?"

"No; but I immediately started for it. It took me three days to make the journey, though I sped with the velocity of a sunbeam. I passed beyond the boundaries of this system, and lost sight of the most distant star that twinkles in these skies, and entered into thick and uninterrupted darkness." Here the shadow paused for a moment; then, resuming with an expressive look, "Oh, brother," it said, "hell is a solemn reality!—After this, I all at once burst into the glories of heaven."

"The Scriptures represent heaven as a glorious city, such a one as was never seen on earth, and by other splendid and beautiful imagery. Is this entirely figurative," inquired the dreamer, "or is it a literal description?"

"Partly literal and partly figurative," answered the shade. "Heaven is a local residence gloriously fitted up for the abode of saints and angels. All the beautiful imagery of the Scriptures is there seen, though of a spiritual character; such as the trees ever green, the golden streets, etc."

Jonathan then inquired if the saints in heaven knew each other.

The deceased assured him that they did, perfectly. He knew all the patriarchs, prophets, and apostles at sight.

Here the dreamer, satisfied with his examination, rested; when his ethereal visitant, who seemed to be quite as much in the dark about earthly affairs as was his brother in the flesh concerning things celestial, became querist in return, and thus began to interview the slumberer:

"I desire to know how you are getting along in the good work."

"About as we were when you were with us."

"Do the Methodists pay their preachers no better than formerly?"

"No!"

"Oh! what a pity! what a pity! The itinerant plan," the shadow of the old exhorter then went on to say, "is the plan of God. He designs it to take the world, and nothing will prevent it but a want of liberality in our people. You must never locate. If I had my life to live again, I would travel, if I begged my bread from door to door. If I had traveled as I ought to have done, I should have shone much brighter in heaven than I now do. Don't locate, brother; God will support you." He then reached up to the chimney-piece, the dreamer proceeds to relate, and took down a considerable roll of bank-notes of the most beautiful and singular appearance, which he handed to Jonathan, saying, "Here,—these are for you."

Jonathan suggested that perhaps the money had

better go to his own widow, but the shade answered, "No; it is for you. There is a bank in heaven for the support of itinerant preachers, and this is for you;" when the slumbering brother reluctantly reached out his hand and took it. After some loud and animated shouting and singing, the vision ended, and the sleeper awoke.

This saintly interview of Brother Jonathan must not be understood as a humorous invention, devised, by way of novelty, as a hint for higher salaries, but as a circumstance of serious fact and worthy of most sober acceptance.

Among the reverends notable for their early labors along the bor.er are to be found such men as Thomas Wilkinson, John Page, John Watson, Lewis Garret, Benjamin Lakin, Jesse Walker, Samuel Parker, Samuel Doughty, Benjamin Young, Anthony Houston, John Adam Granadd, Jacob Young, Archibald McElroy,—distinguished for his "peculiar aversion to Calvinism,"—and the Bishops Asbury and McKendree. Jarvis C. Taylor has a rather prominent record as "a pretty good poet," and the author of a pamphlet under the inviting title of "News from the Infernal Regions." James Quinn, who "lived and preached like a primitive evangelist," enjoys the distinction, which he shares with his "poor horse Wilks," of having been first to carry the Methodist gospel into the State of Ohio (1799). Four years later, having been appointed, with John Meek for his colleague, to the newly-created "Hockhocking Circuit," embracing the settlements in the valleys of the Muskingum, Scioto, and Hockhocking, he made his permanent abode within its bounds. Benjamin Lakin is known in connection with Peter Cartwright as having been the original pioneer of the Faith in Indiana (1802), among the borderers occupying the lands opposite Louisville. These neighborhoods were formed into a circuit called the "Silver Creek Circuit," and placed under charge of Moses Ainsworth, in 1807. The credit of introducing Methodism into Illinois (1793) belongs to Joseph Lillard; although Hosea Riggs was the first to settle in the State, about five years later.

Methodism was of rapid growth in the back woods,—everywhere except in Western Pennsylvania, throughout the length and breadth of which "Calvinism and Universalism had so intrenched themselves that Methodism could scarcely live,"— its preachers "not hoping to rise above the occupation in the church of hewing wood and drawing water." In 1800 the communion, embracing the entire membership of the border, numbered 2000 souls. In 1802 it was increased to 7200; in 1804, to 9600; and in 1811, to 30,741. Work done quickly, however, is seldom work done well. Members were glued to the surface merely, as would appear, not mortised into the body of belief; so that, while there is room for regret, there is none for surprise, that they should hold in place by an attachment very precarious, and extremely liable to come apart under unfavorable exposure. Three thousand cases of apostasy are reported as having occurred within one year (1812). Perhaps it was from the commonness of a tendency thus to lapse—natural, nay, inevitable, from the "method" by which conversions were made—that, to meet the exigency, it had been found necessary at the outstart to declare against the dogma of the "perseverance of the saints," and not only to confess the possibility of "falling from grace," but to write and register the confession as a doctrine of the church.

And so, keeping up a pretty equal ratio of increase through the years ensuing, the Society has gone on winning and losing, but, in the long run, gaining and growing; and so it lives and flourishes, whether to last for long in the future, as organisms of forced growth seldom can, or to die out eventually, all the sooner for the process, the time to be must determine.

THE PRESBYTERIAN.

(279)

THE PRESBYTERIAN.

I.

OLD REDSTONE—ITS PEOPLE AND ITS PRESBYTERY.

OVER the top-piece of the door of the old house in which he lived, in the "Nether Bow," John Knox, the maker of Presbyterianism, had caused to be written this legend:

𝔏𝔲𝔣𝔢.𝔊𝔬𝔡.𝔞𝔟𝔬𝔳𝔢.𝔞𝔩𝔩.𝔞𝔫𝔡.𝔶𝔬𝔲𝔯.𝔫𝔦𝔠𝔥𝔟𝔬𝔲𝔯.𝔞𝔰.𝔶𝔬𝔲𝔯𝔰𝔢𝔩𝔣.

If the distinguished Scotch Reformer had made search through all the recorded sayings of the wise of all ages, he could not, for his purpose, have hit upon a more comprehensive, a better, or a more beautiful precept. If, as well as across the lintel of his home, he could have had the sentence inscribed over the threshold of the sanctuary in which he preached, and at the same time have made its sentiment the governing principle of the new faith which it was his choice to proclaim, his followers would have been none the worse of it, and himself, perhaps, somewhat the better. But the text seems not to have been understood according to the letter of its rendering; else the First of Presbyterians could never have merited the epithet, scarcely complimentary, of the "Iconoclast," nor his disciples have perpetuated for themselves a fame of reproach for deeds of violence and vandalism done by their hands. Churches would not have been forcibly entered and despoiled; pictures and images sacred to Christian worshipers would have been spared, and monasteries would have been exempt from sack and from pillage.

Whatever tracing may serve for his picture as of to-day,—with which this sketch has nothing to do,—one hundred years ago, when we find our "congregation"alist drifted off from his native shore and anchored far away in an inland wilderness of the New World, we discover a likeness but little altered from the original, notwithstanding generations had passed since its angry population, roused at the blast of their prophet's trumpet, were stirred to riotry in the streets of Perth, and although two centuries had elapsed since the Reformer himself had ended his career and been gathered to his fathers. First among adventurers had he started from the settlements of his people on the James and Rappahannock, and foremost among squatters, crossing the ridges of intervening mountains and penetrating to the "Yough" and Monongahela, had he hewn out his little clearing and planted his cabin, on the levels and slopes drained and made fertile by their floods. Still the legitimate, unadulterated issue of the race to which he belonged, the characteristics of the progenitor were inherited in the successor; his tough energies, eager to be employed, seeking that occasion for exercise among the savages which more fortunate forbears had found in their feuds among old neighbors.

Backwoodsmen were "crack" men all, as it well became them to be; but at handling an axe or poising a rifle, at leveling a tree or laying a Mingo, at willing with a purpose and doing what was to be, whole-heartedly, till all done and well done, better, at best, than the Scotch-Irish Presbyterian wore not buckskin nor domiciled in logs on the border. Did forests, dense and deep, encumber the ground which he would reduce to cultivation? Inch by inch he hacked his way in through the timber, till patches at first of fat soil growing into fields, then widening into farms, were laid bare, and the labor that Hercules might have halted at was accomplished. Were murderous assaults essayed against him by the savage? He was ready to meet him, in his own way and on his own terms: behind trees, a hundred yards between, at "Hy Spy,"—the style of dueling current in those days,—with a rifle; openly and face to face, at throwing-distance, with a tomahawk; or grip and grip, with a knife. Besieged in his cabin, he would hold at bay his score of dusky assailants outside, discharging death through the loop-holes, while his wife moulded the bullets and his stripling son picked the flints; amid all comporting himself as composedly as though a bull's-eye were his target, and a shooting-match on an after-harvest holiday the occasion. In his lexicon there was no such word as fear,—no such word as fail. His practical belief was that virtue goes by inheritance, and that with man, the son, in his degree, as with God, the Father, in his, all things were possible; that, not in a conditional sense but an absolute, it was practicable to say to a mountain, "Be thou removed, and be thou cast into the sea," and to see it done; in fine, that miracles were not mysteries, but may-be's,—difficult, no doubt, of achievement, but, under a living consciousness of one's omnipotence, feasible.

But the Presbyterian was not only remarkable for his qualities of faith and courage. All the severer, or what may be termed the more strictly masculine, virtues besides, were permeating elements, as well, in his character. He was honest. Averse to aught that savored of disingenuousness or dissimulation,—of hypocrisy or fraud,—his opinions were never liable to misapprehension, nor his conduct, if he knew it, open to misconstruction. As he thought, he spake,—"the word the cousin to the thing" always; as he spake, he meant; and as he meant, so, to the letter, he lived. He was just. Accepting certain maxims, hereditary in his house since the days of the Marys,—or of Moses, for that matter,—as of settled incontrovertibility, he made them the rule of his reasoning and of his judgments. The rule may have been hard, but it was wholesome; he could quote you the text for it, and he was true to the text. Wrongs done had to be righted to the fullest degree of compensation. If a man caused a blemish in his neighbor, as he had done so was it to be done to him. It was bounden duty to duplicate a crime—lawfully to perpetrate over again that which in itself was unlawful—in order to atone for it; to smite for having smitten; to maim for having maimed; to murder for having murdered. Such was his standard of equity; even-handed assuredly, and impartial, as was becoming, in accordance with the economy of ancient dispensation, in which he delighted, and to which he adhered with loyal fidelity. So, examined strictly on each, down through the whole catalogue of moralities,—examined, that is, in the light of the olden ordinances,—he might be represented as of righteous reputation in all, unimpeachable, irreproachable. Like the young Judean in the gospel, he knew the Commandments, and kept them. He did not commit adultery; he did not kill; he did not steal; he did not bear false witness; he defrauded not; he honored his father and his mother.

But there his virtues ended. Perfect as he strove to be, and as, according to the law, let it be conceded, he was, yet, measured by the purer standard of the gospel, was he lamentably wanting. As the law knew not charity, neither did he. How could he be generous and at the same time just? To show mercy was, to the extent of the showing, without authority to abate the punishment dutifully due the offender, thus becoming an offense in itself. To forgive absolutely was to forget all obligation and to sin unpardonably. Under cloud of such a conviction, he stood veiled impenetrably apart, as it were, from all the warmer, kindlier, brighter influences of heaven. With the tender growth indigenous to it ever as it peeped to the surface plucked up by the roots, his heart, weary at length of the ineffectual struggle, ceased its efforts, sunk into unproductiveness, and so remained, a blighted, ruined, wreck-strewn waste. He had no feeling. His nerves were steel; "his blood was very snow-broth." Hard, uncompromising, compassionless, the very virtue—the *summum jus*—in which he gloried, was the vice—the *summa injuria*—that told most to his shame.

The Presbyterian had a religious character as well as a moral; not less marked,—not less thoroughly imbued with the spirit of the law,—not less in accord with the temper of the gospel.

A reverend orator, now occupying a high position as a theological teacher in a leading school of the sect, on a certain occasion once made "Protestantism" the theme of a popular discourse. In the discussion of his subject, he undertook to make it appear that the antagonistic feature implied in its title was the one of highest order and of most praiseworthy merit in the reconstructed system of which he appeared as the champion,—in other words, arguing, upon the presumption, apparently, that whatever is, in religion, is, always has been, and always must be wrong, that therefore the oftener the "protest" the purer the profession. In proof of his point he started back with the genesis of history, quoting his examples from the patriarchs (strangely overlooking, however, the still earlier instance in the garden of Eden), and so, from the Luther of the Flood, coming down, through the prophets, the apostles, and the martyrs, to John Knox of Edinburgh. Why he stopped short of Beecher—or Brigham Young—did not satisfactorily appear.

The early religionist of the Monongahela Valley was of like mind, precisely, with the Princeton Professor. His conviction seemed to be that the worst and most dangerous enemy, if not, indeed, the only one, which the church had to contend against, was the church itself; that the surest way to prove a faith perfect was to pick flaws in it; that to point out its weaknesses was to show its strength, and—coming down to the practical belief at the bottom of the whole—that to despitefully treat the world of believers outside his own elect circle, and to cast contempt upon their usages, was, as the Nether Bow motto had it, to "lufe God above all, and his nichbour as himself." Chiefly was it his duty to protest against all, in creed, or custom, or ceremonial, that appertained to the Roman Catholic Church,—that Scarlet Woman, and Mother of Harlots and Abominations of the earth. Did she, out of deference to a taste which she thought it not derogatory to her Christian character to gratify, build her temples after an artistically ordered plan, and with an eye to architectural beauty? Turret and spire, and arch and column, were heathenish devices, therefore, and decorated walls and carved woods and dim religious lights idolatrous inventions, contrived to captivate the carnal sense and allure infatuated souls to their eternal undoing. Square walls instead, and squat roofs, inclosing interiors bare, utterly, of ornament, and as dull, comfortless, and wretched as possible, composed the edifices of worship, presumed only to be consistent with a proper idea of devotion. In the observance of the "popish" Sunday was it lawful to engage in such innocent diversions as, contributing to rest and relaxation, would make the day one to be looked forward to eagerly through the week, and to be enjoyed heartily and sincerely when it came? The very idea of "rest," in any reasonable sense, lay under rigid ban of the "protest." To walk abroad in wood or field, to sing (unless a psalm of Rouse), to read (except a treatise on Justification, or a dissertation on the Decrees), to talk (unless upon some topic drawn from the Confession of Faith), to laugh from any cause, and, indeed, to eat (except cold meats of Saturday's cooking), were sins, one and all, of rankest odor, that smelt to heaven. Dispensation was granted for but one indulgence: "Monongahela" was not prohibited, and the Presbyterian could take his toddy when he pleased —hot or cold—without offense. For writing hymns and singing them on the Lord's day, Zinzendorf, the Moravian, and his daughter were arrested and fined in the sum of six shillings. In fact, to such an extent was the reformatory process carried that Christ was almost protested out of Christianity, and the anomalous but scarcely singular coincidence succeeded of extremes meeting, and Gospeler and Jew uniting on a common basis of belief and practice.

And yet the Presbyterian was guilty of glaring inconsistencies. He censured the presumption of Rome in claiming to be the only true church, and yet was quite as exclusive himself, holding no communion with any one outside of his own persuasion. It was punishable misdemeanor to attend a Methodist meeting. To refuse to have his child baptized by a "lawful minister" subjected the unruly member to a fine, by way of expiation (for pardons had their purchase-price outside of Babylon as well as in it), of two thousand pounds of tobacco. It was a cruel, despotic wrong, which neither God nor man could excuse, to burn John Rodgers at the stake, and yet it was a law "of universal and perpetual equity," as orthodoxy did not hesitate to preach, and quote the Scripture for (Deut. xiii. 9, 10), "to put to death any apostate seducing idolater or heretic who seeketh to thrust away the souls of God's people from the Lord their God." He contended for a Bible without note or comment, insisting that "God was his own interpreter, and He would make it plain," and yet, notwithstanding, thought the "gilt" of a confession indispensable for the "refined gold" of the word, which the believer was forced to accept as solid coin, conscience or no conscience, on peril of excommunication. To show reverence to the Cross through one sense was gross idolatry, while to adore it through another was orthodox and proper. He might not *look* upon that sacred emblem without sin, and yet, most rightfully and piously (but out of the sanctuary only at first, until Rouse, after a convulsion that shook the church to its centre, was set aside for the hymn-book), he could sing, or *hear* sung, "Jesus, I my cross have taken," or, "Simply to thy cross I cling," or, "Here it is I find my heaven, while upon the cross I gaze." So in his lighter social occupations and amusements. To participate with a lady, at a neighborhood gathering of an evening, in a jig, a fling, or a hornpipe, was scandalously indelicate and immoral, while to "hold," and to "bundle," as the since-discarded but then all-prevalent customs were on the border, was harmless and allowable. A Virginia reel was a "session"able enormity, but a deacon might dance at the selfsame diversion under the fiction of "Peeling the willow,"—kiss his partner, too, at the end of it, if he pleased,—and not provoke the whisper of a protest.

The Presbyterian could not be charged with negligence in the religious training of his children. While nurselings still, and ere able to articulate the syllables of their task distinctly, they were taught to repeat devoutly, bent at their mother's knees, or at the bedside, and regularly as the hour for retiring came with each night, "Our Father which art in heaven." Nor, besides, were their seats allowed to be vacant at the "family exercise," when, morning and evening, that service was conducted, the father reading, and copiously commenting upon, some chosen portion of Scripture, leading in the singing of a psalm, and delivering a prayer remarkable for its orthodoxy, its legality, and its length. On weekdays no additional observances —excepting, of course, the "grace" at meals— were exacted. Bible and psalm-book were laid carefully aside betweenwhiles, one upon the other, in their corner, by sacred appropriation, of the shelf, balanced at the opposite end by "Baxter's Call to the Unconverted," or "Alleine's Alarm," and the "Pilgrim's Progress." The moral obligation of Work was tantamount, in its place, to the spiritual one of Worship, and, as in one case so in the other, the youths of the household had to take and bear their proportionate share. "Sabbath," however, was the day especially devoted to educational purposes. School-hours began before breakfast, and, without a moment (except a stolen one) of intermission or relaxation, were continued until bedtime. Study, close, hard, dry, as incomprehensible subject-matter could make it, was the inflexible law, submission to which, enjoined by parental authority, was enforced by such threatenings of divine indignation for neglect as, striking terror to the soul of the pupil, proved all-sufficient to insure it. The discipline was stringent, but it was effective; so effective that scarce a boy or girl of " evangelical " begetting was to be found on the border but that, with Madge Wildfire, could say "the single carritch, and the double carritch, and justification and effectual calling, and the Assembly of divines at Westminster," through each particular " act " and " work," and prohibition and requirement, from cover to cover, without a stumble.

Fifty-two good whole days at cramming out of three hundred and sixty-five, repeated year after year until the student had attained a parental age and relation himself, ought to have left him at the end quite competent to pass examination. And it did. He understood all mysteries and all knowledge quite as well as Paul,—perhaps a little better. Indeed, so complete was his theological schooling —so thoroughly (to put it in another shape) had he familiarized himself with the sinuosities and circuities of his channel of passage to the celestial shores—that he felt himself entirely qualified to sail his own craft; as he would have attempted and been perfectly content to do, only for the fact that the *law* of the line, in which he was a shareholder and by which he voyaged, demanded the services of a professional pilot at the helm. To preside in the pulpit, to pronounce the benediction, to administer the sacraments, must be done, according to statute, by the minister, licensed, called, and ordained for the discharge of those offices.

The settlement of Western Pennsylvania may be said to date from 1752, when Christopher Gist, with eleven other pioneers and their families, chose out places and built them cabins at what is known as Mount Braddock, lying west of the Youghiogheny, and about midway between Connellsville and Uniontown, in Fayette County. The early emigrants were exposed to sufferings that made their lot a sorely trying one. The forests were infested with roving bands of savages, armed with knife and rifle, and abroad everywhere for massacre and plunder. Who stepped beyond the threshold of his door went out at the peril of his life. Men were slain in the fields; women, as they went to the springs for water, were seized and butchered or carried captive into the wilderness. Dwellings were burned, property was destroyed or stolen, and, in short, disasters and misfortunes visited upon him so sweeping and disheartening as might well have served to deter the borderer from a new attempt to establish himself in so inhospitable a region. But the iron will of the Covenanter, used in other lands to maintain itself under hardest pressure of adversity, was not of a texture likely to yield to the circumstances, grievous as they were, of his new situation. Crushed to earth, he rose again. Out of the ashes of his ruin sprang up himself in certain reappearance, with the finer perfumes of his nature lost, perhaps, like a rose subjected to a similar process, but with his other perfections purified rather than impaired in the palingenesis. Miraculous energy such as this was sure to win in the end. The savage, wearying at length of his unsuccessful efforts at dislodging his enemy, ceased his raids, and the pioneer was left in undisturbed possession of his home. Hostilities suspended, adventurers who had not cared to share the perils of the border while they lasted, took heart of the fact, and began to follow as their predecessors had led. Emigrant after emigrant gathered in; clearings multiplied; cabin after cabin was built, until at length, of a still summer twilight, house-dog baying to house-dog, the chain of responses linked across the rolling lands to Old Redstone,—to Turkey-foot,—to Catfish; and down the valleys of the Youghiogheny and Monongahela to the little "Manor," that lay—with a destiny in store for it of which the loiterers in and about it did not dream—wedged in between its rivers, a hundred miles below, under the guns of old Fort Pitt. As early as 1763, at the close of the French War, the settlements had a population of four thousand souls.

At this time the Presbyterian Church in the East began to turn its attention to the West. A meeting of the Synod of New York and Philadelphia, down till 1789 the supreme judicatory of the church, was held, when, the condition of the "distressed frontier inhabitants" being taken into consideration, it was resolved to send out two ministers on a tour of inspection among them. The Reverend Messrs. Beatty and Brainerd were nominated for the mission. According to their report, offered before Synod at its next meeting (1764), they were providentially prevented from fulfilling their appointment, "the whole design of the mission being entirely frustrated by the breaking out of the Indian [Pontiac's] war." Two years later (1766) the appointment of Mr. Beatty, with Mr. Duffield for his colleague on this occasion, was renewed. The savages having abandoned their designs on Fort Pitt and retired beyond the Ohio, the journey could be taken with entire safety, and the two reverend gentlemen started on it accordingly. At the fort they were politely received by Captain Murray, the commandant, who gave them places at his table, provided them with rooms, and furnished them with beds, so that, "on the whole," as a historian of the times relates, "they were as comfortable as could be expected." After a flying visit to the Muskingum, they returned home, the whole tour consuming some six or eight weeks. No particular results are recorded as growing out of the mission. Messrs. Cooper and Brainerd were next commissioned for the service, "to spend at least three months on the frontier;" but, in consequence of ".discouraging accounts brought in by the interpreter, Joseph," they declined to act. Mr. Anderson, shortly afterwards, was proposed to take the field "for twelve Sabbaths," at twenty shillings a Sabbath; but it does not appear from the records that he ever went. Mr. Niles, the next appointee, "failed through sickness." Other emissaries, such as Finley (1771),—who took advantage of the trip to buy himself a good tract of land in Fayette County,—Craighead, and King (1772); Foster (1775) and Carmichael (1776), were ordered out on transient visits, certainly one (Finley), and possibly two of whom, complied, although without seeming to have accomplished anything worthy of mention; and thus terminated the efforts of the church towards the planting of the Faith on the border.

Late in the year 1776 a little band of journeyers might have been seen pursuing patiently the way by which the descent, on its western slope, of Laurel Hill is made. The track they followed was that opened up twenty years before by the unfortunate British officer who, alas! never lived to trace it all back again, and which was long afterwards known, in association with that disastrous expedition, as "Braddock's Trail." A man in the prime of life, with his oldest daughter, still a girl, behind, and his youngest, a child, pillowed before him on a horse, led the way, closely followed by his wife, riding like himself and leading still another horse, on either side of which, packed snugly in creels or baskets slung across the animal and fastened securely to the pack-saddle, were deposited the two remaining children of the family. Thus, one day in the darksome month of November, descended into the valley of the wilderness JAMES POWER, who enjoys the distinction among Presbyterians of having been first of the Black-Robes of their order to establish himself among the settlers of the border and "aid in laying the foundations of the western Zion." Mr. Power undertook this mission not by appointment of the church, but on his own motion, prompted to it, without doubt, precisely as was any other emigrant of the time, by the attractive prospects of the new region, with its fields of plenty and of promise, opened up and reaching forth invitingly for occupation. Indeed, except that we hear somewhat vaguely, of his having baptized a child for Mr. Marquis, at Cross Creek, in 1778, there is no positive evidence that he pursued his profession at all, in any regular way, for several years after his arrival. On the contrary, the date of his first settlement and service as a preacher (at Mount Pleasant) is fixed by Dr. McMillan as late as 1781.

In the mean time the congregations of the frontier, left altogether uncared for, and beginning to realize, as we have seen, the necessity of church organization, decided to take up the work and carry it through on their own account. Meetings were held accordingly. As the result, on the 21st of June, 1779, a Call was made out from the "United Congregations at Buffalo and Cross Creek, to the Rev. Joseph Smith, a member of the Presbytery of New Castle." The Call set forth "the great loss youth sustain by growing up without the stated means of grace, the formality likely to spread over the aged, and the great danger of ungodliness prevailing amongst both: there being divers denominations of people among us" (Ommishes, or Dunkards, Quakers, and Seventh-day Baptists) "who hold dangerous principles, tending to mislead many weak and ignorant people." Submission was pledged to the "due exercise of discipline," and a salary promised of one hundred and fifty pounds, or rather, according to the summing up of the subscription paper accompanying the Call, something over a hundred and ninety-seven pounds, Pennsylvania currency, "money to be made equal in value to what it was in the year 1774," before the depreciation in that class of paper took place. Among others in the list of subscribers occur the names of Andrew Poe and Adam Poe, the famous brothers whose daring adventures furnish the material for many a thrilling story of the border. The

Call was accepted, and, in the year following, Mr. Smith, along with his family, planted himself permanently within the bounds of one of his parishes. Near about the same time the churches at Lower Ten-Mile and Upper Ten-Mile, each distant from the town of Washington the space intimated by their titles, fell under the pastoral care of Thaddeus Dodd, who had bought and was cultivating a farm in the neighborhood; while John McMillan, more noted as a "doctrinal examiner and instructor" than as a preacher, took charge of the congregations at Chartiers and Pigeon Creek. With these four reverend gentlemen for its members, the old Presbytery of Redstone was organized (1781), the creed of the Catechisms established, and the general enginery, invented at Edinburgh, put in motion, by which backwoodsmen were to be trained how, evangelically and soundly, to *"lufe God above all, and their nichbour as themselves."*

II.

THE PARSON OF SEVENTY-FIVE YEARS AGO.

A SKETCH of the Presbyterian Black-Robe of the olden time, to represent its subject faithfully, calls for but little variation in the general outline from the picture already presented of the layman of his **persuasion**. Their features in the main were the same, save that in the case of the officer they were more definitely traced, and betrayed a deeper and more determined outline of development, than in the subordinate. Passing through the same preparatory training, yielding under persistent pressure to the same constraints, that which, taking its bent accordingly, hardened eventually into a *habit* with the latter and ended there, went on, attaining a still more vigorous and overshadowing growth, until it matured into a *profession*, with the former. As a teacher, or preacher, following his vocation up on a chosen line, it became him—of course it would become him—to magnify that line, to show its superiority over all other lines, and by emphatic protestation of his own unlimited confidence in the singular and exclusive advantages of it, to win over customers from competing routes. Very naturally, as a result, his preaching turned chiefly on the points of difference; his religion became a religion of reason, and himself the orator, conscientious, earnest, obstinate, as schoolmen always are, of its philosophy. Mirroring that philosophy all the while, his own mind caught and held fast the likeness of what it reflected, so that at last it became a fixed impression, felt to the core of his being and picturing all the surface of his character.

As the expounder of its ordinances, the Law was with him the subject of absorbing study. It was his meditation all the day; its testimonies were his delight. He measured his steps by it; he ordered his thoughts according to it; he believed, he hoped, he preached, he sung, he prayed by it. The straitest among the "most straitest" of Jewish sects, in the tight days when the Pharisees wore broadest their phylacteries, could not have adhered with a truer or more exact fidelity to its precepts. Its demands admitted of nothing short of plenary and absolute satisfaction. "Thus saith the Lord" settled the question, and was an extinguisher upon all controversy,—a choke-off against whatever plea the sufferer under it might propose to offer in abatement of the decree pronounced. Hence, where the heart of the layman under like influences was as flint, that of the Black-Robe became as adamant. The springs of compassion that should have had source in his bosom, were dried up. "He had no juice but that was verjuice in him."

Of such a mould, one is in no wise surprised, in following up his history, to discover that in all cases of civil disturbance, when, upon one provocation or another, mutinous men were banded together to achieve violently the correction of alleged causes of complaint, the disciple of the Iconoclast was leadingly identified with the movement. Among the terrible incidents of border times, that of the planned attack in the night on a cluster of Indian huts on the Conestoga Creek, when the unconscious slumberers were crept in upon and "shot, stabbed, and hacked to death," and which was but the beginning of a continued series of outrages, has a dark and sorrowful prominence. The Paxton Boys who did it, and who, the blood of their shedding still red and reeking on their hands, quoted Scripture in justification of its doing, were organized in his own parish and from among his own parishioners, by one Presbyterian preacher, and defended afterwards, when all was over, as men "humane, liberal, and moral, nay, religious," by another. Reverend penmen who have written their narratives of olden events, naturally anxious to defend the good reputation of the "missionaries" from the reproach of having had either heart or hand in Tom the Tinker's rising, assert that no sympathy was felt for the malcontents by the Black-Robes; on the contrary, that they opposed the movement "strenuously and successfully." The scene of insubordination lay within the bounds of what had then become (1794) the Synod of Virginia. A party of soldiers on their way out to aid in suppressing the insurrection, arrived in the town of Harrisonburg, where, at the time, the Synod was in session. The occasion seemed to call for an expression of loyalty, and, on the motion of one of the members, an address to the people was proposed, "inculcating obedience to the laws of the country." The prevailing sentiment of the body, as a lively discussion soon revealed, was that "there were wrongs to be redressed, rather than a rebellion to be suppressed." A vote being taken, the address was rejected, and Tom the Tinker had the indorsement of the Synod.

In like manner, as respected questions affecting the interests of humanity,—where Charity which knew not law, on the one side, stood advocate as against the Law that knew not charity, on the other,—the attitude of the Presbyterian was just what, according to his code and creed, it could not but have been. In his own time he was the patron, as his church after him was the apologist, —not to use a stronger term,—of slavery,—the persevering apologist, down until the Samaritans outside, with whom it had no dealing, interposed to rid the nation of the curse. He "could not say that slavery was a sin, without charging the apostles of Christ with conniving at it." So he was ready to testify, as half a century later his professional successors through their General Assembly did testify, and as often afterwards, in much less moderately chosen terms, was ratified by many a divine, who perhaps would scarcely care—possibly might blush—to own it now. For criminals doomed to punishment he manifested no symptom of mercy, no showing of compassion,—unless the offer of his ghostly services at the sharply-closing crisis of their career, in extreme cases, might be so construed. Penance to the full extent of the award must be had, without easement, curtailment, or commutation,—as, in like manner, was demanded by the justice-loving Jew of Venice; as, in like manner, has been insisted upon by the clerical of his own sect ever since and until now. A movement was made, not many months ago, having in view the doing away with capital punishment in the State of Pennsylvania. While the project was pending, a paper was prepared and sent forward to the legislature from the judicatory of one of the branches of the church (the "United Presbyterian"), then in session at Pittsburg, praying against the proposed change, as prompted by mistaken notions of humanity, and as in direct contravention to the law—not of Christ, although affirmed as "of God," but—of Moses.

His ideas of conversion were, of course, in harmony with his views of belief. Faith had its philosophy, which the would-be partaker of its benefits must be thoroughly drilled in before he could hope to enjoy the saving advantage of its exercise. The poor sinner of the gospel whose all of confession was comprehended in two simple words, sufficient as they seem to have been in his day, would not have found them equal to the emergency of his case under the later schedule of conditions: *"Pisteuo Kurie!"* would scarcely have carried him past the pickets, to get where he is gone, by way of the Redstone Presbytery. He must have first been led to understand that he was made a partaker of the redemption purchased by Christ by the effectual application of it to him by the Holy Spirit; that the Holy Spirit applied this redemption by working faith in him, and thereby uniting him to Christ in his Effectual Calling; that Effectual Calling was the work of God's Spirit, whereby, being convinced of his sin and misery, having his mind enlightened in the knowledge of Christ, and his will renewed, he would be persuaded and enabled to embrace Jesus Christ; and that thus, at length, being Effectually Called, he would partake of justification, adoption, and sanctification, the benefits of which were peace of conscience, increase of grace, and perseverance therein to the end.

The "enlightening" operation could be considered as a success only by the overcoming beforehand of obstacles, minutely specified and elaborately described by journalists of the time, who went through with it, and which were wellnigh insuperable. There were the difficulties of the "Imputation of Adam's Sin to his Posterity," the "Strictness of the Divine Law," the fact that "Faith alone was the Condition of Salvation," and numerous others over which the seeker must pass necessarily, and at which it was inevitable that he should stumble,—not to mention the experience, indispensable besides, of a "Sufficient Weanedness from the World," and of the "Mortification of indwelling Corruption," before he could expect to gain "evidence of serious and comfortable exercise." The satisfaction which followed the enlightenment was of its own kind, and quite peculiar to the Presbyterian subject. Moses Tinda Tautamy, the converted Indian interpreter of Brainerd, in his moments of enthusiasm used to testify, "that he never felt better pleased than when his heart echoed to the soul-humbling doctrines of grace, and when he heard of the absolute sovereignty of God, and the salvation of sinners in a way of mere free grace." A refreshing experience it must have been, certainly.

A "call" for the ministry, while not claimed as having been made through special and miraculous revelation of himself by the Almighty, as in the case of the Methodist, was still viewed as of supernatural prompting; the Deity indicating, not in an ostensible way, but through the secret consciousness of the subject, his election to the sacred office. That God *had* a choice, and that this one or that one out of the multitude of less worthy vessels, on some account or other, which often puzzled the inquirer to determine, had been particularly ticketed for distinction, was assumed as a matter of course. The election, although usually signified to the favored subject himself directly, was not unfrequently, however, the result of arrangement entered into with responsible parties before, and, in fact, as a condition of, his existence. He was made to order, as it were; expressly to fill a place for which, among all the living ready-made, the fitting substitute was not to be found. One of the members of the Old Redstone Presbytery thus, we are informed, on their pledge that he should be dedicated to the ministry, was granted to his parents, "like Samuel and John of old," in answer to special prayer.

But the mere "call" was not enough to entitle the candidate to an assumption at once of the functions of the priestly office. A previous course of training, really indispensable to a complete mastery of the difficult mysteries of his faith, was required; embracing in its order a thorough study of the Latin, Greek, and Hebrew languages. Consequently, whatever may have been his position with regard to information derivable from other alien sources, in his own literature, or that of his church, he was well schooled. The distinctive dogmas of his communion, which he was taught to respect as its most sacred properties, were the subjects upon which it was his duty to be accurately informed. As the sinners among whom it must be his destiny, following along the border, to direct his missionary labors, would consist chiefly of Quakers, Sabbatarians, Baptists, and Methodists, he must not only hold correct views, but be able to defend them, of Original Sin, Election, Pedobaptism, and Perseverance. Familiarity with the scriptural languages prepared him not merely to grapple with doctrine in the naked, as it were, but armed him besides with the means of hopelessly confounding the adversary with whom he had to deal; for while the Arminian and the Immersionist, from frequent hearing of controversies common to the time, had caught and could toss back again their single stray terms of "original," their Presbyterian antagonist in return could overwhelm either, or both, with whole sentences of dumbfoundering quotation.

Testimony must be borne to the fact that the Presbyterian was always the faithful friend and zealous promoter of education. The Methodist himself, contemptibly ignorant as he was,—conscious of it, too, and glorying in it,—recognized, in the very attempt of affecting to despise, this feature of excellence in his Calvinistic rival. Scarcely had he planted himself in his new parishes on the border, when he began to turn his attention to that interest. Rev. Joseph Smith, appreciating the want which all the neighborhood experienced, but had not the enterprise to remedy, determined to take the correction of it in charge. Consulting first his wife, and having secured her "cordial acquiescence," he set apart a new kitchen which, as an appendage to his house, he had just built, and, at Upper Buffalo, in 1785, opened in it a classical school, the first of the kind in the West, commencing duty with three young men, Messrs. McGready, Porter, and Patterson, for his pupils. In 1791-2 the institution was transferred to Canonsburg, erected into an academy, and by appointment of the Synod of Virginia, who assumed the control of it, left for management in the hands of the Rev. Dr. John McMillan. The establishment grew in favor, increased in patronage, and acquired a wider and wider renown, until, under charter of the State, as Jefferson College, in 1802, it took its place among the leading seminaries of the land.

And yet, sorrily irreconcilable with such tutorage as it would seem, the Presbyterian Black-Robe was decidedly — confessedly — superstitious. As between his own views on this point and those of his Wesleyan brother, he made the distinction, where it is difficult to detect the difference, that whereas the latter claimed the manifestations with which he was honored as of express matter-of-fact revealment from heaven, his were referable to "a strong and firm persuasion" flowing from an extraordinary "liberty and enlargement of soul." The Rev. Joseph Smith lay, as was supposed, at the point of death. Mr. Edgar, a warm personal friend, was hastening to wait upon him in his extremity; when, as he approached the house, he met an old lady who was considered in her neighborhood as a "Mother in Israel." Mr. Edgar's first natural inquiry had reference to the condition of his sick friend. "He is worse," said the Mother; "but he will not die, *for the Lord hath told me to-day* that He will raise him up, and send him out to the West to preach the gospel;" and, continues the reverend writer who has made memorandum of "this singular but well-authenticated fact," he began to recover from that very hour. This same ministerial gentleman with his wife was returning from a walk, one evening, about sundown, when, in a wood near the town where they dwelt, "they both distinctly heard strains of sweet and melodious music over the tops of the trees, that seemed to them to rise and float away into the distant skies." It was interpreted "as under a special providential direction, and designed, as without doubt it served, to encourage and cheer them in the prospect of setting out at no distant day, with their family of helpless children, to the western wilds." It did not weaken the supernatural aspect of the case that a band, in a military encampment some distance off, was known as a regular custom to serenade the closing day; but it did surprise the historian, as he states in a foot-note, that so excellent a writer as Dr. Mosheim should sneeringly speak of "the pious sort of mistake" that Christians sometimes make in interpreting a "happy coincidence" into a special interposition of Providence. A son of the Rev. James Finley, one of a party of twenty men, was waylaid and attacked by a band of savages. A sharp skirmish took place. Finley, the force to which he belonged being worsted and beginning to retreat, found, when he wanted to fire as he ran, that his gun would not "go off," stopped to pick his flint, and, doing so, fell behind his companions. An Indian leveled his rifle at him, but before he could fire was luckily shot down. A few moments later, by a happy dodge, he succeeded in throwing one of his comrades between himself and a pursuing red-skin, and so escaped, but at the expense of the life of the comrade, who was instantly tomahawked by the enemy. At the same hour, as a comparison of time instituted afterwards made to appear, the father of young Finley, three hundred miles off, felt a "strange and unaccountable impression" that his son was in imminent danger of some sort, and immediately "betook himself to intense and agonizing prayer" for the boy. He continued this exercise for some time, until at length "he felt relieved and comforted, as though the danger was past." Finley, the senior, regarded the escape as a special providence. How the father of the son who was elbowed back and got brained instead esteemed it, we are not informed.

After the expiration of his academical term, the pupil was transferred to some minister, under whose private instruction he pursued his strictly theological studies; Dr. McMillan's lectures being his text-book, with such collateral authorities besides as the clerical libraries, within reach of borrowing, afforded. This system of private tuition—a necessity of the time—had its advantages. The student enjoyed the undivided care and attention of the teacher. What was required, by olden usage in the church, to be learned, he had to learn, and to learn well. There could be no shirking of duty,— no skipping over of half-mastered tasks. Ready to lend assistance when assistance was needed, the instructor, nevertheless, expected, and taught his disciple to expect, that the burden of achievement should rest on his own shoulders, and that if he would bear him worthily up under the pressure, and carry him palmily through, it must be mainly by his own efforts. The consequence was that the close of his apprenticeship found him well prepared for service, and possessed, very naturally, of the fullest confidence in his own sufficient ability to assume, and capably to wield, the responsibilities of his office. But the system had its drawback. Presbyterianism was not born in a manger, nor saluted in its cradle with the songs that angels are wont to employ at the Nativities over which they rejoice. Sprung from a conjunction of the temporal with the spiritual, its character discovered a pretty evenly-balanced share of the family marks of both. If it appeared with an olive-branch in one hand, it came armed with a sword-blade in the other. Its sect in church became its party in state, for one, or the other, or both of which, it could either fight or pray, as inclination prompted or as the contingency invited. Politics and "persuasion" were woof and warp of one piece, and the whole cloth was its religion. That its "professors," therefore, and particularly its preachers, moved by both these powerfully constraining influences, should have manifested a devotion perhaps without a parallel—certainly without its like—to their creed, is not astonishing. Time did not, neither could change of scene or surrounding, of country or of circumstance, alter the cast of their conscience, or qualify their conviction, or modify their confession. As in the beginning, so to the end, they were "*True Blue*" all the time. The master-graduate taught, and the student learned: learning, in his turn he taught again; so that, handed down from generation to generation, the theology that was promulged in the Nether Bow was perpetuated in the study of the Redstone Presbyter. As the result, the pupil came out from his cloister well disciplined, truly, in the tenets of his church, but so impregnated with, and habituated to, its "doctored" atmosphere as to doubt, if not disbelieve entirely in, the presence of a healthy, life-supporting presence at all in any other.

Thus he was outfitted for duty, and so, commissioned, went he forth to fill his professional place in the service,—a redoubtable champion surely, as his Methodist cotemporary was willing to concede, but view-contracted, arrogant, and intolerant, as the same authority, by way of complement, and with an emphasis decidedly more to his relish, was also prompt to testify.

III.

THE SABBATH-DAY, AND HOW IT WAS SANCTIFIED.

BEFORE the Black-Robe had thought it prudent to attempt a permanent settlement among them, the borderers, not willing to await his coming at the expense of a total deprivation of the privileges of worship, had long been accustomed to observe the stated assemblings of themselves together for "exercise" on the Sabbath. These "societies," as they were called, were held in the private dwellings of such families as chose to offer the accommodation, alternating from one to another in regular rotation, and were conducted usually by an elder; the ordinary routine of services being followed, except that a select reading of some appropriate sort took the place of a sermon, and that the delivery of the benediction, as well as, of course, the administration of the sacraments, was dispensed with. Houses of worship began to be erected perhaps as early as 1790. In their construction they differed in no particular from the cabins of the settlers, only in the respect that they were somewhat larger. A few hours' labor was the cheap cost of their erection. Timber necessary for the purpose had but to be felled, cut the desired length, notched at the ends, laid, log upon log, in place, covered with clap-boards, and the sun that at its rising saw the axe laid at the roots of the standing trees out of which the work was to be made, witnessed at its setting the laying of the last "weight-pole" that kept the clap-boards of the roof in position and finished the job. For ordinary Sabbath-day use the meeting-house answered the purpose well enough. In summer-time, when the heat was oppressive within-doors, and on sacramental and other special occasions, when the attendance was unusually large, services were conducted in the open air. Near by the meeting-house, on the slope of a gently-rising hill, a plot of ground was marked off, from which the underbrush was cleared away and the trees cut down, with the exception of here and there an oak or a maple of imposing growth, left to lift its wide-spreading branches as a shelter against the sun. The space thus opened was laid with logs, or slabs, arranged in parallel order across the ascent of the slope, and designed to serve as seats for the congregation. At the lower extremity of this area a platform was erected, six or eight feet wide by ten or twelve in length, and about four from the ground at the front. This platform was boarded up nearly breast-high above its floor, entrance to it being had by means of a short flight of steps and through a doorway left open at one side, while the whole was covered with a roofing of slabs. Intended as a pulpit for the minister, this structure went by the name, along the border, of the "Tent,"—a title still preserved as applied to one of the oldest churches, near Uniontown, in Fayette County, for many years, and down to the date of his death, under the pastoral care of that amiable gentleman and most loyal Presbyterian, the Rev. Dr. A. G. Fairchild.

The meeting-houses were about as comfortless as it was possible to have them. The walls, sometimes "chunked and daubed," sometimes not, allowed of a free passage of air between the logs, the bitter blasts of which, on winter-days, told with tingling effect on the ears, the noses, and the ungloved fingers of the worshipers. Stoves were not permitted in the building. Physicians objected to them on hygienic principles, while professors opposed them as devices of the devil, designed to produce a feeling of ease in Zion, and thus to rob the believer of the benefit of a flesh-afflicting but soul-chastening experience. Certain, among the women especially, of the congregation, either doubting the efficacy of the penance,—"cross" they called it,—or scarcely tough enough to endure it, and willing to risk the consequences, were accustomed to heat stones in the nearest cabin fires, or fill jugs with boiling water, and to convey them clandestinely, carefully wrapped in a fold of their gowns, to their seats, where laid upon the floor they served to keep the feet warm at least, let the rest of the person fare as it might. For ten or twelve years this singular practice was persisted in; and when at length a change was proposed, and by a close vote of the congregations the use of fire was formally authorized, it was at the cost of an opposition so violent as to threaten, while it lasted, the complete disruption of the churches.

No Sabbath-day duty was more strictly enjoined upon the people than that of regular and prompt attendance at public worship. As the appointed hour of service drew nigh, they might be seen filing in along the paths that led Tent-ward through the woods, some afoot, others on horseback,— the riders, if fathers, with an elder son or daughter, sometimes both, mounted behind them, or, if mothers, studded all around with the smaller family jewels,—a babe in the arms, last year's twins in creels, one on each side of the "beast" bestraddled, and, perched *en croupe*, the promising three-year-old of the household closely hugging the maternal waist, as a dependence both needed and relied upon to maintain the mastery of his situation. The husband rode in advance of the wife. Arrived at the outskirts of the sanctuary precinct, or edge of the uncleared woods, the former dismounted, and, after fastening his horse with a tie of the raw-hide hitching-strap attached to its bridle, doubly knotted and carefully tested, to a sapling or the lower branch of a tree, turned to look to the making fast, in like manner, of that of the latter, who, meanwhile, drawing rein at the side of a stump for the easier execution of the task, had, alone and unassisted, succeeded in safely landing herself and the entire of her infant *impedimenta* in charge. Here, too, the pedestrians—the younger folk generally of the settlements—halted as they came, the men ostensibly to interchange neighborly greetings with each other, but more likely, as observing ones among the elders shrewdly suspected, to cast sly glances askant at the girls, who, having walked barefoot from their homes, to save the wear and tear of leather, took advantage of the partial screen afforded by the bushes to draw on the stockings and shoes with which, wrapped up in handkerchiefs and carried under their arms, for wearing at "meeting," as the mannerly custom was, they had not failed to come provided.

The ascent of the minister into the pulpit was the signal for the congregation to assemble. Soberly and solemnly the members advanced, the men and the women falling into separate lines, and, with very much the air of prisoners moving to their doom, marching down the aisle or passage dividing the auditory, these filing to the right and those to the left,—for it was not lawful that the sexes should worship together,—and edging in between logs as they went, until all were seated. Among the attendants, however, were not a few who preferred to decline the offered accommodations of the sanctuary. These were composed of the less reverent youths of the parishes, upon whom the reins of discipline were not so tightly drawn at home as they should have been, much to the detriment of their proper deportment abroad, and of a sort of Arab class wandered in from the mountains,—men with unshorn beards, shaggy heads, and faces hard as iron and brown as its rust,—who, disliking close quarters, were not to be drawn into a crowd when free elbow-room could be had outside of it. Holding back, near enough to hear and to see, but clear of the consecrated limits, they stationed themselves, leaning indolently against the trees or lolling at half-length on the ground. Both classes—all of the one, and many, that is, of the other—came furnished with powder-horns and bullet-pouches, and armed with rifles; the latter, because it was the regular habit of their lives, from which they never deviated, and the former, really, perhaps, to be ready for any chance shot that might offer at a wild turkey or a deer on the way, but professedly for the more orthodox purpose of protecting the congregation against surprise from the Indians,—who, by the way, so far as we are informed, never offered to interfere with them. In fact, if they had been so inclined, much the easier and safer plan, as well as the one more in accordance with their style of doing things, would have been to waylay the church-goers singly and separately on the road to and from—rather than in a body, watchful and expectant, at—the Tent.

After a short introductory invocation, the exercises of the day were opened with the singing of a psalm. Recited first at length from the pulpit, the task was taken up immediately after by the precentor, or clerk, an officer second perhaps, but only second, in importance to the minister, who occupied a seat, constructed for his exclusive use, right under the sacred desk. The stanzas were delivered line by line by this officer, who had his professional way of doing it, commencing at a pitch perhaps a fifth above the natural key of his voice, drawling out the syllables in a sort of sing-song recitative, and so regulating the intonation as to leave the last-spoken word at the pitch precisely with that of the note next in order, whatever it might be, in the suspended melody. So nicely were the two renderings dovetailed into each other that they might have passed as solo and refrain, or chant and response, of one musical performance. In his selection of an air the clerk had a dozen out of which to choose. These were known as the "Twelve Tunes of David," copies of which, carefully produced in angular characters variously shaped to indicate the different notes (fa, sol, la, mi) of the gamut, and elaborately illuminated as to the text, were among the properties of all competent precentors. To these melodies the faithful adhered, and to the exclusion of all others, with scrupulous fidelity. Later down a few years, when, captivated by their novelty, some of the more daring among the leaders undertook to introduce certain "fugue tunes," caught up from emigrant Yankees passing through on their way to Marietta,—like "Coronation," for instance, which, by the way, became immensely popular soon after,—the attempt excited intense opposition, and for some time, like the stove-question, threatened seriously a downright schism in the churches. The first plunge into the melody was made by the clerk alone, the voices of the congregation dropping in one upon another in after-succession with an effect which, while it increased the volume, so retarded the progress of the music that it required the fullest exertion of the lung-power of the leader, always chosen with special reference to his superior qualities of chest, to keep the chorus up to time, or anything like it. The style of singing was unique. The rendering of the lines proper was prefaced by a snatch of nasal "voluntary"—so, for lack of a better term, to distinguish it—closely resembling the prolonged sounding of the closing consonants of the present participle,—ng,—and not unlike the drone of a bagpipe before the stops are operated upon. Fairly plunged into the text, the task of struggling through went on, word mortising into word, note gliding through vague and wayward flights into note, until the end of the passage was reached. Usually, almost uniformly, in fact, at first, the congregation, men, women, and children, all sang in unison, following in various octaves the air of the melody. Now and then a clerk, happily possessed of more accomplished parts than distinguished the general, would veer off into the base; but the diversion was not often attempted, and was prudently limited to the few closing notes of the verse; when, in the case of misadventure, ticklishly probable, in the experiment, the stop of the strain would cleverly cover up the failure. Later on, about the time of the introduction of the fugue tunes, the singing of "parts" began to be introduced; in the apportionment under the new order of arrangement, the men sustaining the air, and the women, or detachments of them, serving on the "tribble," answering to what is known in these later days as the tenor. Parceled off in this way, the effect may be more readily conceived than described of the singing of a hymn like Mear or Dundee, the burden of it borne by the multitudinous baritone of one side of the congregation, and the accompaniment, in soprano, by the other; the voices of these latter soaring at a giddy height among the "fifths" (making their escape chiefly through the nose), and maintaining that elevation, with as little variation as a decent respect for the harmonies permitted, down to the very close,—quieting lingeringly and reluctantly into silence even then.

The psalm ended, a "portion of Scripture" was read, selected usually either from the Old Testament or the Epistles of the New, each verse of the chapter so chosen, in its order, undergoing a close analysis and critical exposition, rather more to the edification than to the entertainment of the congregation. This exercise was followed by a prayer, particularly worthy of mention on account of its length, —often consuming thirty minutes or more in the delivery; its breadth,—covering all subjects conceivably within the scope of desire, except those, perhaps, that appear in "Our Father" in the Sermon on the Mount; and its depth,—penetrating to the very bottom of profoundest doctrines, and defining according to Westminster science, and making clear so as to come within the comprehension of their Author, the dark and difficult significance of his own mysteries. After the prayer came the second psalm of the service. This praise-offering differed from the first in that, as read from the sacred desk, and before being taken hold of by the clerk, it was subjected, sentence by sentence, to a searching note-and-comment process by the preacher. The special aim of this labor was to show the "evangelical" character of David the Hebrew, and to illustrate how eminently appropriate for devotional purposes in a Christian meeting-house was the psalmody composed for priestly rehearsal in a Jewish synagogue.

But the sermon, next in order, was the feature of the service. If the people felt it, as they evidently did, to be so, so, still more evidently, did the minister. Having the scriptural authority to that effect, it was his duty, as well as his delight, "to magnify his office;" and as the sermon, best, if not alone, of the round of exercises, afforded a ready range for the purpose, he made the most of the chances, in it and attending it, to do that justice to himself and his profession. After the singing of the psalm, the pause of a moment or two, usually occurring between performances, was allowed to lengthen out materially, the parson consuming the interval, very much at his leisure, and with a quiet show of preparation that was very impressive, in turning over the leaves of his Bible, dog-earing a page here and there for convenience of reference, or producing and assorting his notes, or (although this was less ostentatiously done) in fortifying the inner man with a draft of sufficient cordial from the little brown jug that seldom was wanting in its own appropriate nook behind the breast-board of the pulpit. These preliminaries disposed of, to the desired effect of stimulating the attention and whetting the expectation of his listeners, he arose to his feet, stripped himself of his coat, if the day happened to be warm, and in his shirt-sleeves stepped forward to his place at the desk. Inviting the attention of his hearers, he then announced his text, indicating, first, the book, chapter, and verse, and again, the more certainly to impress it upon the congregation, the verse, chapter, and book, reversely, where it was to be found. Promptly, in return, each member of the flock produced his own private copy of the Bible, with which he always came provided, and, with a sound like the rustle of leaves stirred by a summer wind, or the flutter of birds' wings as a flight of them is about to light among the branches, turned over the pages in search of the passage, to make sure that it was rendered true to the letter in the reading. As among the sacred writers, the lawgiver and the prophets stood first in the esteem of ministers, the epistolary authors next, and the evangelists, rather distantly, last. The sayings of our Lord, as gathered from his lips and as recorded in the books of Matthew, Mark, Luke, and John, were of account certainly, but of account only as they tallied, or could be made to seem to tally, with the utterances of Moses or the mystical vaticinations of Isaiah, or as they stood the test of the criticisms of Paul. Out of these higher authorities, therefore, it was the favorite custom of the preacher to choose his subject of discourse. In the treatment of his topic he followed the old regular routine of his fathers in the profession,—setting forth the same proposition in the same terms, pursuing the same line of argument in the same methodical manner, quoting the same proofs in defense of the same positions, and arriving, through the same series of heads, sub-heads, inferences, and practical observations, at the same conclusions; very much in the same manner, with the same degree of animation, and to the same convincing, and about the same spirit-cheering, effect that would have attended the attempt, had it been made, at a solution of a question in calculus, or one of the more intricate of the problems of Euclid. To go through with all this called for time, so that, although one and a half and two hours sometimes sufficed, three were not regarded as an extraordinary allowance for the performance. The audience lingered out the siege with more than the patience that could have been expected. If the elders of the congregation, when their backs, which were without support, grew weary, and the crook'd hinges of their knees became cramped from long sitting, rose to their feet during the service, it was only to relax their joints with a walk to window or door, if in the meeting-house, or simply to stand for sake of change, if on the Tent-ground, resting them for a time against sill or jamb in the one case, or leaning, still listeningly and devoutly, with palms planted, hand over hand, on the knotted heads of their stout hickory walking-sticks, in the other. The younger hearers kept up a wakeful attention as long as they could, the better to sustain them at it nibbling the while at shreds and ends of slippery-elm bark, peppermint, and sassafras-root, or gnawing at bits of biscuit. But even these expedients spent their virtue ere long, when, after many a nod dropped more and more decisively, followed by as many a less and less alarmed start of recovery, the drowsy influence prevailed, and the captured senses settled into a repose that was thenceforth to know no balk nor break through all the dull while the sermon lasted. The women, less restless than the men, if not quite so attentive, sat the performance out with the perseverance of saints. If the day proved warm and the atmosphere close, they employed their folded handkerchiefs as fans, or, unprovided with those conveniences, the leafy extremities of the slender twigs which they had used on their way to "meeting" to brush off the flies from the necks and the flanks of their horses. But for this exercise as a counter-recourse, the influences together of weather and "word" would have been insupportable, and the strongest of flesh, the most willing of spirit, must have sunk exhausted under them. Except the mothers—not a few, nor far between-times freshly in that way—among them; in which case tired nature found a sufficient diversion in the frequently-recurring attentions required by their nurslings, whose cravings and whose necessities had to be cared for, of course,—as they were, right openly, and without a thought of impropriety, in the presence of the whole congregation.

Meanwhile a spirit of impatience, in smart contrast with the forced repose of the people, began to manifest itself among the "beasts," standing hitched in close neighborhood to each other, along the outer lines of the Tent-ground. Fagged by the toils of the Sabbath-day's journey that brought them there; with hanging heads, and drooping ears, and eyes half closed; leaning their weight on three legs for the relief of the remaining one, loosely depending and resting at ease on the toe, as it were, of its hoof; showing scarcely a sign of life, except an occasional quiver of the skin on flank or foreshoulder, to shake off the flies that swarmed about them when they became too annoying,—the drowsy animals had stood out the opening services in a well-behaved and most orthodox manner. But rest, in due time, wrought its work, and, rousing from the dreamy, indolent mood into which they had settled, the creatures, refreshed, were now themselves again. Wearying soon from idleness, as before from exercise, they became restless and fretful; switching their tails at the troublesome insects whose stinging assaults were no longer to be passively endured, stamping their feet, and swinging round their heads with great stretches, sometimes to the very shank of a hind-leg, lifted to shorten the effort, to bring their teeth to bear relievingly, or their noses, upon some particularly irritated spot of attack. Hitched to neighboring trees, pairs of cross-grained geldings, on terms of forbearance hitherto, seeming to have discovered sudden cause of misunderstanding, threw back their ears, made dashes with open teeth at each other, and, finding their career checked by the tightened tether before quite within nipping distance, reversed their tactics, and, turning rear to rear, with angry screams joined skirmish with their heels. Mares, appearing to have awakened all at once to the consciousness of their absence, began to call, in tones indicative of alarm, for their offspring. Prompt at the summons, the colts, bleating as they ran, came racing from abroad in the woods, whither they had wandered; in the confusion attending the common rush, making for the wrong dams, and meeting with such repulses, when they began to make themselves at home, as to send them skipping away, their mouths, the while, going through the motions, but without the voice—too completely shocked by surprise to find it—of a protest at the unmotherly treatment. Stallions, stationed prudently at more distant posts, caught the contagion of excitement, champed their bridle-bits, pawed the ground madly with their feet, tramped in circles round and round the saplings to which they were tied,—winding themselves up, and then unwinding back again, in the process,—leaped, now with plunges that made their straightened raw-hide fastenings twang to cracking fairly under the strain, now stood with lifted crest in breathless pause, now gave vent to their suspended respiration in a blast through their nostrils, sharp and shrill as the shriek of a trumpet, and now crowned the proceeding with a neigh, long, and fierce, and loud, that sped pealing and reverberating abroad till the forest rang in all its shelters, far and near, with the echo.

Amid all these untoward circumstances, the

minister, wholly unconscious, or at all events regardless, of them, proceeded with his discourse. It was the sinner's own affair whether he would hear or whether he would forbear; but as for himself, it was his business to preach, and, like a faithful servant, once entered upon his task he was bound to see it through. Holding fast to the line of his argument, step by step plodding along he followed it up. If the sound of his voice happened to be lost for a time, **swallowed up** by a wave of tumult rolled in from the disturbed verge **of the camp,** no matter; a proof missed, more or less, of the **proposition, for** instance, that "all mankind sinned in Adam and **fell** with him in his first transgression," left the elucidation of it none the less complete on that **account. Told** over and over so often, his people had heard the story to little purpose if now they were to lose the chain of it by the simple dropping of a link. And so the work went on, slowly, steadily, surely,—one great section of it after another dissected, desiccated, and, as was proper with the meat of doctrine, made dried-beef **of** to insure its keeping, ere laid at length away; and so, like the "going—going—gone" of an auctioneer, followed the warning calls, delivered with the due delays between, of, " In the last place,—finally,—in conclu**sion,"** when with the closing thump of "Amen!" the hammer fell, and the sermon was ended. A prayer, long enough, but brief compared with the one that went before it, succeeded, followed by a psalm, after which the benediction was pronounced, and the morning service closed.

Dismissed, the congregation slowly retired in close procession from their seats, scattering, when quite outside the precincts of the sanctuary, in various directions. Some went to look after their horses, to see that they had not slipped their headstall, and that their fastenings were secure; or, perhaps, to "piece" them on nubbins of corn, brought along in their pockets for that purpose, just as on the same grain, ground, and baked into "dodgers," did the mothers their children, and from the same tenderly considerate motive. Some withdrew in pairs, or groups of three and four, and, seeking the shade of a tree, whittled with their heavy-bladed, horn-handled jack-knives at the tough knots on their walking-sticks, talking the while of the weather and the crops; of the flocks and herds that filled their pastures,—their hogs, their cattle, and their horses,—and, as likely as not, going through the preliminary negotiations of a "swap," which to-morrow or next day would see consummated, before all was over. Some retired to the graveyard, picking their course along pathless ways, wading knee-deep in heavy, rank grasses, and forcing a passage through thickets of thorn and patches of blackberry-bushes to the spot of their search, where, pausing and leaning over the rough stone planted to mark the place, they paid their tribute of sorrow to the memory of some loved one,

—husband, or wife, or child,—whose all of what once had been left—and that was its ashes—lay buried there. Women in couples wandered off, slowly strolling, and pausing often on various trifling pretenses,— to reach a leaf, standing on tiptoe to do it, or stooping to pluck a flower,—but quickening their paces as the straggling bushes intervened to veil their retreat, until the utmost limits of the clearing were passed, and themselves, hid from view, were lost amid the cover of the copses. But the centre of general attraction was the "Spring." Thither, sooner or later during the "intermission," all were accustomed to repair. Those that thirsted drank of the water, the more attentive youths of the flock standing, gourd or earthen bowl in hand, in turn at the fountain, and dispensing the element to the rest in waiting,—blushing to the brows when the customer happened to be one, young and fair, of the opposite sex, herself crimsoning to the bosom in return as she tremblingly received the proffered vessel from his hand. Lingering as they came and drank, the visitors tarried, so that ere long quite a large proportion of the congregation was assembled at the spot. Seated on stones or reclined on the grass rested the elders, puffing their pipes, and through the smoke looking dreamily on, while their sons and daughters, in separate companies that would not mingle, and yet could not keep apart, found pastime, the former in delving amid the soil for roots of sassafras and calamus, and the latter, perchance, in gathering sprays of spearmint, tramping the beds in which it grew, and crushing the plants as they did so, till all the air around was odorous with their perfume.

The blast of a horn blown from the Tent by the clerk, as the man naturally presumed to be best in wind for it, gave signal when the half-hour of intermission was up. At the call the worshipers, laying aside all levities—alas for the levities!—of walk and conversation, resumed their serious deportment, and in solemn procession took up their return to the sanctuary. Again were they to be seen seated in their places. Again the minister mounted the pulpit, stooped to a kiss of the little brown jug, and rose to his place at the desk. Again psalm, prayer, and sermon were delivered in their order, but with less of prolixity now; and again, as the sun's rays fell slanting down through the tree-tops on the summits of the hills that lay towards his setting, was heard the welcome end-all to the exercise, long delayed, but reached at last, of the benediction. Meeting was over. The last duty of the day's dismal catalogue was discharged, and with a sense of relief which it would have been rank crime against heaven to confess, even to their own consciences, but which was felt nevertheless, the worshipers scattered towards their various homes, thanking God in their hearts, though the devil may have had the credit of the suggestion, that another Sabbath with its "sanctifications" was gone, and that a good week's allowance was theirs, ere its next return, of rest,—rest that was real in comparison,—rest at the axe, the plow, and the mattock; chopping in the forest, furrowing in the field, or grubbing in the clearing.

IV.

THE LONG SABBATH, AND THE GREAT BUFFALO SACRAMENT.

THE Great Day, holiest among the hallowed of the year, and honored with special observance by the Presbyterians of the border, was the "Long Sabbath," as it was popularly called, or the Sabbath of the Sacrament. The strong right arm of him who led, preparing the way of the "New Departure," had made bare itself with mighty effect to the lopping off of idolatrous superfluities of worship, so that his followers now, of the round of ceremonials that used to give variety and lend attraction to a Lord's-day's services, had but this single spared, sadly-mutilated remnant left. But as a mother, bereft of all beside of her offspring, hugs to her bosom with a therefore more jealous liking the darling that only remains, so the Presbyterian clung to his Communion—the one Settime, the sole Solemn Feast, that he could call his own—with the concentrated whole of his soul's devotion.

The Sacrament, as the common rule of the time, was celebrated but once a year. A minister had usually, however, two congregations under his care, so that, having to provide for the spiritual necessities of both, the ordinance occurred twice under his administration—once to each parish—during that term. The ceremonies of the season lasted through five days. The opening one—Thursday—was consecrated to fasting, humiliation, and prayer, and was observed, especially in the first particular, with scrupulous fidelity. It was the New-Dispensation "Day of Atonement" borrowed bodily from the Old; and not Moses himself could have honored it more strictly in accordance with his own law, save in the offer of the offering by fire, perhaps, of the young bullock, the ram, and the seven lambs, than did his loyal follower on the border. The sermon of the day was long beyond ordinary; prayerfully prepared, and particularly, as an exhibit of the "grounds and reasons" for the fast should be; and powerfully adapted, so the assurance comes down to us, as a strengthening exercise towards making more successfully the ascension of the mount of ordinances on the ensuing Sabbath. Friday was not so devoutly observed. Few, except those who intended to "take the sacrament," went to meeting, the rest remaining at home and pursuing, but only with a half-hearted sort of energy, their usual labors. Saturday followed in the same way, the "seculars" doubtfully on duty at work, and the saints having the worship to themselves. After the preaching on this day, the session of the church was accustomed to meet to examine applicants for membership and to distribute "tokens" among those that were entitled to commune. These "tokens" were small pieces of flattened lead, about the size of the copper coin, then in circulation, known as the "half-cent," and stamped, to make them valid, with the initials—B. C., for instance, indicating "Buffalo Church"—of the congregation to which they belonged. The "token" was regarded for many years as an "element" excellent of virtue, and quite as essential to an orthodox celebration of the Supper as the bread and the wine. It went into disuse finally, as later and somewhat more liberal generations sprang up to take the place of their fathers, but never while a gray-beard of the old stock lingered to protest against the innovation.

The Sabbath, however, was The Day, by eminent distinction, of the group, and enjoyed the special honors of the season accordingly. Not only did all the members of the congregation, converted and unconverted, make it a point to be in attendance at the meeting-house, but distant fellow-believers from other parishes, ten, fifteen, twenty miles away, gathered in, so that the exercises, opening half an hour earlier than usual, witnessed, when begun, such an assemblage as the sanctuary usually had scarcely the capacity to accommodate. The Black-Robe in charge had always from two or three to half a dozen of his ministerial brethren to assist him at the services; while the clerk, extending his invitations on a similar scale of liberality, not to be behind in supporting the dignity of his office, was to be seen surrounded by half the precentors of the Presbytery. The offering of the introductory prayer was attended to by one of the reverend aids; the reading of the psalm, by another. The delivery of the discourse, or *Action Sermon*, as it was called, devolved upon the pastor. A third assistant afterwards took up the exercise of *Fencing the Tables*, or, as with propriety it might be termed, " Boxing the Compass" of the creed. This was a performance preliminary to the dispensation of the Sacrament, in which, taking the Ten Commandments for his text, the preacher entered upon an exposition that, beginning with the first, was sustained—the rest, one by one, following in their order—until the list entire was disposed of. Eminent account was made of the decalogue as covering the whole ground of qualification for church-membership, and so rigorously were the tables "fenced" in the enumeration of the sins forbidden in each commandment, that it was commonly remarked by the profane (and without dissent, either, on the part of the reverend biographer who chronicles the fact), that "the preacher never stopped till he had solemnly debarred from the ordinance every one of his people, and himself to boot."

These preparatory services discharged, the baptismal ceremonies came next. All the children of believers born within the year, to the very youngest, where it was possible for the parents to appear with them, were expected to be present to undergo the rite. A long dissertation preceded the "sprinkling," in which were dwelt upon, particularly, the points in controversy between the more prominent sects of the time: first, that is, as to whether infants were proper subjects of the ordinance; and second, whether the mode in vogue among Presbyterians of applying it was the scriptural one; both of which were affirmatively demonstrated to the entire satisfaction of all concerned. It was not only recommended to the parents at the same time, but required of them by solemn vow, that they should conscientiously perform all their duty in the religious training and nurturing of their children; especially attending to their instruction in that faultless digest of only genuine doctrine, the Shorter Catechism. As a test of their fidelity to the promise thus given, it was the custom of the minister to call at least once a year on each of the families in his charge, and put the children to the "question" (in more senses than one), who were expected, and seldom failed, to be ready for the ordeal.

Then followed "the Sacrament." Tables made of logs with the upper side hewn down so as to leave a flat surface, and supported either on blocks of wood or legs of sapling-stocks cut the right length and straddled apart, two at each end, to make a steady work of it, were arranged lengthwise along the central aisle or passage, and again transversely across the open space in front of the pulpit. Other logs, dressed in a similar way, but narrower and lower, and designed to serve as seats, ran parallel-wise along either side of the table. On the centre of the transverse table, and consequently at the head of the other,—widened somewhat for the purpose,—stood the vessels containing the sacred symbols. These latter were covered with white linen napkins, as, in cloth of the same material, was the board itself (neatly folded and pinned at the corners); prepared—the spotlessness of the fabric, and the creases, marked by the iron, with which it was barred, showing with what an eye to tidiness—for the occasion. Taking his station at this point of the table, the exercises of the Feast were opened by the pastor with an address, the most noticeable feature of which was its elaborate laying bare of the kindred enormities of transubstantiation and impanation, as heretically entertained by Romanists and Lutherans; both of which, the people were assured, it became them as good and true communicants utterly to repudiate. Next in order a psalm was read, during the singing of which, to some melancholy tune, such as "Coleshill," or "Communion," or, when the metre admitted of it, "Windham," a portion of the church-members rising to their feet and filing into line marched into and along the aisle, the men on one side and the women on the other, until the leaders reached the end of the table, where they seated themselves,—their followers dropping successively into place likewise, side by side, as they approached, until the benches were filled. The singing then ceased; whereupon two of the elders arose, and, commencing at the rear of the board, started along the lines to collect the tokens; pretty much as a car-conductor does, passing among his passengers to lift their tickets for the trip. Served with the customary formalities, more or less tedious as the minister officiating chose at his pleasure to order it, this first installment of communicants retired at length, under cover of Coleshill resumed; while a second, at the same time,—the counter-files edging side-wise past each other as they came and went along the narrow aisle,—moved forward to occupy their vacated places. The same proceeding was repeated over and over again, so that there were, not unfrequently, six or seven tables filled and administered to before all were served who were entitled to the privilege. At the close of the meeting the preachers and the elders were accustomed to assemble in a little group by themselves and have a private entertainment of their own, on a more liberal scale, over the elements that were left of the Supper, not, of course, to gratify a carnal appetite, but merely to show, practically, their contempt of the old notion, which they had just heard denounced from the pulpit, of the fact of a Real Presence in the Sacrament, or that the bread and wine were anything other, holier or better, than they ought to be.

It seems almost incomprehensible how out of a series of exercises so frigid and formal it should be possible for other than correspondingly formal and frigid effects to proceed. The intellectual and the emotional are not in such relations of sympathy that the tender susceptibilities of the one should melt responsively to the dull logic (which it does not comprehend) of the other. And yet we have the evidence that the miracle could happen; that a homily of Smith's or Macurdy's could arouse to enthusiasm as well as a harangue from Finley or Cartwright, and that the imperturbable predestinarian could be brought to his raptures as well as the impressible Methodist. Shortly after the Cane-Ridge revival, a very similar movement started in one of the Presbyterian parishes of Western Pennsylvania. It created intense excitement at the time, and—not only because of the extraordinary manifestations which attended it, but as the opening scene of a revival that spread through all the settlements, and continued, more or less powerfully, to prevail through some four years, to the material building up of the Redstone Zion— has become memorable in the annals of the church. The occasion is associated with the place in which it occurred, and is known in the narratives of the time as the GREAT BUFFALO SACRAMENT.

On the last Sabbath of October, 1802, the communion of the congregation at Cross Roads took place, which was attended with such gracious displays of divine power as to induce the brethren to make an appointment for the administration of the same ordinance, two weeks later, at the church of Upper Buffalo. Very remarkable exercises had attended the services at Cross Roads, in the presence of an unusually large assembly, the fame of which was carried far and wide throughout the region; so that when the announcement was published that the celebration was to be repeated, the people everywhere were eagerly ready to attend. With the dawn of the day before the appointed Sabbath—Saturday—began to pour in the worshipers, the tide keeping increasingly up until much the largest assembly which had ever been seen at a religious meeting in Western Pennsylvania, numbering about ten thousand, was collected on the ground. Among the rest were fifteen ministers. Houses in the neighborhood were hospitably thrown open for the accommodation of attendants; horses were stabled in the barns, and the wants of both—beasts and owners—abundantly supplied while food and fodder lasted. Tents, with which they had prudently come provided, were erected by some, while others camped in the woods, under booths of bushes hastily heaped together for a shelter. On Saturday afternoon two of the ministers preached at the same time,—one in the meeting-house, the other in the tent. Exercises, consisting of preaching, exhortation, prayer, and praise, were resumed in the evening and kept up through the night. Two discourses were delivered, simultaneously again, on Sunday morning, one in the church, as before, and one in the open air. The Sacrament, with its customary formalities, was then administered, nearly a thousand communicants participating in the ceremony. The Reverend Elisha Macurdy, well remembered yet by many on the scene of his early labors, as in the closing days of his life he used to appear, after having officiated at the first table, at the request of one of his brethren, took a position at a short distance from the meeting-house, and, while the rest of the tables were still being served, began to preach to the crowd that soon collected about him. He selected for his text the second Psalm, and delivered the discourse, entirely unpremeditated, as we are assured, which proved the eventful one of his life, and which has ever since been famously known in clerical circles as "Macurdy's War Sermon." The effect produced upon his audience was overwhelming,—literally, almost, in point of fact, like a discharge of musketry. He "popped them down," as the saying among the thoughtless and wicked was, "like pigeons," the scene appearing "like the close of a battle, in which every tenth man had fallen fatally wounded." It was the old experience told over again of Cane-Ridge, the same mysterious agency breaking out and working in the same mysterious way. Some fell to the earth suddenly; some sunk gradually; some lay quiet and silent; some were violently agitated; some, seeing the spiritual glory, rejoiced hopefully, while others groaned in pain, sorrowing and thirsting for the water of life. The work continued with unabated interest on through Monday and until the evening of Tuesday, the people lingering fondly as long as they might at the place where so much of God's power had been manifested in their presence

Not to let the awakening subside, nor to fail of putting it to the best advantage while it lasted, the meeting at Buffalo Creek was followed up by similar ones, held, one after another, in all the various churches of the region. Each in its turn was a success, the interest which had been aroused keeping up unabatedly from first to last. Crowds gathered at all, from all quarters of the country,—from the Forks, from Salem, from Congruity, from Chartiers. The church at Cross Roads was so packed with hearers that the preacher, unable to force an entrance at the door, had to use a ladder and climb in to his pulpit through a back window of the building.

A remarkable feature of the revival, viewed in connection with its peculiarities of manifestation, was the character of the preaching, not only under which it started, but by which, afterwards, it was sustained. The sermons were purely doctrinal. The source and the supply of the enthusiasms of the season were the Confession of Faith and the Catechisms. The doctrine of Justification by Faith, we are assured, was much insisted upon; also that of Sanctification by the Word and Spirit of God, and the manner of receiving Christ and walking in Him, as set forth in the Holy Scriptures and the Standards of the church. That "men of information, of strong nerves and vigorous understandings," to say nothing of women and children, should have been overcome—"popped down like pigeons" —by orthodox knocks such as these, is certainly astonishing, and is about the best evidence that could be quoted in proof of the presence of a supernatural agency in the work.

That there was an influence more than human astir was generally conceded among the members; but whether it emanated from above, or proceeded from below, was a controverted point. One would suppose that the simple fact of there being room to doubt the question ought to have settled it. To say that "the devil could *not* have been its author," seems rather like an intimation that there was plausible reason to suspect he was, and to try to prove the proposition only strengthens the doubt.

Outside the communion, among "the opposers of the revival," the excitement was attributed by many to the terrific character of the preaching, the vehement appeals to the conscience, and the protracted exercises; all calculated, as was alleged, to produce just such an effect on persons of weak nerves and delicate constitutions. As against this solution, it was retorted that the deists who offered it ought to be ashamed of it, especially as not a few of their own number, fortified against impression by the writings of Bolingbroke, Hume, Voltaire, and Paine, had, nevertheless, been brought down among the rest. Could such a miracle be ascribed to anything else than the finger of God?

Others accounted for it on the ground of "Sympathy." In rejoinder to this theory, it was urged that sympathy can only communicate as it has been communicated to; that it never could have *begun* such a work, and that the work having ceased though but for an hour, it could not have brought it again into operation. One person falling might have brought another sympathizing neighbor down with him, but what occasioned the first prostration? The merit of the invention of this argument belongs to the Rev. Doctor George A. Baxter, the then President of Washington College.

A more philosophical and better-sustained view,

as its author claims, was that the bodily affection was the result of the mental excitement arising from the influence of the Spirit and truth of God upon the consciences of those who were its subjects. As violent gusts of passion, sudden surprise, strong mental impulses in which either joy or sorrow predominates, produce sometimes injurious, occasionally fatal, bodily results, why might not similar effects proceed from the similar influence of religious excitement? And yet the inventor of the argument confesses to having encountered a difficulty in it,—this, that there were instances of pungent exercise of mind where the generally accompanying physical symptoms were entirely wanting. The difficulty was an insuperable one, for an exception to the rule was an extinguisher to the argument, as the projector of it upon final reflection concedes, and it was abandoned. No explanation could be settled on that was entirely satisfactory, although the general conviction soon grew to be that the outsiders, or "opposers," had, as near as could be, the sensible view of it.

As the results of this remarkable outpouring of the Spirit, we are informed that many hundreds of persons, of both sexes and of all ages, were brought under deep conviction of their sins. A considerable proportion of these—one hundred and twenty-five at the congregations of Cross-Roads and Three Springs alone—were converted, as it was hopefully believed; but there were numerous cases among them, unhappily, of apostasy. On the whole, notwithstanding the large accessions claimed, the church does not seem to have afterwards held the Buffalo style of sensation in particular esteem; for, with the exception of a brief run of very unsatisfactory experience at the Anxious Bench, which occurred about a generation later, when similar scenes, though on a less extravagant scale, were acted over again, she has cautiously steered clear of it altogether.

V.

THE EARLY LABORERS IN THE BORDER VINEYARD.

OF those who enjoy distinguished mention, as eminent on one account or another among the Presbyterian Black-Robes of the border, the choice of renown attaches to the half-dozen who were foremost to take the field,—Power, McMillan, Finley, Smith, Dodd, and Clark. These "missionaries" appeared on the scene of their future labors nearly simultaneously,—entering almost abreast, as we are told, upon the mighty harvest,—and continued thenceforward as faithful co-workers in the cause to the end. As conglomerately, so to speak, the Rock upon which the Western Zion was founded, their fame rates high, in the estimation especially of the generation that succeeded them; nor among the children's children will their names be forgotten while frontier legends, told at family firesides, may hold their power to charm, or while the local histories last, to invite a perusal, in which they are written. We have already alluded to most of them, but a somewhat more particular reference may not be out of place.

JAMES POWER emigrated with his family to the West in 1776. He did not take the regular charge of a congregation for some years, but served as a sort of missionary pastor, dividing his time among the churches at Mount Pleasant, Unity, Laurel Hill, Dunlap's Creek, Tyrone, and Sewickley. Five years later he was installed as the regular pastor over the flocks of the two folds at Mount Pleasant and the neighboring field of Sewickley. In 1787 he ceased his connection with the latter-mentioned people, and, on a salary of one hundred and fifty pounds a year, devoted his exclusive services to the former. Here he remained until the spring of 1817, when, in consequence of the infirmities attending old age, he retired, resigning his charge to the care of the Rev. A. O. Patterson. Thirteen years afterwards he died.

Mr. Power was a man of medium height, slenderly built, and of erect stature. In his dress he was plain and neat; easy in his manners; courteous in his deportment; of a mild disposition; a dignified minister in the pulpit, and a genial gentleman, though rather a precise one, out of it. He had a sweet voice, and spoke with great ease and no little eloquence. His favorite portion of the Scriptures was the Psalms; handling them often at the desk,—always, in fact, when favorable occasions tempted him to aim at telling effects in his lectures. His parishes extended over a reach of thirty miles, every family in which it was his rule to visit at least once during each year. Besides these pastoral calls, it was his custom to assemble the people, men, women, and children, of different neighborhoods, from time to time, and put them through a course of examination on doctrinal faith; requiring them to repeat the Assembly's Catechism from beginning to end, together with the proofs from the Bible, and the explanations of Fisher. In addition to his other virtues, faithful chroniclers have not neglected to note the fact that he was a good rider and an excellent judge of a horse; always, with an eye to the protection of his dress, selecting one with such a step as would not cast mud or dirt, while traveling, on his person. Professionally, Mr. Power's labors could not be said to have been rewarded with remarkable results; although it is claimed for him that he was successful in edifying Christians, instructing the young, and improving the morals of the community.

JOHN McMILLAN was born of North-of-Ireland parents, at Fagg's Manor, Chester County, Pennsylvania, in 1752. He commenced his classical studies at the academy, somewhat celebrated, of his native place, under the charge of the Rev. John Blair, which he further pursued at the grammar-school at Pequea, and finally completed at Princeton College, in New Jersey, at the time presided over by the Rev. Dr. Witherspoon. He studied theology privately under the direction of Dr. Smith, at Pequea, was licensed by the Presbytery of New Castle in 1774, and entered upon his border mission, taking charge of the congregations at Chartiers and Pigeon Creek, in the fall of 1778. Mr. McMillan was a man of stern and forbidding aspect; of an uncommonly dark complexion, and with a countenance sharply marked and strikingly expressive in every feature. His manners were "studiedly" —perhaps it would be nearer the mark to say vulgarly—plain. He was clownishly careless as to his personal appearance, being usually dressed, as chroniclers, seeing fun but no farce in the fact, inform us, like the Jack of Spades, with boots on like a ten-gallon keg. It is scarcely characterizing his common walk and conversation too severely to say that they were ungentlemanly. General Morgan having ridden to church one day in a carriage, the first vehicle of the kind ever seen in the neighborhood, Mr. McMillan manifested his ill-bred impertinence by contemptuously remarking in his sermon that "people might travel on the *broad road* in fine carriages, as well as on horseback or afoot." In a quarrel with one of his professional brethren, the Rev. Mr. Birch, he denounced him as "a liar, a drunkard, and a preacher of the devil." Mr. Birch entered suit against him for slander, on which he was tried before the civil court of Washington County, and convicted. The plea that the language had been used in a sort of Pickwickian sense, secured a reversal of the decision in the Supreme Court, to which it was appealed, but could not shake the opinion of the honorable-minded among the people, that the expression was grossly unbecoming, and such as no circumstances could justify, especially in a minister of the gospel.

As a preacher, Dr. McMillan was of no marked reputation. There was little or no action in his delivery. He seldom moved an arm or lifted a hand, by way of gesture, in the pulpit. His voice was harsh, and his sermons, while always sensible, pious, and full of matter, were severely plain and simple. . He was much in the habit of repeating himself; but his exhortations, though heard ever so often, always, somehow, we are assured, seemed fresh to the hearer. As a teacher he was a greater success than as a preacher; so that, although there was reason to be thankful for three wide-spread and powerful revivals that occurred under his ministry, the church confesses to a deeper sense of gratitude for the hundred, more or less, of young men taken in hand and trained for the pulpit under his private tuition. He lived to the ripe old age of fourscore-and-one, his death taking place at Canonsburg in 1833, up almost to the very date of which he continued, with his mental and physical faculties but little impaired, in the active prosecution of his professional labors.

JAMES FINLEY, an Irishman, born (1725) in the county of Armagh, in the province of Ulster, emigrated to America while yet a boy; was taught in the languages and sciences at Fagg's Manor; ordained to preach in 1752, was the first minister to set foot on western soil, although rather on a mercenary tramp (having "an eye on certain good tracts of land") than a missionary one; moved to the border with his family in 1783, and permanently settled there, as the pastor of Rehoboth and Round-hill congregations, some two years afterwards. Mr. Finley is described as a fat, fidgety, red-faced little fellow in black, good-natured, and quite a favorite among his people. He was a man who, while duly attentive to spiritual affairs, was, at the same time, not forgetful of temporal ones. It was possible, as he saw it, to serve God, and yet, without disparagement to his loyalty, to lend some little allegiance to Mammon too. To have a faith was no reason why he should not have a farm, or, for that matter, several farms,—one for each of his half-dozen of promising boys. The only points in Mr. Finley's history which tradition has laid hold of as worthy of mention are that he was a man of eminent piety, and an excellent pastor; that he visited much among his people, and that he was particularly remarkable for his attention to the catechetical instruction of the youth of his congregation. In his own family it was his custom to call his children and slaves together and put them through the same training, regularly every Sabbath evening. His forte does not seem to have lain so much in bringing sheep into the fold as in keeping them there when they were in. He was conservative rather than aggressive; better satisfied to hold fast to the bird in the hand than to run any risk by reaching after others in the bush. And so he lived, his parish his world, he all in all to his people, his people all in all to him; and so he died.

JOSEPH SMITH, a Marylander, of Nottingham in that State, was born in 1736, received his literary education at Princeton, studied theology under Dr. Samuel Finley, at Nassau Hall, and in 1767 was licensed to preach the gospel. He visited Washington County in 1779, where he remained for some time, breaking the bread of life to these people "in the wilderness." A few months later he received a call from the congregations at Buffalo and Cross Creek, which he accepted, moving out to take charge of them in the year following. Mr. Smith was tall and slender in person, of fair complexion, an expressive countenance, and with eyes that were piercingly brilliant, but which, like the celebrated Whitefield's, squinted. This peculiarity served him in profitable stead, however, giving him an increased power over his audience; as, look where he might, each hearer felt that his eye was on him, and, taking the notice in good faith, accepted the appeal that went with it, never doubting, as personal to himself. His voice, promptly adjustable to any style of eloquence,—" now like the thunder, and now like the music of heaven,"—was perfectly at home alike on the "terrific" as on the "pathetic,"—when in glowing rhapsodies he pictured the attractions of heaven, or when, "arrayed with divine and awful majesty, he uncovered the bottomless and wide-extending pit of woe, whose billows of fire are ever lashed into fury by the almighty breath of an incensed Saviour!" He was more particularly strong, however, on the "terrific,"—"that kind of preaching that drives a man into the corner of his pew, and makes him think the devil is after him;" on which account he was generally known as "Hell-fire" Smith along the border. As a deviser of innocent contrivances "to catch flanking-parties and strolling individuals in the gospel net," and as an "eagle-eyed spy and scouter upon the trails of the enemy," capturing them singly and in squadrons, he was eminently skillful and successful. In the Christian warfare upon which he was entered, he made it his mission to conquer,—peaceably when he could, forcibly when he must; accepting the latter alternative, as it happened, unhesitatingly and boldly, for "he feared none of the devil's emissaries on this side of hell." He was of a particularly devotional temper of mind, observing closely not only the regularly-appointed seasons of fasting, humiliation, and prayer, but privately, in his own family and on his own account, setting apart others, and keeping them quite as religiously. It was, also, a common custom with him to seize occasions in the night for intercessory exercises; at which times he would leave his couch and kneel upon the floor,—in the winter season and when the nights were cold, keeping for his comfort, as he did so, a cloak always hanging ready to wrap about him, at the foot of his bed.

Hell-fire Smith may with propriety be said to have been the Lion of the Tribe of the Redstone Judah. Wind and will and muscle are potent elements in the church as well as out of it, and there was a larger share of all of them lodged in that long, lank frame of his than in the persons of the whole remaining of his co-presbyters put together. He had scarcely planted himself among the people of his charges before a lively "gale" of grace was started in both congregations. Keeping in steady blast through the mean time, the gale reached its height at the May Sacrament of 1787, at Cross Creek, after which it subsided considerably, still continuing, however, to sustain a vigorous current, as long as life was spared the inspirer of it to keep it in motion. He died, after a twelve years' service in the settlements, on the 19th of

April, 1792; sorely to the sorrow and seriously to the apprehension of his people, who, a mourning cotemporary informs us,—

> "——trembled when this Pillar fell,
> Lest God, who his ambassador withdrew,
> Should take away his Holy Spirit too."

THADDEUS DOD, educated at the College of New Jersey, and ordained by the Presbytery of New York in 1777 or '78, moved in the year following with his family to the West, where he settled, in charge of the two congregations of Upper Ten-Mile and Lower Ten-Mile, each about the distance implied by their names from the town of Washington. Mr. Dod is described as a young man of sallow complexion, slender figure, black hair, and with eyes that were dark, keen, and penetrating. Intellectually he was possessed of only ordinary ability, although he had not failed, by diligent use of the means of improvement that were within his reach, to make the most out of his faculties that they were capable of. He made himself a thorough master of the Greek, Latin, and Hebrew languages. His preferences, however, ran rather in the line of the exact sciences. The Dods of the day were famous for their mathematical heads, and Thaddeus did no discredit to the connection. He could explain every line and figure on Gunter's scale; and that his pupils, when he had them, might do so, perfectly, too, it was required of them that they should make copies of this ingenious contrivance to carry about with them in their pockets, so as to be conveniently at hand at all times for study,—which they did, carving them out of pieces, neatly prepared for the purpose, of dogwood. Mr. Dod, known throughout the parishes as the "Son of Consolation," was a man in whom the crowning Christian virtue shone more conspicuously than in any other of his brethren,—in fact, in whom alone of the whole Presbytery it may be said to have shone particularly at all. He was modest and unpresuming in his manners, gentle in his speech, and deeply devout and spiritual in his nature. But Providence had never, evidently, designed him for the pulpit. Mathematics was his mission. He seemed himself to be conscious of the fact, and before he had been many years in the service began to turn his chief attention in that direction. In 1782 he opened the first classical and scientific school in the West. Seven years later he was appointed principal of the academy at Washington, which position he continued to fill until the old court-house in which it was kept was destroyed by fire. He died in the spring of 1793.

JOHN CLARK, born "somewhere" in the State of New Jersey, educated at Princeton, and licensed by the Presbytery of New Brunswick, after having spent much the better part of his life in unprofitable service among various folds in his own and the neighboring Presbytery of Philadelphia, moved to the Redstone region in 1781, and, then in the sixty-fourth year of his age, took charge of the united congregations of Bethel and Lebanon. Mr. Clark had not experienced a halcyon time of it while tending his flocks in the valleys of the Delaware, and this was undoubtedly the chief inducement which tempted him to hazard the fortunes of his declining years among a strange people and in the new settlements of the border. The big white wig he wore—quite a novelty on the frontier—has kept the memory of him from perishing, more than anything else. Concerning him as a preacher, except in the general, matter-of-course particular that he was "solemn and impressive," little or nothing is known. His church had its attendants on Sabbath-days, but whether they were not attracted there by the performances, regularly to be expected, of two of his slaves famous for their singing, rather than by his preaching, is a point which at least will admit of dispute. Perhaps the cause may have been benefited somehow by his labors, but, if it was, no one seems to have discovered it. His death is mentioned as having taken place in 1797.

The Redstone settlements, even at this early period in their history, must have been a remarkably inviting field for missionary enterprise, notwithstanding the perils and privations, so elaborately and so compassionately made note of by historians, which attended the occupation of it;

because we discover that at a very early date other missionaries were out on their own account, to share the labors and to participate in the profits of the same vineyard. The fact that some of these may have been pronounced impostors, and the rest, all of them, regarded as informally, one way or another, in the service, while it may indicate a lack of strict fidelity among them, somehow, to their church, cannot but be accepted nevertheless as an evidence of their zeal. Participating alike in the risks of the mission, and subject equally to its hardships, they are as justly entitled to mention as any of their regularly commissioned and respectably recognized cotemporaries. A certain Mr. Barr, we are told, gained admission into the Presbytery shortly after its organization. Where he labored we are not informed. His connection with the Presbytery lasted some three or four years, when, it having become too plainly apparent that he was a hinderance rather than a help in the cause, he received his dismissal. Thomas Cooly, a "wandering star" from the Presbytery of Charleston, South Carolina, as he claimed, illuminated the congregations for some time, but serious doubts began to be entertained at length of his orthodoxy. He was called up to undergo an examination on "experimental religion and cases of conscience," in which he failed satisfactorily to sustain himself. It was afterwards ascertained that he was out under forged credentials, when, instead of being stripped of his robe of office, he was merely transferred, on his own petition, to the Presbytery of Carlisle. Two Irishmen, father and son, of the name of Morrison, filled pulpits here and there for awhile, but they proved vexatious and troublesome, and it was not long until, according to a peculiar expression of the time, they were "hated out" of the settlements. Mr. Hughey, an importation from Ireland, —Presbytery of Derry,—was also found prophesying among the people. He was regarded by the Redstone regulars as a slippery adventurer, loose in his belief, and altogether unworthy of confidence. Being accustomed to officiate at weddings, Presbytery, not liking the interference, took the matter up, and, after due deliberation, resolved that, "as many difficulties arose from marriages celebrated by Mr. Hughey," who had no authority civil or ecclesiastical to perform the same, "such marriages be discountenanced, and people cautioned against them as unlawful." The Derry divine, cut off from his most profitable source of income, soon retired, and was heard of no more among the churches. The next and last prominent of the repudiated was "a man of the name of Birch," who has already been referred to in connection with the McMillan slander suit. Mr. Birch was an Irishman, and a regularly ordained Presbyterian minister. He was charged by his brethren as being deficient in "experimental knowledge;" in fact, as destitute of piety. It was also suspected of him that he was addicted to the too free use of liquor. On these accounts, when he applied for admission into the Presbytery he was rejected. If Mr. Birch was in the habit of manifesting in his daily life anything like as little of the genuine spirit of piety as was exhibited when that application was made by the ecclesiastical body into which he asked to be received, then was the judgment that excluded him a most just and righteous one. Dishonored thus in his own country, the discarded prophet next laid his application before the Presbytery of Baltimore, where he fared better,—that *fag-end* of the Presbyterian Church, as it was contemptuously styled by its border sister, admitting him, by a "gross irregularity," into its body. Mr. Birch still continued on duty in the West. We do not hear that he accomplished much by his labors, but there is no evidence that the after-course of his life justified the scandalous accusations of Mr. McMillan, or could be referred to as vindicating the angry charges of complaint against the Presbytery that adopted him.

As the scenes of his earliest labors, the Presbyterian Black-Robe had invariably fixed upon fields selected out of country quarters. All the churches to which reference has been made were situated in the various settlements planted along the watercourses and intermediate uplands included in what are now known as Washington, Fayette, Westmoreland, and the south-of-the-river strip of Alleghany Counties. The towns which had sprung up here and there, Greensburg, Uniontown, Brownsville, Washington, Florence, and the like, were entirely destitute of the means of grace, except as very rarely, now and then, in a missionary way, it may have been dispensed to them by the pastors of the neighboring rural churches. From the time, in 1756, when Charles Beatty, acting for a few months as chaplain among the troops at Fort Pitt, was accustomed to induce attendance at worship by making the distribution of whisky rations a part of the service, down for thirty years, there was not a priest of any persuasion, nor church, nor chapel, in Pittsburg. The whole town, as a distinguished Virginia visitor of the time has testified, was likely to be damned without benefit of clergy. In 1786 an interest seems to have awakened in the spiritual welfare of the slovenly Scotch and Irish inhabitants of the place, and a congregation was organized, over which the Rev. Samuel Barr was settled by Presbytery as the pastor. Mr. Barr had not been long in his place before trouble arose between him and his people. It was alleged against the latter that they would not hold themselves amenable to church discipline; that they devolved upon their pastor the responsibility of collecting his salary; that the elders among them indulged too much in drinking and card-playing and being idle with women; that they were untruthful and covetous; and that by circulating false reports they had made it impossible to worship God in a peaceable manner on the Sabbath-day. On the other hand, it was retaliated by the elders that their minister had not done his duty by his people; that he had not visited their families, nor examined them in their Catechism; that he had collected money in Philadelphia and New York and rendered no account of it to the trustees or anybody else in the church; that he never tried to use discipline; and that he, as well as his officers, was addicted to card-playing and night-reveling. A trial of the case being had before Presbytery, the elders were sustained, and Mr. Barr, after a three years' term of service, was relieved of his charge. Upon assuming his pastorate, a church "of squared timbers and moderate dimensions" was erected for the accommodation of his flock. This humble structure was the original First Presbyterian Church of Pittsburg. In course of time around it were piled—itself remaining undisturbed meanwhile—the brick walls of another edifice, considered as very imposing in its day, but which grew to be despised, too, in after-years, and was torn away to give place to the temple which, of far costlier construction, has since been reared, and still stands, with its two stone towers planted square and broad upon its old foundations, the pride of the worshipers that gather at its gates.

For two years after Mr. Barr's retirement the congregation remained without a pastor. In 1793

Mr. Mahon, a licentiate of the Carlisle Presbytery, undertook to supply the pulpit; but, like his predecessor, his "experimental acquaintance with religion" was not what Presbytery, after having put him through an examination, thought it ought to be, and within about a year his connection with the church was dissolved. Mr. Semple followed next; but, the civil law proving more to his taste than the ecclesiastical, he abandoned the pulpit and took to the bar. The congregation, failing, after so many attempts, to secure the services of a sound man, declined now to experiment further, and through a long interim were shepherdless altogether. In 1800 Mr. Steele made a venture at the vacancy. His brethren had grave doubts about his orthodoxy; but, after two trial sermons preached in their hearing,—meanwhile, however, being allowed to officiate as a "supply,"—he was finally admitted, *speciali gratiâ*, into the Presbytery. A call was then (1802) placed in his hands, and the First Church of Pittsburg had a pastor.

With the occupation of Pittsburg the "missionary" labors of the church may be said to have terminated. Satan had here intrenched himself behind his last defenses, and when these were stormed and taken his sovereignty was ended. Presbyterianism had conquered the situation. It only remained for her to protect herself in the possession of her properties,—to call in her "watchmen to set on her walls," to lengthen the cords of her tents and strengthen her stakes; and to this work were her energies thenceforth directed. How she met the responsibility, with what success, through what chances, and changes, and modifications in her experience, her faith, and her customs, and whether, consistently, for worse, or at clash, for better, with the example of the olden time, her after-history, which falls not within the province of this sketch, and her living self, as she stands to-day, will best illustrate.

THE END.

LIST OF PUBLICATIONS

OF

J B. LIPPINCOTT & CO.

PHILADELPHIA.

Will be sent by mail, post paid, on receipt of the price.

The Albert N'Yanza. Great Basin of the Nile, and Explorations of the Nile Sources. By Sir Samuel White Baker, M. A., F. R. G. S., &c. With Maps and numerous Illustrations, from sketches by Mr. Baker. New edition. Crown 8vo. Extra cloth, $3.

"It is one of the most interesting and instructive books of travel ever issued; and this edition, at a reduced price, will bring it within the reach of many who have not before seen it."—*Boston Journal.*

"One of the most fascinating, and certainly not the least important, books of travel published during the century." *Boston Eve. Transcript.*

The Nile Tributaries of Abyssinia, and the Sword-Hunters of the Hamran Arabs. By Sir Samuel White Baker, M. A., F. R. G. S., &c. With Maps and numerous Illustrations, from original sketches by the Author. New edition. Crown 8vo. Extra cloth, $2.75.

"We have rarely met with a descriptive work so well conceived and so attractively written as Baker's Abyssinia, and we cordially recommend it to public patronage. . . . It is beautifully illustrated."—*N. O. Times.*

Eight Years' Wandering in Ceylon. By Sir Samuel White Baker, M. A., F. R. G. S., &c. With Illustrations. 16mo. Extra cloth, $1.50.

"Mr. Baker's description of life in Ceylon, of sport, of the cultivation of the soil, of its birds and beasts and insects and reptiles, of its wild forests and dense jungles, of its palm trees and its betel nuts and intoxicating drugs, will be found very interesting. The book is well written and beautifully printed."—*Balt. Gazette.*

"Notwithstanding the volume abounds with sporting accounts, the natural history of Ceylon is well and carefully described, and the curiosities of the famed island are not neglected. It is a valuable addition to the works on the East Indies."—*Phila Lutheran Observer.*

Cottage Piety Exemplified. By the author of "Union to Christ," "Love to God," etc. 16mo. Extra cloth. $1.25.

"A very interesting sketch."—*N. Y. Observer.*

Stories for Sundays, Illustrating the Catechism. By the author of "Little Henry and his Bearer." Revised and edited by A. CLEVELAND COXE, Bishop of Western New York, and author of "Thoughts on the Services," etc. 12mo. Illustrated. Tinted paper. Extra cloth. $1.75. FINE EDITION. Printed within red lines. Extra cloth, gilt edges. $2.50.

"We are glad to see this charming book in such a handsome dress. This was one of our few Sunday books when we were a school-boy. Sunday books are more plentiful now, but we doubt whether there is any improvement on Mrs. Sherwood's sterling stories for the young."—*Lutheran Observer.*

"The typography is attractive, and the stories illustrated by pictures which render them yet more likely to interest the young people for whose religious improvement they are designed."—*N. Y. Evening Post.*

An Index to the Principal Works in Every Department of Religious Literature. Embracing nearly Seventy Thousand Citations, Alphabetically Arranged under Two Thousand Heads. By HOWARD MALCOM, D.D., LL.D. SECOND EDITION. With Addenda to 1870. 8vo. Extra cloth. $4.

"A work of immense labor, such as no one could prepare who had not the years allotted to the lifetime of man. We know of no work of the kind which can compare with it in value."—*Portland Zion's Advocate.*

"The value of such a book can hardly be overestimated. It is a noble contribution to literature. It meets an urgent need, and long after Dr. Malcom shall have left the world many an earnest pen-worker will thank him, with heartfelt benedictions on his name, for help and service rendered."—*Boston Watchman and Reflector.*

The Geological Evidences of the Antiquity of Man, with Remarks on the Origin of Species by Variation. By SIR CHARLES LYELL, F.R.S., author of "Principles of Geology," etc. Illustrated by wood-cuts. Second American, from the latest London, Edition. 8vo. Extra cloth. $3.

This work treats of one of the most interesting scientific subjects of the day, and will be examined with interest, as well by those who favor its deductions as by those who condemn them.

The Student's Manual of Oriental History. A Manual of the Ancient History of the East, to the Commencement of the Median Wars. By FRANCOIS LENORMANT, Sub-Librarian of the Imperial Institute of France, and E. CHEVALLIER, Member of the Royal Asiatic Society, London. 2 vols. 12mo. Fine cloth. $5.50.

"The best proof of the immense results accomplished in the various departments of philology is to be found in M. Francois Lenormant's admirable *Handbook of Ancient History.*"—*London Athenæum.*

Thoughts on the Services. Designed as an Introduction to the Liturgy, and as an aid to its devout use. By RT. REV. A. CLEVELAND COXE, Bishop of Western New York. 18mo. Cloth. 80 cents. Extra cloth, gilt edges. $1.13. Turkey super. gilt edges. $3.

—— *Fine Edition.* 12mo. Tinted paper. Extra cloth, gilt or red edges. $1.75. Turkey antique. $4.

Coleman's Manual on Prelacy and Ritualism. The Apostolical and Primitive Church, Popular in its Government, Informal in its worship. By LYMAN COLEMAN, D. D. 12mo. Tinted paper. Extra cloth. $2.

"It is a complete refutation of the claim of Episcopacy, that it is derived from the primitive Church. It establishes the fact that the primitive Church was distinguished for simplicity in government, and that the polity and ceremonials of prelacy had no place in it. It is a book which should be carefully and thoroughly studied by our ministers and intelligent people."—*Presbyterian Banner.*

"Professor Coleman has contributed if not the ablest anti-ritualistic argument of any of the disputants, certainly a very able one."—*Chicago Even. Journal.*

The Closing Scenes of the Life of Christ. Being a Harmonized Combination of the Four Gospel Histories of the Last Year of our Saviour's Life, forming a complete Scripture Narrative, with occasional Notes, Dissertations and Tabular Views, and Outlines of a New System of Bible-class Instruction. By D. D. BUCK, D. D., with an Introductory Essay by W. D. WILSON, D. D., of Hobart College, Geneva, N. Y. 12mo. Tinted paper. Cloth. $1.50.

"We commend Dr. Buck's book to the earnest attention of Sunday-school teachers, and indeed to all students of the sacred Scriptures."—*Sunday-School Times.*

The Beauty of Holiness; or, The Practical Christian's Daily Companion: being a Collection of upward of Two Thousand Reflective and Spiritual Passages, remarkable for their Sublimity, Beauty and Practicability; Selected from the Sacred Writings, and arranged in Eighty-two Sections, each comprising a different theme for meditation. By the editors of "Truths Illustrated by Great Authors." Fifth edition. 16mo. 536 pp. Cloth. $1.50. Cloth, beveled boards, gilt top. $1.75.

"An admirable and admirably arranged selection of texts from the Bible under various appropriate heads, such as Affliction, Associates, Blessedness, Charity, Diligence, Duty, Faith, Love, etc. The book is beautifully printed in large, clear type, and is an excellent one for use in family devotions, and also in the pulpit and conference-room."—*The Liberal Christian.*

Preparation for Death. Translated from the
Italian of Alphonso, Bishop of S. Agatha. By Rev. ORBY SHIPLEY, M. A. Square crown 8vo. Tinted paper. Extra cloth, red edges. $1.75.

"But at the same time many of the pages of this book teem with rich spiritual matter, and many of the prayers may be well studied as models."—*Presbyterian Banner.*

"As to the contents, their merits have long since been settled, deeply and lovingly, in all hearts whose needs and tastes make welcome the precious ore outpoured for us through the long ages by those who have dug earnestly in the exhaustless mine of communion with God."—*Charleston Courier.*

Mizpah. Friends at Prayer. Containing a Prayer
or Meditation for Each Day in the Year. By LAFAYETTE C. LOOMIS. 12mo. Beautifully printed on superfine tinted paper, within red lines. Fine cloth. $2. Extra cloth, gilt edges. $2.50.

"A beautifully printed volume with colored border. The plan of the work consists in 'an evening meditation' for each day of the year; with appropriate Scripture references for morning and evening. The meditations are well and piously written, and will, we doubt not, accomplish great good."—*The Lutheran Observer.*

Blunt's Key to the Holy Bible. A Key to the
Knowledge and Use of the Holy Bible. By J. H. BLUNT, M. A., author of "Household Theology," etc. 16mo. Extra cloth. $1.

"Is a compact history of Holy Scripture, showing how, when and by whom it was written, with what purpose, what was its writers' inspiration, how it is to be interpreted, and what are the Apocrypha of the Old and New Testaments. There is an Appendix of peculiar Bible words, with their meanings, and a good Index. ... On the whole, this is a singularly well-executed work, of great value in many respects."—*The Philada. Press.*

Pulpit Germs. Plans for Sermons. By Rev. W.
W. WYTHE. 12mo. Tinted paper. Extra cloth. $1.50.

"This book is intended as an aid to clergymen in the preparation of their sermons—not as a labor-saving apparatus for drones, but as an incentive to study. It contains 455 texts, upon each of which the leading heads or skeletons of a discourse are supplied with occasional subdivisions under such heads. The utility of the work is obvious."—*San Francisco Times.*

"The book is unquestionably the best and most unexceptionable of its kind we have met with."—*The Prot. Churchman.*

Evidences of Natural and Revealed Theology.
By CHAS. E. LORD. 8vo. Toned paper. Extra cloth. $3.50.

"This volume bears the marks of careful study and clear thinking. ... The book is a calm, serious and valuable contribution to the theological literature of the age."—*N. Y. Observer.*

"Dr. Lord is a calm, clear and careful writer, and this volume is a valuable contribution to theological literature.

"... As a summary treatise upon natural and revealed theology, or as a manual for use in schools and higher institutions of learning, this book has few, if any, superiors. It will therefore be welcome to the general reader of religious works and useful to the cause of education."—*N. Y. Times.*

The Christian Worker; A Call to the Laity. By
REV. C. F. BEACH. 16mo. Cloth. $1.

PUBLICATIONS OF J. B. LIPPINCOTT & CO.

LIPPINCOTT'S PRONOUNCING DICTIONARY

OF

BIOGRAPHY AND MYTHOLOGY

Containing Memoirs of the Eminent persons of all Ages and Countries and Accounts of the Various Subjects of the Norse, Hindoo and Classic Mythologies, with the Pronunciation of their Names in the different Languages in which they occur. By J. THOMAS, A. M., M. D. Imperial 8vo. Published in Parts of 64 pages. Price 50 cents per Part. In two handsome vols. Per vol., extra cloth, $11. Sheep, $12. Half Turkey, $13.50.

This invaluable work embraces the following peculiar features to an eminent degree:

I. GREAT COMPLETENESS AND CONCISENESS IN THE BIOGRAPHICAL SKETCHES.
II. SUCCINCT BUT COMPREHENSIVE ACCOUNTS OF ALL THE MORE INTERESTING SUBJECTS OF MYTHOLOGY.
III. A LOGICAL SYSTEM OF ORTHOGRAPHY.
IV. THE ACCURATE PRONUNCIATION OF THE NAMES.
V. FULL BIBLIOGRAPHICAL REFERENCES.

"I have taken the trouble to look out a large number of names, such as seemed to me good tests of the compass, sufficency and accuracy of the biographical notices. The result has been in a high degree satisfactory. So far as I have examined nobody was omitted that deserved a place, and the just proportions were maintained between the various claimants to their page, or paragraph, or line. The star of the first magnitude was not shorn of its radiance, and the scarcely visible spark was allowed its little glimmer."—*From* DR. OLIVER WENDELL HOLMES.

"It is a work which I shall be glad to possess, both on account of the fullness of its matter, and because the pronunciation of the names is given. I have had occasion, from the other works of Dr. Thomas, to be convinced of his great exactness in that respect. The work will be a valuable addition to the books of reference in our language."—*From* WILLIAM CULLEN BRYANT.

"I can speak in high terms of the thoroughness and accuracy with which the work has been prepared. It is a storehouse of valuable and trustworthy information. The pronunciation of the names, which is systematically given, will add much to the usefulness of the work."—*From Prof.* JAMES HADLEY, *Yale College.*

"I think that the work when completed will supply a real want. I was especially pleased with the sensible and learned preface of the editor, and am persuaded that he has chosen the true system of orthography. From what I know of Dr. Thomas, I feel sure that he will give us a book that may be depended on for comprehensiveness and accuracy, the two great *desideranda* in such an undertaking."—*From Prof.* JAS. RUSSELL LOWELL.

"It is the most valuable work of the kind in English that I have seen."—*From* GEN. R. E. LEE, *Washington College.*

Special Circulars, containing a full description of the work, with specimen pages, will be sent, post-paid, on application.

Subscriptions received by the Publishers, and the Parts forwarded to subscribers by mail, post-paid, as issued, on receipt of the price (50 cents) for each part.

Agents wanted in all parts of the United States on liberal terms. Address the Publishers.

PRESCOTT'S WORKS.
CROWN OCTAVO EDITION.
COMPLETE IN FIFTEEN UNIFORM VOLUMES.
EACH VOLUME WITH PORTRAIT ON STEEL.

Prescott's History of the Reign of Ferdinand and Isabella the Catholic. Three vols. 8vo.

Prescott's Biographical and Critical Miscellanies. With a finely engraved steel Portrait of the Author. One vol. 8vo.

Prescott's History of the Conquest of Mexico, with a Preliminary View of the Ancient Mexican Civilization, and the Life of the Conqueror, Fernando Cortez. In three vols. 8vo.

Prescott's History of the Reign of Philip the Second, King of Spain. In three vols. 8vo.

Prescott's History of the Conquest of Peru, with a Preliminary View of the Civilization of the Incas. In two vols. 8vo.

Prescott's Robertson's History of the Reign of the Emperor Charles the Fifth. With an account of the Emperor's Life after his Abdication. In three vols. 8vo.

Each work sold separately. Price per vol., cloth, $2.50; half calf, neat, $3.75; half calf, gilt extra, marble edges, $4.25; half Turkey, gilt top, $4.50. Complete sets, printed on tinted paper, handsomely bound in green or claret-colored cloth, gilt top, beveled boards. Price, $40.

CHAMBERS'S BOOK OF DAYS.

The Book of Days: A Miscellany of Popular Antiquities in connection with the Calendar, including Anecdote, Biography and History, Curiosities of Literature, and Oddities of Human Life and Character. In two vols. royal 8vo. Price per set, cloth, $9; sheep, $10; half Turkey, $11. Edited under the supervision of ROBERT CHAMBERS.

This work consists of

I.—Matters connected with the Church Calendar, including the Popular Festivals, Saints' Days, and other Holidays, with illustrations of Christian Antiquities in general.

II.—Phenomena connected with the Seasonal Changes.

III.—Folk-Lore of the United Kingdom: namely, Popular Notions and Observances connected with Times and Seasons.

IV.—Notable Events, Biographies and Anecdotes connected with the Days of the Year.

V.—Articles of Popular Archæology, of an entertaining character tending to illustrate the progress of Civilization, Manners, Literature and Ideas in those kingdoms.

VI.—Curious, Fugitive and Inedited Pieces.

The work is printed in a new, elegant and readable type and illustrated with an abundance of Wood Engravings.

www.ingramcontent.com/pod-product-compliance
Lightning Source LLC
Chambersburg PA
CBHW020306240426

43673CB00039B/715